Journal on Policy and Complex Systems

Volume 5, Number 2 • Fall 2019

Also from Westphalia Press
westphaliapress.org

JOURNAL ON POLICY AND COMPLEX SYSTEMS

Volume 5, Number 2 • Fall 2019

Mirsad Hadžikadić & Liz Johnson, editors

Westphalia Press
An imprint of Policy Studies Organization

Journal on Policy and Complex Systems
Volume 5, Number 2 • Fall 2019

Westphalia Press
An imprint of Policy Studies Organization
1527 New Hampshire Ave., NW
Washington, D.C. 20036
info@ipsonet.org

ISBN: 978-1-63391-496-4

Cover and interior design by Jeffrey Barnes
jbarnesbook.design

Daniel Gutierrez-Sandoval, Executive Director
PSO and Westphalia Press

Updated material and comments on this edition
can be found at the Westphalia Press website:
www.westphaliapress.org

TABLE OF CONTENTS

Editor's Letter

This issue of the Journal of Policy and Complex Systems includes an extended version of eight papers selected from those presented at the Complexity and Policy Studies conference held on April 15-17, 2019 in Washington, DC. Two regular papers complete the issue.

These papers offer a modeling approach to a range of policy issues, ranging from conflict (Kaufman, Kaufman, & Diep—multi-group conflict; Salami & Karp—Kurdish conflict), business (Ogibayashi—reproducing business cycles and evaluating effects of tax reductions; Morales-Martinez & Lee—effects of immigration on the US economy; Wilson—evaluating healthcare systems), and child sex trafficking (Khataera—targeting demand versus supply) to social capital (Frieson—dynamics of critical realism), law (Moskaleva & Zohdy—unintended consequences of legal reforms), and theoretical and methodology considerations (Goode & Pires—error reasoning in complex systems; Davis—modeling uncertainty in policy analysis).

This range of methodological considerations and applications in various domains attests the health of the field of complexity-driven policy. The Journal of Policy and Complex Systems continues its effort to build this new discipline at the intersection of policy and complexity. Current events in politics, technological innovations, and business cycles provide the best justification for the advent of this interdisciplinary field.

We encourage potential authors to submit their contributions to the Journal of Policy and Complex Systems and help us build a discipline that can address the challenges of the changing world.

Best regards,

Mirsad Hadžikadić
Editor, *Journal of Policy and Complex Systems*

Este número de Journal of Policy and Complex Systems incluye una versión extendida de ocho documentos seleccionados de los presentados en la conferencia Complexity and Policy Studies llevada a cabo los días 15 y 17 de abril de 2019 en Washington DC. Dos documentos regulares completan el tema.

Estos documentos ofrecen un enfoque de modelado para una variedad de cuestiones de política, que van desde conflictos (Kaufman, Kaufman y Diep - conflicto multigrupo; Salami y Karp - conflicto kurdo), negocios (Ogibayashi - reproducción de ciclos comerciales y evaluación de los efectos de las reducciones impositivas ; Morales-Martínez y Lee - efectos de la inmigración en la economía de los Estados Unidos; Wilson - evaluación de los sistemas de salud) y el tráfico sexual infantil (Khataera - focalización de la demanda versus la oferta) al capital social (Frieson - dinámica del realismo crítico), ley (Moskaleva y Zohdy - consecuencias no deseadas de las reformas legales), y consideraciones teóricas y metodológicas (Goode y Pires - Razonamiento de errores en sistemas complejos; Davis - modelado de incertidumbre en el análisis de políticas).

Este rango de consideraciones metodológicas y aplicaciones en varios dominios atestigua la salud del campo de la política basada en la complejidad. El Journal of Policy and Complex Systems continúa sus esfuerzos para construir esta nueva disciplina en la intersección de la política y la complejidad. Los acontecimientos actuales en política, innovaciones tecnológicas y ciclos económicos proporcionan la mejor justificación para el advenimiento de este campo interdisciplinario.

Alentamos a potenciales autores a que presenten sus contribuciones a Journal of Policy and Complex Systems y nos ayuden a construir una disciplina que pueda abordar los desafíos del mundo cambiante.

Atentamente,

Mirsad Hadžikadić
Editor, *Journal of Policy and Complex Systems*

本期《政策与复杂系统》期刊共收录十篇文章，其中八篇选自2019年四月15日至17日华盛顿特区举办的“复杂性与政策研究”会议。另外两篇是常规论文（regular paper）。

这些文章为一系列政策议题提供建模方法，议题包括冲突（作者Kaufman、Kaufman、和 Diep研究了多集团冲突；作者Salami 和Karp研究了库尔德人冲突）、商业（作者Ogibayashi 研究了商业周期复制和减税效果评估；作者Morales-Martinez 和 Lee研究了移民对美国经济造成的影响；作者Wilson 研究了医疗体系评估）、儿童性贩卖（作者Khataera 研究了需求与供应）、社会资本（作者Frieson 研究了批判性现实主义的动态）、法律（作者Moskaleva 和Zohdy研究了立法改革带来的意想不到的结果）、以及理论考量和方法论考量（作者Goode 和Pires研究了复杂系统中的误差推理；作者Davis研究了政策分析中建模的不确定性）。

这一系列有关方法论在不同领域中的考量和应用，验证了由复杂性驱动的政策领域的发展状态。《政策与复杂系统》期刊持续努力建设这一与政策和复杂性相关的新学科。当前的政治事件、技术创新、商业周期都为这一学科间领域的出现提供最佳证明。

我们鼓励有兴趣的作者为《政策与复杂系统》期刊投稿，帮助我们建立一个能应对不断变化的全球挑战的学科。

献上最好的问候，

Mirsad Hadžikadić

编辑

《政策与复杂系统》期刊

Multi-Group Conflict Paths: Anticipatory Scenarios of Attitudes and Outcomes

Miron Kaufman

Professor, Department of Physics, Cleveland State University

m.kaufman@csuohio.edu

Sanda Kaufman

Professor, Department of Urban Studies, Cleveland State University

s.kaufman@csuohio.edu

Hung The Diep

Professor, Laboratoire de Physique Théorique et Modélisation, Université de Cergy-Pontoise, France

diep@u-cergy.fr

Abstract

We explore intractable social conflicts in various contexts where unexpected outcomes can be costly and/or violent. We extend a network model of two-group conflict dynamics to multiple groups. We study the time dependence of the groups' mean attitudes, using mean-field theory. We incorporate contextual characteristics that alter the group dynamics. We find that in time, regardless of initial conditions, the paths followed by the groups' mean attitudes converge to a multi-dimensional attractor. Small differences in initial conditions do not diminish or diverge exponentially over time, but instead generate stable oscillations. We offer examples for which the model could be used to construct scenarios of conflict paths in time and we examine how context changes might affect these paths and in-group attitudes. The scenarios can inform the strategies that groups might select to contend with each other.

Keywords: social networks; social physics of conflicts; group cohesion; intra- and inter-group interactions; group decisions; collective behaviors

Rutas de conflicto multigrupo: Escenarios anticipatorios de actitudes y resultados

Resumen

Proponemos explorar conflictos sociales intratables en varios contextos donde los resultados inesperados pueden ser costosos y/o violentos. Extendemos un modelo de red de dinámicas de conflicto de dos grupos a múltiples grupos. Estudiamos la dependencia del tiempo de las actitudes medias de los grupos, utilizando la teoría del campo medio. Incorporamos algunas características contextuales que alteran la dinámica del grupo. Encontramos que, con el tiempo, independientemente de las condiciones iniciales, los caminos seguidos por las actitudes medias de los grupos convergen en un atractor multidimensional. Pequeñas diferencias en las condiciones iniciales no disminuyen ni divergen exponencialmente con el tiempo, pero generan oscilaciones estables. Ofrecemos ejemplos para los cuales el modelo podría usarse para construir escenarios de caminos de conflicto en el tiempo, y examinamos cómo los cambios de contexto podrían afectar estos caminos y las actitudes dentro del grupo. Los escenarios pueden informar las estrategias que los grupos podrían seleccionar para competir entre sí.

Palabras clave: redes sociales; física social de los conflictos; la cohesión del grupo; interacciones intra e intergrupales; decisiones grupales; comportamientos colectivos

多群体冲突路径：态度和结果的预期场景

摘要

我们提出探究不同背景下难以应对的社会冲突，在这些背景中出乎意料的结果/后果可能代价高昂和/或伴随暴力。我们为多个群体提供了有关两群体间冲突的动态网络模型。我们使用平均场理论，研究了群体平均态度的时间依赖。我们融入了一些能改变群体动态的情境特征。我们发现在时间情境里，不论初始情况如何，群体平均态度的路径会向一个多维度的吸引子汇聚。初始情况中的小差异不会随时间推移而成倍减少或分散，但都会产生稳定振动。我们提供了实例，证明该模型能被用于建构时间情境里的冲突路径场景，我们还检验了背景变化如何能影响这些路径及群体内的态度。这些场景能影响一系列可能被群体用于相互竞争的策略。

关键词：社会网络; 冲突之社会物理学; 团队凝聚力; 团队内部互动与团体之间互动; 群体决策，集体行为

1. Multi-Group Social Conflicts

Social conflicts are waged among groups with shared histories, identities, values, interests, and attitudes regarding specific social issues (Felson & Tedeschi, 1993; Oberschal, 1978). The groups are not necessarily internally homogeneous, however, regarding how conflicts should be addressed. As if in response to Fink's (1968) early call for interdisciplinarity in conflict research, scholars from several fields have studied social conflict dynamics, consequences to individuals and societies, and approaches to conflict management (Coser, 1967, 1998; Dahrendorf, 1958; Rubin, Pruitt, & Kim, 1994).

Some conflicts among specific groups flare up and then abate. For example, the "Yellow Vests" protest movement in France, begun in October 2018, shows signs of waning several months later. In contrast, other conflicts last over longer periods—years, decades and even centuries. In some instances, conflicts that seem to have been resolved resurface (Goodman, 2019). The Northern Ireland conflict between Unionist and Republican groups has been held as an example of successful negotiation. The "Good Friday" agreement of April 1998 appeared to put an end to a long period (at least 30 years) of violent strife. However, in 2018, there were signs of this conflict erupting again, perhaps triggered by border disputes related to Brexit (Watson, 2018).

The Northern Ireland conflict illustrates key intractability characteristics (Coleman, 2003): it spanned decades during which the two groups interacted at times violently and stemmed from a mix of irreconcilable value or moral differences, high-stakes distributional issues, and/or domination issues (Burgess & Burgess, 2003). There are numerous other examples of such deep-seated, long-lasting conflicts, including between North and South Korea, China and Tibet, Greeks and Turks in Cyprus, Bosniaks, Serbs, and Croats in Bosnia, Hindus and Muslims in Kashmir, Hutus and Tutsis in Rwanda, and Flemish and Walloons in Belgium. Pruitt and Olczak (1995) called these conflicts "seemingly intractable" in recognition of the fact that historically even the longest lasting conflicts eventually end, although often those who started the strife did not live long enough to see it. In all these examples, we can identify two or more directly involved groups, as well as other groups interested in the conflict outcomes that intervene indirectly.

A key characteristic of intractable social conflicts is their complexity. The opposing social groups are embedded in broader, ever-changing social systems with which they are interlinked. With more than two groups, the enemy of one's enemy may well turn out to be one's enemy too. Therefore, not only are intractable conflicts resistant to resolution, they are also resistant to prediction even in the short run. Neither the disputing groups nor their would-be helpers can foresee when even seemingly insignificant acts or events can trigger reactions that lead to conflict escalation and violence. Sometimes reports in the media, spreading quickly (Menczer, 2016), can set off serious confrontations.

Intractable social conflicts can be managed in several ways, including direct negotiations, intervention through mediation, legal tools, dialogue, and military means. Their effectiveness depends on the specific characteristics of the groups involved, contextual factors, expected consequences of continued strife and costs of intervention, and the groups' readiness[1] to address their differences, whether peacefully or violently. These approaches entail risks, not least because of the difficulty of predicting consequences of various courses of action on complex systems in continuous slow or rapid flux. Nevertheless, all involved—direct and indirect stakeholders, interveners, and researchers—need to understand and manage such conflicts in order to avert destructive and even catastrophic consequences. As history and current events show, these consequences range from turbulence, which may cause economic losses and social unrest, to acute ethnic strife and loss of life, which can stay local or spread across nations.

Managing specific conflicts requires information about the stakeholders, their interests, the history of their past interactions, their cultures and ways of handling conflicts, the current institutional context and other specific case-based details. It is also necessary to equip the stakeholders and interveners with tools to anticipate and explore possible futures they can link to actions they might undertake in the present. This enhances their ability to construct effective strategies and helps interveners to persuade disputants to engage with each other peacefully.

To agree to a specific move toward agreement or to accept/reject a specific approach to managing their conflict, groups need to evaluate the possible results of alternative courses of action and the paths that lead to these results. For example, the conflict involving North and South Korea, their neighbors, and the United States has deep roots in the past 70 years, with episodes of severe violence and millions of victims on all sides. In the most recent flare-up in 2017-2018, parties traded threats of mass destruction. In the ongoing stage,

1 Zartman (2000) called this conflict "ripeness."

the key active participants—those making overt, observable, and behind-the-scene moves (North Korea, China, and the United States)—need to assess the consequences of trusting each other and making concessions that risk endangering one or more parties.

The parties to the North Korean conflict have information that stems chiefly from the fraught history of their past encounters. On the one hand, these encounters have undermined mutual trust and willingness to take any risks, and they have all but eliminated direct communications. On the other hand, all should expect the same (poor) results from continuing on the confrontational path. Switching to a different strategy might be helpful, but it is difficult to predict with any level of confidence what might work. The parties could proceed on a trial-and-error basis, testing limited actions and mutual responses to them to rebuild trust. However, conflict trajectories are path-dependent: by the time parties are engaged in one direction, they may practically eliminate other, more mutually desirable trajectories they did not foresee. If they could play out the future under different decision scenarios, the parties might be able to choose wisely and reduce some of the risks (Lempert, Popper, & Bankes, 2003).

In this and other conflicts around the world, all parties might value insights into possible outcomes, were they to adopt a different approach or stay the course. The North Korea conflict is complex because it is embedded in shifting broader global conflicts and power struggles among the direct and indirect stakeholders, as well as contending with intra-national (intra-group) politics. The current negotiations may take some time, during which emergent factors may alter the interests and calculus of the parties. For instance, the United States and China have other differences that are not independent of the Koreas situation; and, instead of waiting for North Korea to denuclearize, Japan might seek nuclear capability, altering the regional balance. The international context is likely to change in other ways too, as may key decision-makers, for example, due to elections in the democratic countries or coups in others. Therefore, predicting outcomes by extrapolating from the past or current situation is likely to be misleading. Instead, anticipatory tools, such as scenarios, may be helpful in exploring the range of possible futures (Diep, Kaufman, & Kaufman, 2017; Kaufman, Diep, & Kaufman, 2019; Kaufman & Kaufman, 2013, 2015; Kaufman, Kaufman, & Diep, 2017; Weaver et al., 2013).

To examine the paths and outcomes of multiparty, complex, intractable conflicts, we adapt to them some statistical physics tools. Our approach belongs to the developing field of sociophysics, consisting of applying physics models to various aspects of social processes (Barnes & Wilson, 2014; Galam, 2012; Godoy, Tabacof, & Von Zuben, 2017; Schweitzer, 2018; Stauffer, 2003; Wilson, 1969). The sociophysics approach to modeling intractable conflicts is illustrated by Liebovitch et al. (2008) and Kaufman and Kaufman (2013). Such models rely on finding analogies between physics and social dynamics, to identify patterns and trajectories of complex social systems. Assessing the range of future possibilities is precisely the kind of input that decision-makers in a particular situation need to consider when constructing engagement strategies. According to Bernstein, Lebow, Stein, and Weber (2000), "Knowledge of structure and process also allows conscious and far-reaching transformations of social systems" (p. 51)—a statement that undermines point predictions and instead supports the attempt to understand interactive systems in order to intervene and change course when necessary.

With regard to the Korea conflict, few will hazard to predict the outcome of current negotiations surrounding North Korea's nuclear arsenal, especially given the difficulties that have already occurred since 2017. However, exploring possible trajectories of this three-group system—North Korea, China, and the United States—may provide those who are managing this conflict with means to explore consequences of their choices.

Models drawn from statistical physics are helpful in representing social systems with some key characteristics corresponding to physics terms. Such are social groups whose members interact with each other, akin to a system of particles. This correspondence is possible because in both physical and social systems, the complex interactions among numerous components at one level evolve self-organized patterns at a higher level of observation (Buchanan 2007; Castellano, Fortunato, & Loreto, 2000). Social interactions have been modeled in this manner in areas ranging from culture dynamics to information dissemination, transportation flows, and social conflict. In negotiation theory, many characteristics of two-party negotiations—interactions processes, level of cognitive and interaction burdens, and outcome complexity—change meaningfully with the addition of even one more party (Kaufman, Ozawa, & Shmueli, 2017). Moreover, with three or more groups, there is the possibility that ad-hoc, shifting coalitions will emerge. To explore this multi-group effect, we extend here Diep et al.'s (2017) dynamic two-group social conflict model to multiple groups and to the study of intractable conflicts that extend over long periods. We explore the possible paths a conflict might take on the way to long-run outcomes, using a mean field approach borrowed from statistical physics. To enhance applicability to social systems, we relax some of the conservation and symmetry rules that prevail in physical systems, but not necessarily in social ones. Besides paths, we examine outcome patterns and in-group attitudes using three groups and discuss some examples of such conflicts where the model could be used to gain insights into conflict management strategies. We conclude with some ideas for further refining the model.

2. Modeling Three-Group Conflicts

Intractable social conflicts have different histories, characteristics, causes, and interaction patterns that we should consider when trying to understand and account for intricate webs of contributors to recurrence, escalation, or de-escalation. Although the predictive ability of such models decreases relatively quickly with time and hinges on correct model specification, insights into contributors to intractability can be derived. In contrast to such explanatory models, our model is anticipatory: it looks into the future to derive possible directions these conflicts might take, based only on the dynamics of intra-group and inter-group interactions in time. Its purpose is to enable a mapping of sorts for possible conflict trajectories (scenarios) that parties in conflict need to consider in preparing their engagement strategies.

We assume that when groups are locked in social conflict, they are not necessarily internally homogeneous regarding how the conflicts should be addressed. At any moment in time, within each group, individuals may adopt (within a range) a number of frames about the issues at stake and differing attitudes with respect to the ways out. The members of each group interact to persuade each other of their points of view. Thus, at any point in time, the average stance of a group reflects this mutual persuasion process and can shift in time even without any input from external effects. We assume the groups to be homophilic (Aiello et al., 2012; McPherson et al., 2001), because inside each group members share characteristics,[2] such as ideology or perspective on the conflict; they tend to communicate mostly or only with each other and not with individual members of other groups.

The groups may interact with each other as well. One group may either persuade another group to form a coalition or reject the overall position of another group with opposing views. In the North Korea example, the United States may want to rally China against the North Korean position of continuing the development and testing of nuclear weapons, but China and North Korea also share some interests. The United States, Mexico, and the Central American countries of Guatemala, Honduras and El Salvador are waging a conflict over population migration, with Mexico at times helping its southern neighbors and sometimes assisting the United States in stemming the flow of migrants. Great Britain and the European Union are locked in a post-Brexit conflict, with obstacles to agreement involving Ireland. In the United States, before national elections, Republicans and Democrats tend to polarize and each of these two groups tries to attract independents. Within Bosnia and Herzegovina (BiH), three ethnic groups—Bosniaks, Serbs, and Croats—are in a latent conflict that flares up at times, such as preceding elections, with a different pattern of inter-group relationships than in the other examples.

We begin here by modeling three-group conflicts, such as the United States, North Korea, and China (US-NK-C), BiH, or the United States, Mexico, and Central American (US-M-

2 McPherson et al. (2001) described homophily as "similarity breeds connection."

CA) examples. As in Diep et al.'s (2017) model for two-groups conflicts, we assume that each individual in each group has an attitude s with respect to a specific conflict, as to whether or not (and how) to proceed in dealing with the other groups to attend to the conflict. Attitudes s range between -Mn and Mn (the ranges may differ between groups, but here we take them to be the same for all three groups). When individuals' attitudes are close to the lower bound, -Mn, they have a loose attachment to their own group's stance and therefore tend to be the most open to compromise. Conversely, when attitudes s are close to the upper bound, Mn, the individuals are strongly attached to their group's goals. They tend to shun concessions and instead are willing to engage in confrontation to defend their group's stance. Individuals whose attitudes s are close to 0—the midpoint of this range of attitudes—respect their group's values, but they are also ready to make concessions to resolve their conflict.

Each individual interacts with every other individual inside their own group, forming a homophilic network of members. Each individual within a group acts with intensity J to persuade others to his/her stance. Each individual is also the target of others' efforts to sway him/her. The three groups (networks) form a multiplex when they interact with each other. Thus, the individuals' attitudes within one group are affected, indirectly by the "average" attitudes of the other groups, even though individuals do not necessarily communicate across groups. This is the case in the US-NK-C and BiH examples.

As group members interact with each other and consider the opposing groups' attitudes, their own group's resulting preference average at any time t is sn (n=1, 2, 3). In each group n, the intensity with which an individual tries to persuade others. This intensity, which in physics terms is analogous to "negative energy," is Jn*s*sn. Similarly, the inter-group intensity of interaction K, the result of an individual's consideration of an opposing group's stance, is also analogized to negative energy. We consider it proportional to the product between that individual's preference s and the mean value of the preferences of the other groups' members: K12*s*s2 + K13*s*s3 for an individual in group 1, where K12 and K13 represent the individual's interpretation of what the average attitudes in groups 2 and 3 mean in the context of the ongoing conflict. The three-group model thus has nine parameters:[3] three intra-network couplings J (the links among members in each group) and six inter-network couplings K.[4]

In our dynamic model, the changes in preferences are captured by assuming that the intensity of interactions involves the product of individuals' preferences at a current time and

3 The two-group model had four parameters; an n-group model would have n^2 parameters, quickly escalating computational and representation impediments.

4 The links between any two groups are not necessarily symmetrical: for example, K12 may be different from K21. In this respect, social networks composed of individuals with agency differ from physical networks, which behave according to Newton's third law.

average preferences of the groups at an earlier time. This lag represents the delay between individuals' persuasion efforts in one period and the effects likely to emerge later.

To represent the homophilic linkages among group members, we consider them as nodes in a Renyi-Erdös network. The mean of preferences s of each group is proportional to the exponential of the negative energy representing the intensity of interactions:

$$s1_{t+1} = \frac{\sum_{s=-M1}^{M1} s e^{s(J1s1_t + K12s2_t + K13s3_t)}}{\sum_{s=-M1}^{M1} e^{s(J1s1_t + K12s2_t + K13s3_t)}}$$

$$s2_{t+1} = \frac{\sum_{s=-M2}^{M2} s e^{s(J2s2_t + K21s1_t + K23s3_t)}}{\sum_{s=-M2}^{M2} e^{s(J2s2_t + K21s1_t + K23s3_t)}}$$

$$s3_{t+1} = \frac{\sum_{s=-M3}^{M3} s e^{s(J3s3_t + K31s1_t + K32s2_t)}}{\sum_{s=-M3}^{M3} e^{s(J3s3_t + K31s1_t + K32s2_t)}} \quad (1)$$

The time lag between persuasion efforts and their effects is introduced in equations (1) by assuming that the preference s at time t + 1 interacts with the averages s1, s2, and s3 evaluated at a previous time t. The "delay time" units become the measure for time.

3. Results: Attitudes, Conflict Paths, and Outcomes

To illustrate the model's capabilities, we consider a situation where the upper limit of the attitudes s is the same for all three groups: M1 = M2 = M3 = 3.[5] Then, to characterize qualitatively the behavior of the time dependence of s1, s2, and s3, we need to plumb a nine-dimensional space, which is very challenging. Therefore, we show next a few examples of qualitatively different time evolutions of conflicts, by selecting specific values for the K and J parameters.

We take K12 = - 0.2, K21 = 0.2, K13 = 0, K31 = 0.2, K23 = 0, K32 = 0.2 and weak intra-group couplings J1 = J2 = J3 = 0.15, meaning that inside each group, members are not very active in persuading each other (as might be the case in the Brexit dispute). Then, the mean attitudes exhibit oscillations of decaying (to zero) amplitude (Figure 1).

For stronger intra-group couplings J1 = J2= J3 = 0.25 and same values for all inter-group couplings the oscillations are sustained with an am-

5 This means the full range of attitudes is from -3 to 3 for all groups. However, this might not be a realistic assumption in specific cases. The model can be adapted to the study of such cases.

plitude that does not decay to zero in the long run (Figure 2).

In the (s1, s2, s3) phase space, there is an attractor or limit cycle (Figure 3): trajectories starting from different initials conditions approach the attractor over the long run.

Because of the existence of the attractor, differences in the initial conditions values do not decay to zero (as for stable fixed points), nor do they diverge (chaos, strange attractor) after a long time. This is shown in Figure 4.

When we further increase the intra-group couplings, the oscillations period increases and the sinusoidal dependence changes drastically (Figure 5).

The shape of the corresponding attractor approaches a rectangle (Figure 6).

For J1 = J2= J3> 0.617, the attractor is replaced by a stable fixed point, i.e. s1, s2, and s3 approach fixed values, independent of initial conditions.

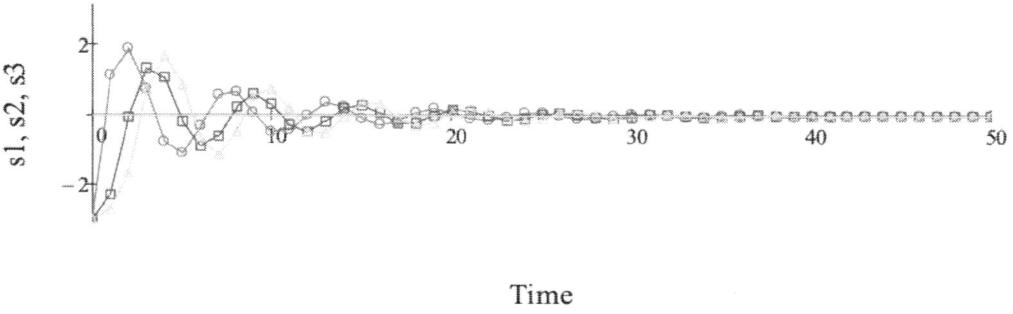

Figure 1.
J1 = J2 = J3 = 0.15, K12 = - 0.2, K21 = 0.2, K13 = 0, K31 = 0.2, K23 = 0, K32 = 0.2.

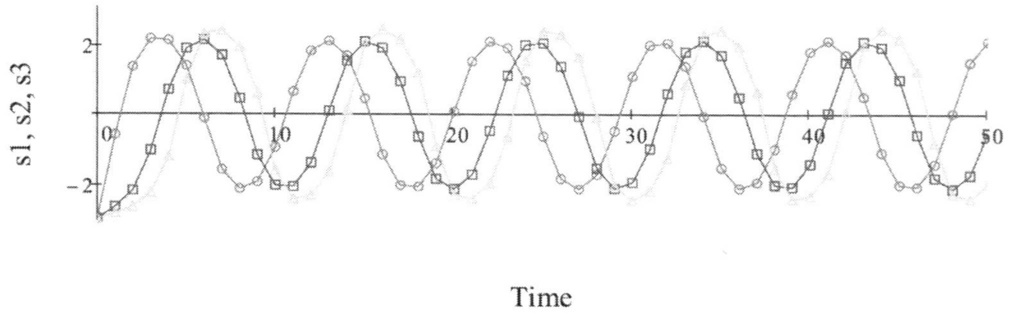

Figure 2.
J1 = J2 = J3 = 0.25, K12 = - 0.2, K21 = 0.2, K13 = 0, K31 = 0.2, K23 = 0, K32 = 0.2.

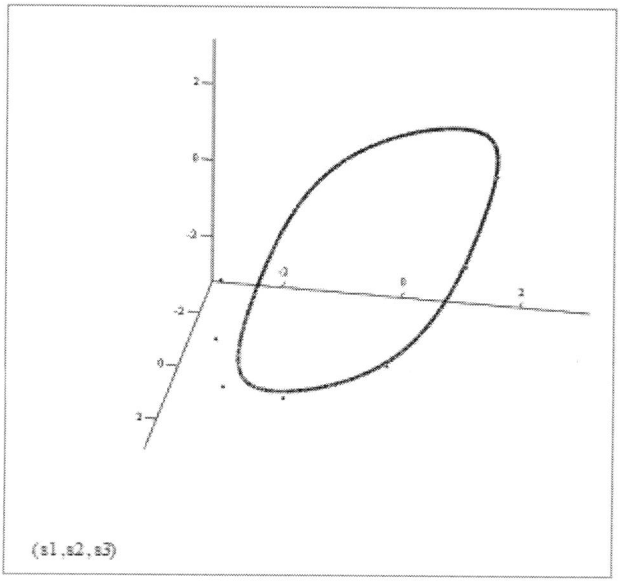

Figure 3. Attractor for trajectories starting at different initial conditions.
J1 = J2 = J3 = 0.25, K12 = - 0.2, K21 = 0.2, K13 = 0, K31 = 0.2, K23 = 0, K32 = 0.2.

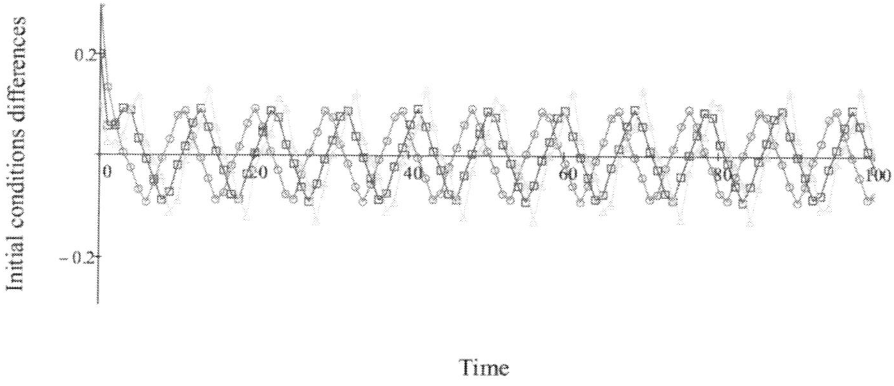

Figure 4. Small differences in initial s1, s2, s3 as function of time follow sustained oscillations.
J1 = J2 = J3 = 0.25, K12 = - 0.2, K21 = 0.2, K13 = 0, K31 = 0.2, K23 = 0, K32 = 0.2.

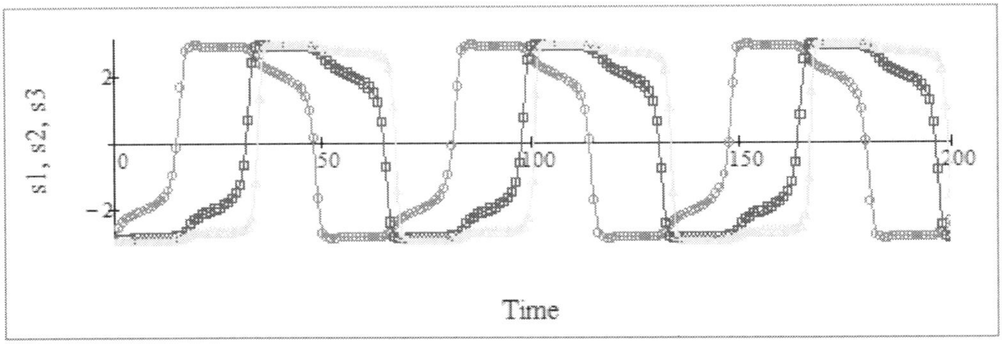

Figure 5.
J1 = J2 = J3 = 0.6, K12 = - 0.2, K21 = 0.2, K13 = 0, K31 = 0.2, K23 = 0, K32 = 0.2.

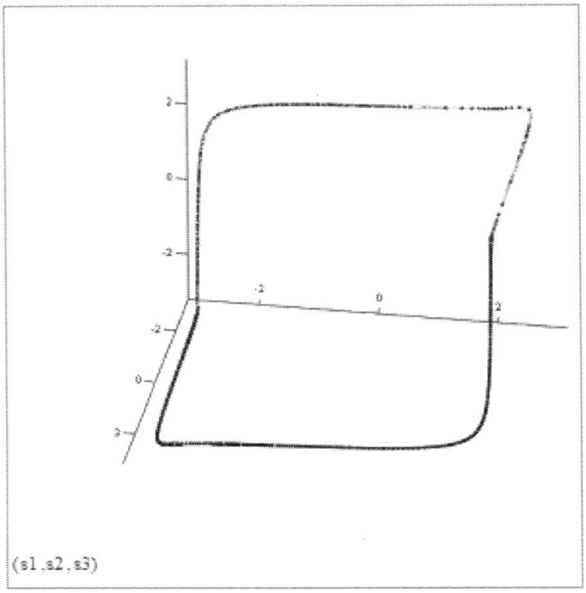

Figure 6. Attractor.
J1 = J2 = J3 = 0.6, K12 = - 0.2, K21 = 0.2, K13 = 0, K31 = 0.2, K23 = 0, K32 = 0.2.

How can the model be populated with real data and used to study a specific conflict? We have already used poll data to assess initial intra-group attitudes and linkages and inter-group linkages in the two-group model (Diep et al., 2017) that explored 2016 conflicts surrounding Brexit and the U.S. elections. The same approach can be used in multiple-group situations. For example, we used an in-depth attitudinal survey in Bosnia and Herzegovina (Prism Research, 2013) to assess intra-group and inter-group linkages and derive a range of scenarios (Kaufman, et al., 2019). Our sensitivity tests indicated that the scenarios would not change meaningfully within a range of values for each of our parameters.

For BiH, we examined three different "temperature" levels—low, medium, and high—to capture the effect of the international context on this conflict. The temperature T is incorporated in the model as each coupling, J and K, is inversely proportional to T. We found that as external events and interventions (such as European Union actions) became more salient, corresponding to "higher temperatures," the conflict scenario became more protracted. This may be true in general, though the factors that raise the temperature in each specific conflict may differ. In the US-NK-C example, we would expect the temperature to rise and long-run divergences between the United States and North Korea to increase if countries affecting this relationship (Japan or Taiwan) make unilateral moves. Conversely, we may see a drop in temperature corresponding to a de-escalation in the relationship between the United States and Mexico over the migration issue if economic considerations lead Mexico to discourage entry of United States-bound migrants at the U.S. border.[6] The scenarios offer some insights into what it would take (including "temperature factors") to alter the conflicts' trajectories.

4. Conclusions

We have proposed a statistical physics dynamic model of interacting networks to represent multiple groups in conflict and derive scenarios of possible conflict paths and patterns of outcomes, given data that allow estimation of the intra- and inter-group attitudes and linkages. We have discussed some examples involving three main groups. Our assumptions with respect to ranges of attitude values and symmetries can be relaxed, if warranted, for specific cases.

Intractable conflicts tend to recur and cycle among a number of possible outcomes, which our model can uncover. The more numerous the possible outcomes among which the conflict cycles, the more intractable it may be in the sense that it is more difficult to settle on any choice when there are many. The fewer the possibilities, the likelier it is that one outcome may emerge. Thus, the model reveals the novel possibility of different degrees of intractability and allows us to distinguish them in specific cases. The presence of the limit cycle (Figures 3 and 6) expresses a new type of sensitivity to initial conditions: in-between stability and instability (chaos). If the interactions are only between neighbors (short range), chaotic behavior emerges (Kaufman et al., 2019).

The relatively simple quality of the model has both advantages and limitations. The advantages derive from the model's simplicity, yielding interesting anticipatory results usable in specific

6 This has indeed occurred in 2019.

cases to explore different strategies with a relatively small investment in data. It allows us to ask "what if" questions and explore consequences for paths and outcomes of various anticipated changes in context and in circumstances that drive individual and group attitudes. The results are relatively easy to communicate to stakeholders and interveners, which is not always the case with more intricate models.

The same simple quality is also a limitation: this model is not of the explanatory kind, but is rather anticipatory. Our two-group model produced scenarios that were realized in the Brexit and U.S. elections cases, but did not explain what social and political factors led to them. Similarly, our exploration of the BiH conflict yielded scenarios consistent with reality, without offering causal linkages among the many historical, political, and economic factors that likely contributed to the 2018 election outcomes. Those searching for the causes of various intractable conflicts will not find them here. Instead, this is an "as if" model that produces results by different means than direc links between causes and their effects which are difficult, if not impossible, t(discover in complex systems.

An added limitation of this model is the quick rise in the computational difficulty as we add groups. To get around this challenge, we explored specific value regions rather than plumbing the entire parameter space. In other cases with multiple groups, we may be able to examine paths and outcomes if some groups are sufficiently aligned that we can consider collapsing them into one group. That can be done in the US-M-CA dispute, where, for purposes of exploring migration scenarios, we could consider the three Central American countries to comprise one group, even if in reality they differ along many dimensions.

We plan to refine and continue to develop the multiple group model. We are considering the introduction of principal-agent effects, as we add a layer of negotiators to the disputing group layers. We will explore leadership effects and situations where an entire group takes the position of its leader (as in dictatorships), as opposed to groups who may diverge from their leaders' positions (as in democracies), resulting in strong or impaired cohesion levels between group members and their respective leaders. We also plan to examine sparse networks, where not every individual interacts with every other in the group. We will also work to unpack "temperature" by identifying specific components that can be affected by disputants or interveners.

References

Barnes T. J., & Wilson M. W. (2014). Big data, social physics, and spatial analysis: The early years. *Big Data & Society, 1*(1). doi:10.1177/2053951714535365

Bernstein S., Lebow, R. N., Stein J. G., & Weber S. (2000). God gave physics the easy problems: Adapting social science to an unpredictable world. *European*

Journal of International Relations, 6(1), 43-76.

Buchanan M. (2007), *The social atom.* New York, NY: Bloomsbury.

Burgess, H. & Burgess G. M. (2003). What are intractable conflicts? *Conflict Information Consortium.* Retrieved from the Beyond Intractibility website: http://www.beyondintractability.org/essay/meaning-intractability.

Castellano C., Fortunato S., & Loreto V. (2009), Statistical physics of social dynamics. *Reviews of Modern Physics, 81*(2), 591-649.

Coleman, P. T. (2003). Characteristics of protracted, intractable conflict: Toward the development of a metaframework-I. *Peace and Conflict: Journal of Peace Psychology, 9*(1), 1-37.

Coser, L. A. (1967). Continuities in the study of social conflict. New York, NY: Free Press.

Coser, L. A. (1998). *The functions of social conflict* (Vol. 9). London, England: Routledge.

Dahrendorf, R. (1958). Toward a theory of social conflict. *Journal of Conflict Resolution, 2*(2), 170-183.

Diep, H. T., Kaufman, M., & Kaufman, S. (2017). Dynamics of two-group conflicts: A statistical physics model. *Physica A: Statistical Mechanics and its Applications, 469,* 183-199.

Felson, R. B., & Tedeschi, J. T. (Eds.) (1993). *Aggression and violence: Social interactionist perspectives.* Washington, DC: American Psychological Association.

Fink, C. F. (1968). Some conceptual difficulties in the theory of social conflict. *Journal of Conflict Resolution, 12*(4), 412-460.

Galam S. (2012), Sociophysics: A physicist's modeling of psycho-political phenomena. New York, NY: Springer-Verlag.

Goodman, P. (2019, April 15). Inequality fuels rage of 'yellow vests' in equality-obsessed France. *The New York Times.* Retrieved from https://www.nytimes.com/2019/04/15/business/yellow-vests-movement-inequality.html

Godoy, A., Tabacof, P., & Von Zuben, F. J. (2017), The role of the interaction network in the emergence of diversity of behavior, *PLoS ONE 12*(2): e0172073. doi:10.1371/journal.pone.0172073

Kaufman, S. & Kaufman, M. (2013), Tipping points in the dynamics of peace and war. In A. Colson, D. Druckman, & W. Donoghue (Eds.), *International negotiation: Foundations, models and philosophies* (251-272). Geneva, IL: Republic of Letters.

Kaufman, S., & Kaufman, M. (2015). Two-group dynamic conflict scenarios: "Toy model" with a severity index. *Negotiation and Conflict Management Research, 8*(1), 41-55.

Kaufman, M., Kaufman, S., & Diep, H.T. (2017). Scenarios of social conflict dynamics on duplex networks. *Journal on Policy and Complex Systems, 3*(2), 3-13.

Kaufman, M., Diep, H. T., & Kaufman, S. (2019). Sociophysics of intractable conflicts: Three-group dynamics. *Physica A: Statistical Mechanics and its Applications, 517*, 175-187.

Kaufman, S. Ozawa, C. & Shmueli, D. (2017). Multiparty negotiations in the public sphere. In C. Honeyman & A. Schneider (Eds.), *The negotiator's desk reference* (pp. 413-430). St. Paul, MN: DRI Press.

Lempert, R. J., Popper, S. W. & Bankes, S. C. (2003). *Shaping the next one hundred years: new methods for quantitative, long-term policy analysis.* Rand Corporation. Retrieved from https://www.rand.org/pubs/monograph_reports/MR1626.html

Liebovitch L. S., Naudot V., Vallacher R., Nowak A., Bui-Wrzosinska L., & Coleman P. (2008). Dynamics of two-actor cooperation-competition conflict models. *Physica A: Statistical Mechanics and its Applications, 387*(25), 6360-6378.

Menczer, F. (2016). The spread of misinformation in social media. In *Proceedings of the 25th International Conference Companion on World Wide Web* (pp. 717-717). International World Wide Web Conferences Steering Committee. doi:10.1145/2872518.2890092

Oberschal, A. (1978). Theories of social conflict. *Annual Review of Sociology, 4*(1), 291-315.

Pruitt, D. G., & Olczak, P. V. (1995). Beyond hope: Approaches to resolving seemingly intractable conflict. In B. B. Bunker & J. Z. Rubin (Eds.), *The Jossey-Bass management series and The Jossey-Bass conflict resolution series. Conflict, cooperation, and justice: Essays inspired by the work of Morton Deutsch* (pp. 59-92). San Francisco, CA: Jossey-Bass.

Prism Research. (2013). *Public opinion poll results: Analytical report.* Office of the UN Resident Coordinator in Bosnia and Herzegovina.

Rubin, J. Z., Pruitt, D. G., & Kim, S. H. (1994). *Social conflict: Escalation, stalemate, and settlement* (2nd ed.). New York, NY: McGraw-Hill Book Company.

Schweitzer, F. (2018), Sociophysics. *Physics Today, 71*(2), 40. doi:10.1063/PT.3.3845.

Stauffer, D. (2003), Sociophysics simulations. *Computing in Science & Engineering 5*(3), 71-75.

Watson, T. (2018, September 14). Brexit could 're-ignite conflict' in Northern Ireland. *BBC.* Retrieved from https://www.bbc.com/news/uk-northern-ireland-45513462

Weaver, C. P., Lempert, R. J., Brown, C., Hall, J. A., Revell, D., & Sarewitz, D. (2013). Improving the contribution of climate model information to decision making: The value and demands of robust decision frameworks. *Wiley Interdisciplinary Reviews: Climate Change*, *4*(1), 39-60.

Wilson A. (1969), Notes on some concepts in social physics. *Papers in Regional Science, 22*(1), 159-193.

Zartman, I. W. (2000). Ripeness: The hurting stalemate and beyond. *International conflict resolution after the Cold War*, *2*, 225-250.

Modeling the Kurdish Conflict with GIS

Khadijeh Salimi, Ph.D Candidate

Graduate Program in International Studies, Old Dominion University

Ksali001@odu.edu

Dr.Regina Karp, Director

Graduate Program in International Studies

rkarp@odu.edu

Acknowledgment

I would like to show my gratitude to the Dr. Erika Frydenlund, Research Assistant Professor, for her comments on an earlier version of the manuscript that greatly improved the manuscript.

ABSTRACT

The Kurdish dream of having an independent state has changed the borders of the Middle East, which might change more in the future. The objective of this study is to propose a model that will show how theoretically-derived may factors may influence the expansion of Kurdish movement across Iraq, Syria, and Iran. To propose this, I assume that Kurdish ethnicity, central government hegemony, distance from the center of the Kurdish movement (Arbil), and religion are four factors (independent variables) that may affect this expansion. A Geographic Information System and, more specifically, Weighted Overlay Scenario Base Modeling was used in this study to model the possible Kurdish conflict area. The results of the model support the existing research in the field; Kurdish ethnicity, having a weak central government, and religious tensions are all important factors which prohibit or facilitate Kurdish conflicts.

Keywords: Kurds; ethnic conflict; Middle East; GIS modeling; policymaker; computational social science

Modelando el conflicto kurdo con SIG

Resumen

El sueño kurdo de tener un estado independiente ha cambiado las fronteras de Oriente Medio y podría cambiar más en el futuro. El objetivo de este estudio es proponer un modelo que muestre cómo los factores de poder derivados teóricamente pueden influir en la expansión del movimiento kurdo en Irak, Siria e Irán. Para proponer esto, supongo que la etnia kurda, la hegemonía del gobierno central, la distancia desde el centro del movimiento kurdo (Arbil) y la religión son cuatro factores (variables independientes) que pueden afectar esta expansión. En este estudio se utilizó un sistema de información geográfica y, más específicamente, un modelo de base de escenario de superposición ponderada para modelar la posible zona de conflicto kurdo. Los resultados del modelo respaldan la investigación existente en el campo; La etnia kurda, tener un gobierno central débil y las tensiones religiosas son factores importantes que prohíben o facilitan los conflictos kurdos.

Palabras clave: Kurdos; Conflicto étnico; Medio este; Modelado SIG; elaborador de la política a seguir; ciencias sociales computacionales

用地理信息系统对库尔德人冲突进行建模

摘要

库尔德人梦想拥有属于自己的独立国家，这个梦想已改变了中东边界，并有可能在未来促成更多改变。本文目的是提出一种模型，该模型将展示由理论得出的因素，将可能如何影响库尔德向伊拉克、叙利亚、伊朗扩张的运动。为此，我将库尔德民族、中央政府霸权、与库尔德运动中心的距离（Arbil）、宗教假设为四种可能影响扩张运动的独立变量因素。本研究运用了一种地理信息系统，准确的说，是一种基于场景的加权叠加建模，来模拟潜在的库尔德冲突区域。模型结果支持该领域的现有研究；库尔德民族、（拥有）实力不济的中央政府、宗教紧张局势都是能制止或促进库尔德冲突的重要因素。

关键词：库尔德人；民族冲突；中东；地理信息系统建模；决策者；计算社会科学

Introduction

The Kurdish dream to have an independent state can be traced back to post-World War II. The emergence of new countries like Iraq, Syria, and Turkey, after the collapse of the Ottoman Empire, changed the borders of the Middle East. However, British policymakers divided similar ethnicities in different countries during the process of defining the new nations derived from the Ottoman Empire. One of those ethnicities was the Kurds, who were split among those emerging countries.

Ethnicity is a broad concept constructed from certain features, such as language, skin color, religion, race, culture, etc.. Thus, ethnicity is a kind of social distinction which shapes the identity of ethnic groups and their political processes. (Ashcroft, Griffiths, & Tiffin, 2013) defined an individual's ethnic group as a solid identifier that cannot be denied or taken away by others.

(Bates et al., 2003) defined ethnic conflict as an extended period of violence by ethnic minorities to challenge a central government and pursue significant change in their status. An ethnic minority is a group of people who experience systematic discrimination and domination, such as the Kurds. The Kurdish independence movement is an ethnic conflict within the Middle East. (Hill & Rothchild, 1986) and (Gurr, 1993) argued that ethnic and political conflicts act like a contagion. (Sadowski, 1998) claimed that the behavior of neighboring countries influences the behavior of each geographic unit. In other words, in our interdependent world, social and political events are not isolated and might be influenced by other societies (Klingman, 1980).

Thus, it is important to study the Kurdish conflict because an Iraqi Kurdistan movement is not only a matter of Iraq's territorial integrity; in addition, Kurds in Iraq influence other Kurds in the area in an effort toward their dream of having a separate province. This is a matter of national security for Iran, Syria, and Turkey; this then is a matter of regional and international security. Policymakers of those mentioned countries are worried about this area, but they are not alone: superpowers like Russia and the United States have their own policy objectives in these regions. Thus, it is timely and important to study the Kurdish conflict because a Kurdish nationalistic movement has changed and will further change the borders in the Middle East.

The objective of this study is to propose a model that explains the expansion of Kurdish ethnic conflict. To address it, I consider four factors (independent variables): Kurdish populated areas, the control of a central government, distance from the center of the Kurdish movement, and religion.

Literature Review

In this literature review, there are four primary schools of thought studying ethnic conflict factors.

The first group of scholars have claimed that being a member of an ethnic minority causes ethnic conflict. Members of an ethnic minority group might take political action to oppose the majority and to improve their status and interests (Yusoff & Sarjoon). It is important to differentiate between being a member of an ethnic minority and being that ethnicity. (Eriksen, 2002) contended that ethnicity is not a pivotal source of ethnic conflict, but that conflict occurs when an ethnicity becomes a minority (Yusoff & Sarjoon). Thus, ethnicity, such as white people in colonial Africa and Asia who are not facing discrimination, are not considered an ethnic minority (Osaghae, 1998).

The second group of scholars have asserted that ethnic conflict happens due to the globalization. Because globalization increases the awareness of people and different cultures, people learn about different cultures while communicating and interacting with other people; this causes a clash of civilizations. (Fox, 2002) and (Russett, Oneal, & Cox, 2000) found no statistically significant relationships between ethnic conflict and cultural difference. This debate has divided scholars into two groups; I agree with the former and believe that globalization raises sub-nation awareness.

The third group of scholars believed that religion played a crucial role in the ethnic conflict. (Arjomand, 1993) argued that religion is an essential factor of modern social and political phenomena (cited in (Eisenstadt, 1993). Indeed, (Fox, 2004) showed how religion could impact ethnic violence. Fox (2004a) also provided us with the knowledge of how religious grievances and discrimination influence ethnic conflict because religion is an integral part of an ethnic group. (Rummel, 1997) asserted that when the political power is dependent on one social group, such as religion, then ethnic violence is more probable.

The fourth group asserts that ethnic conflict has a direct relationship to the economic situation of a state. In other words, this group believes ethnic conflict happens when a group of people feels that they are marginalized from accessing economic and natural resources (Humphreys, 2005). Thus, economic inequality causes conflict. (Davies, 1962) also emphasized the role of economic inequality and how it led to ethnic violence. However, studies by scholars such as (Besançon, 2005) and (Nagel, 1974) have provided us with the insight that there is not always a link between economic deprivation and violence and that there are poor states that also experience ethnic violence.

So far, I have mostly discussed the factors that facilitate ethnic violence. However, government and policymakers often try to prohibit, regulate, or restrict the conflict inside their territory. Thus, I need an anti-conflict factor to control these pro-conflict factors. (McGarry & O'Leary, 1994) discussed eight different macro-methods to monitor and deal with ethnic conflict: genocide, forced mass population transfer, partition and/or secession, integration and/or assimilation, hegemonic control, arbitration (third-party intervention), federalism, and consociationalism. They believe that the most common method to regulate an ethnic conflict, in contrast, to eliminate the ethnic minority in a multi-national state, is hegemonic control. In other words, the authoritarian government enforces coercive power to control multiple cultures in their territories.

Pro- and anti-Kurdish conflict factor. In this section, I define the four theoretically-informed assumptions regarding my independent variables that influence Kurdish conflict:

> *Being Kurdish.* (Yusoff & Sarjoon) showed us how simply being of an ethnic minority leads to ethnic conflict. Kurds are one of the biggest marginalized ethnic minorities in the world. In addition, the Kurdish independence movement is rooted in Kurdish nationalism as an attempt to build an independent country for Kurds. On the other hand, (Huntington, 1993) explained how globalization increases ethnic awareness of Kurdish identity and raises nationalism, which later causes conflict. As a result, being Kurdish is a crucial factor for joining the conflict. In other words, this movement is rooted in Kurdish nationalism. Thus, cities that do not have a Kurd population probably do not participate in this movement, although there might be some infrequent exceptions. For example, Kurds are sometimes recruited by Iranian or Iraqi central governments to fight against the independent Kurd movement (Van Bruinessen, 1986). Thus, I assume being Kurd makes it more probable to join the independence movement.
>
> *Being Sunni Muslim.* Although Kurdish nationalism is strong, it does not outweigh the religious differences among Kurds. Kurds are mostly Sunni Muslim, but some practice Shia Islam, Yezidi religion, and Alevism. Religious difference is a cultural factor that has resulted in the perception of dissimilarity among Kurds, which later caused separation among them. This difference is doubled when it comes to Shia and Sunni Muslims in the area. As (J. Fox, 2004) suggested, religious discrimination is another factor that facilitates conflict. Most of the Kurds in these three countries are controlled by a Shia government; they thus perceive discrimination and would like to improve their situation. As (Glavin, 2015) mentioned, the hatred between Shia and Sunni Kurds has played an important role in Kurds' separation; a clear example are the Iranian Shia Kurds who began recruiting from the Iranian government and fought against the Sunni rebellion

Kurds just one year after the revolution. (Rubin, 2007) mentioned that religious and tribal ties are an obstacle for Kurdistan solidarity. In other words, the hatred between Shia and Sunni Kurds is enough to prevent Kurd unity. However, if nationalism increases among Kurds in the future, this might change. Thus, religion also plays an important role, and religious differences are perceived as dissimilarity among Kurds, which later could hamper Kurdish unity. As a result, I assume being a Sunni Kurd makes it more probable to join the movement.

Government hegemony. According to (McGarry & O'Leary, 1994), more hegemonic control results in more ethnic minority regulation, and less hegemonic control results in more ethnic violence. The overthrow of Saddam Hussein's regime was the turning point in the independent Kurdish province. Kurds got control of many territories that many had dreams of inhabiting. As (Nader, Hanauer, Allen, & Scotten, 2016) asserted, Baghdad's ability to control Kurdish independence is limited. Another factor was the Arab Spring, which provided incredible opportunity for Kurds in Syria. After the overthrow of rulers in Tunisia and Egypt, Assad had to withdraw many of his forces from Kurdish areas to control the rebellions, and this gave Syrian Kurds a chance for independence. In contrast, Iran has a strong central government, which cannot admit the Kurdish movement. Thus, a country such as Iran, with a strong central government, has more control over its territory in comparison to Iraq and Syria, which have weak central governments. Consequently, in Iraq and Syria, the Kurdish people have more power to protest. It should be mentioned that this study considers central government power.

Distance from Arbil (center of Kurdish conflict). I do not consider the economic hypothesis from the literature review as an independent factor because Iraq has huge oil reserves. As a result of the U.S. invasion of Iraq, Kurds gained control over rich oil resources in Iraq; however, they recently lost control of Kirkuk (Billon, 2015). Iraqi Kurdistan gains considerable revenue by connecting to international oil companies and selling oil to other countries. Thus, Iraqi Kurds who are pioneers of this movement do not perceive economic inequality. In contrast, Iranian Kurds who live in poor areas and have no access to natural resources have also protested against the central government and caused unrest in Kurdish areas. Thus, assigning a value for either area causes bias toward the other. Instead, I propose a new factor: the distance from Arbil. I assume if Kurds want to be one state, Iraqi Kurdistan will send aid and support to other Kurds (troops and economic resources). Thus, being close to the center of Iraqi Kurds' power (Arbil) make it easier to receive aid to fight against the government and to cooperate with Arbil. Also, it makes it harder for the central government to have complete control on that area. In contrast, it is much easier to suppress the Kurd conflict when it comes to the area far from their power center.

Method

This study covers Kurdish ethnic conflict in the regions that include Iran, Iraq, and Syria. Data were collected from scientific articles and GIS data sources. Through a literature review, I found that religion, being Kurdish, and the power of the central government to control Kurds are all principal factors that play roles in the process of becoming engaged in the conflict. I also add a final factor: the distance from Arbil because Arbil is the center of the movement, which might send aid (both economic and military) to other Kurdish areas.

Most of the study of ethnic conflict focuses on large-N size studies and country-level datasets. However, this study uses Geographic Information System (GIS) modeling to explain and test the roboustness of existing theories in the field. GIS computational results and analysis are visualized in maps below, which are useful tools for seeing uncovered information that is impossible to realize as tabular datasets. Using GIS enables policymakers and modelers to look at the same problem from another angle, and it is one additional test beyond those that are sociological or anthropological to demonstrate why or how a theory may hold.

A case study analysis was performed employing Weighted Overlay Scenario Base Modeling. Overlay is a technique that gives us the opportunity to reclassify all datasets to a common scale. I use this technique because my independent variables are diverse and, consequently, related datasets are dissimilar in scale. For example, for distance, I have a range of kilometers, and for religion, I have Sunni and non-Sunni. Applying the overlay technique provides me the opportunity to reclassify those datasets to a standard scale for analysis; for this study, I use 0-5. Moreover, the overlay method enables modelers to study and analyze different layers of input at the same time, which results in deep understanding and analysis of a phenomenon. Indeed, Weighted Overlay Scenario Base Modeling enables modelers to create different scenarios for an event. This is very beneficial in the case of conflict studies and scenario development. Different scenarios give policymakers the opportunity to realize the consequence of a phenomenon and understand what the more probable outcome is. Moreover, this method bounds outcomes to a plausible range, and it enables us to put a weight on our factors to find their influences.

Proposed model. Building the model is a two-step process. The first step is to create one shapefile that encompasses all three countries. I found data to build three separate shapefiles for Iran, Iraq, and Syria along with boundaries and states. Because the sources of data files are different and the files have different projections, first I transferred all three files to the same projection and then merged them into one shapefile. The second step was to find geospatial data for the four independent variables. Then, I put a value on the independent variables. In other words, based on the existing literature, I picked the data, assigned a numeric value to them, and finally joined these values to the shapefile that I built in the first step. In what follows, I explain the process of allocating numeric values to the independent variables.

I set the value of 0 for provinces located under control of a strong government. 0 means it is hard for the area to cooperate with the Kurdish movement. This group includes all of Iran's provinces, some of Syria's provinces under the control of central government, and some of Iraq's provinces. In addition, I set the value of 1 for regions located under the control of a weak government. For this purpose, other provinces not mentioned above can efficiently cooperate with the Kurdish if they are so inclined.

To evaluate inclination, I consider both being Kurdish and having the same religion. Thus, I placed the value of 0 for non-Sunni Muslim provinces and the value of 1 for Sunni Muslim-populated provinces. I assume that cities populated by Sunni have more inclination to join the Kurdish movement because they perceive some similarity based on religion. In contrast, this inclination declines in cities that are dominated by non-Sunni Muslims.

Similarly, I set the value of 0 for non-Kurdish populated provinces and 1 for Kurdish-populated areas. I assume that somebody should be Kurd or consider her/himself Kurd to join the movement, and vice versa.

Finally, I identified the distance for all provinces to Arbil and classified the distance in five classes. I then set the value of 1 (farthest) to 5 (closest) based on the province's distance. This reflects the fact that it is much easier for the closest cities to join the movement because they can receive more assistance from Arbil in a shorter time.

At this step of model building, I have four polygon shapefiles: religion, distance, government, and Kurdish populated areas that needs to be transfered to raster shapefiles. After transferring all four to raster shapefiles, I reclassified all four shapefiles to 1-5 since they are supposed to be in the same measure; a shapefile has 5 classes.

Computational Results and Discussion

I weighted data based on the percentage of the influence in three different scenarios:

First scenario. In this scenario, I set the same weight (25%) for all four independent variables. I assume here that the central government, distance from Arbil, religion, and being Kurdish have a similar influences.

Second scenario. In this scenario, I assume as this movement is an independent Kurdistan movement, that nationalistic factors have a higher percentage of influence. As a result, I increased it to 60%. Also, I assumed that government power is a crucial factor for suppressing this movement. Thus, I changed it from 25% to 30% and decreased the percentage of distance and religion to 5%. Therefore, I assumed that the central government, distance from Arbil, religion, and being Kurds have a similar influence.

Third scenario. In this scenario, I assumed that because this movement is an independent Kurdistan movement, the nationalistic factor is essential. I had to weight this in a way that did not cause bias and underestimate other factors like religion and distance. As a result, I weighted 50% for being Kurd and 10% for both religion and distance. Also, I assumed government power to be a crucial factor for suppressing this movement, so I used 30% here.

Table 1. Computational Scenarios

	Weights		
Variables	Scenario 1	Scenario 2	Scenario 3
Government Control	25%	30%	30%
Distance from Arbil	25%	5%	10%
Religion Tension	25%	5%	10%
Being Kurdish	25%	60%	50%

The computational results, based on scenarios shows the possible Kurdish conflict provinces, are provided in Figures 1-3.

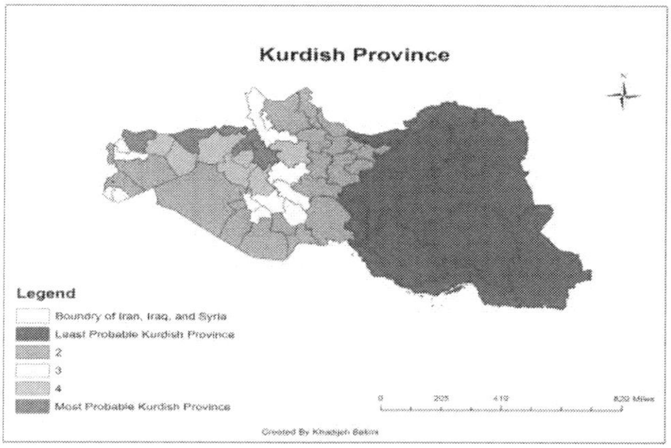

Figure 1. Scenario 1 map.

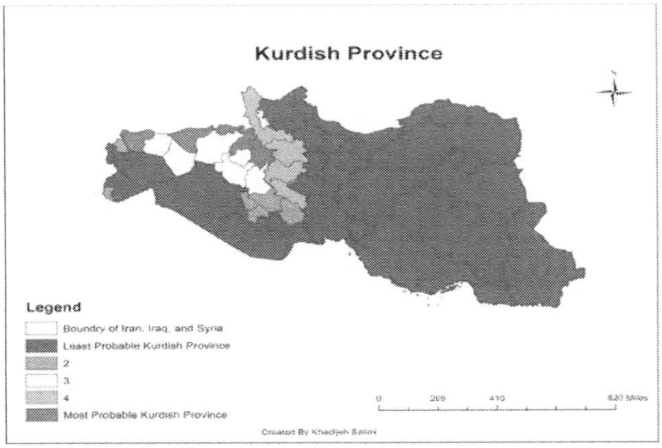

Figure 2. Scenario 2 map.

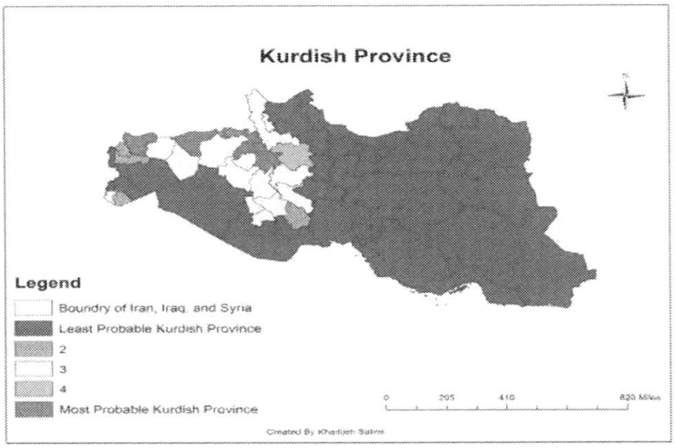

Figure 3. Scenario 3 map.

Putting equal weight on all four factors underestimates the importance of government control and being Kurdish and overestimates the importance of distance. In the first scenario, the northern part of Iraq—such as As-Sulaymaniyah, Arbil, and Dihok—and almost all northern parts of Syria—like Hasaka and Aleppo—are most probable to become engaged in the conflict. According to Figure 1, many parts of Iran—such as Sanandaj, Kermanshah, Ilam, and Azarbayejan Gharbi—and most parts of Iraq—like Al_Qadisiyah, Wasit, Babil, and Maysan—and parts of Syria—such as Idlib, Hamah, and Dara—have some potential to become engaged in the conflict, although Kurds do not populate those cities. This means equal weighting is not correct and underestimates the role of government and Kurdish nationalism while overestimating the role of distance. Thus, I decided to place more emphasis on the government and Kurdish population factors.

Table 2. Computational Results: Provinces by Tiered Probability of Conflict

Probability Rank	*Scenario 1*	*Scenario 2*	*Scenario 3*
First	Iraq: As-Sulaymaniyah, Arbil, Dihok Syria: Hasaka and Aleppo	Iraq: As-Sulaymaniyah, Arbil, Dihok Syria: Hasaka and Aleppo	Iraq: As-Sulaymaniyah, Arbil, and Dihok Syria: Hasaka and Aleppo
Second	Iraq: Diyala, Salah ad-Din, and Ninawa Syria: Ar-Raqqah and Deir AZ Azwr Iran: Sanandaj	Iran: Sanandaj, Ilam, Azarbayejan Gharbi, and Kermanshah	Iran: Sanandaj
Third	Iraq: Al-Qadisiyah, Wasit, Babil, and Maysan Syria: Idlib, Hamah, and Dara Iran: Kermanshah, Ilam, and Azarbayejan Gharbi	Iraq: Diyala, Kirkuk, Salah ad-Din, and Ninawa Syria: Dayr AZ Zawr and Ar Raqqa	Iraq: Diyala, Kirkuk, Salah ad-Din, Wasit, Al- Qadisiyah, Karbala, and Ninawa Syria: Dayr AZ Zawr, Ar Raqqa, and Dara Iran: Ilam, Azarbayejan Gharbi, and Kermanshah
Fourth	Iraq: Al-Anbar, Al-Basrah, An-Najaf, Karbala, and Al-Muthanna Syria: Rif Dimashq, Homs, Damascus, As Suwayada, and Tartus Iran: Tabriz, Ardabil, Rasht, Zanjan, Qazvin, Karaj, Tehran, Qum, Arak, Hamadan, Khoram Abad, and Ahwaz	Iraq: Wasit, Babil, Maysan, and Al-Qadisiyah Syria: Hamah, and Dara	Iraq: Maysan Syria: Suwayada and Hamah
Unlikely	Iran: Gorgan, Bojnoord, Mashhad, Semnan, Birjand, Zahedan, Bandar Abbas, Kerman, Yazd, Esfahan, Shahre Kurd, Shiraz, Bushehr, Qeshm, and Kish	Syria: Center and South Iran: All other provinces	Iraq: The whole Center Syria: The whole Soth Iran: All other Provinces

In the second scenario, the northern part of Iraq—such as As-Sulaymaniyah, Arbil, and Dihok—and most of the north part of Syria—such as Hasaka and Aleppo—are most probable to engage in conflict. Some Iranian cities—like Sanandaj, Ilam, Azarbayejan Gharbi, and Kermanshah—also have a good chance to become engaged in the conflict (Figure 2). However, putting a 60% weight on being Kurdish likely overestimates the importance of Kurdish identity and underestimates the role of religious tension among Shia and Sunni Kurds, especially in Iran. Thus, I decided to increase the weight of religion.

In the third scenario, northern Iraq—including As-Sulaymaniyah, Arbil, and Dihok—and the northern parts of Syria—including Hasaka and Aleppo—are most probable and only Sanandaj in Iran, populated by Sunni Kurds, has a good chance of becoming engaged in the conflict (Figure 3). However, the computational results show the same results as Scenario 2 in the highest probability and one city (Sanandaj) in the second rank. This overlap in results between Scenarios 2 and 3 is important because it means that the theory is likely robust to changes in the weighting factors. These provinces are likely to enter conflict no matter what.

It is important to mention the most recent situations at the time of writing as covered in global news indicate that Kurds have control over Afrin, Raqqa, Qamishli, and Hasaka in Syria, as well as control over As-Sulaymaniyah, Arbil, and Dihok (Chughtai, 2019). This is a cursory validation of the computational results. Indeed, Kurds in cities like Sanandaj, which the results show has a good chance of engaging in conflict, has, in reality, been continuously engaged in the conflict with the central government, but still does not have not control over the cities. The only exception in the results is Aleppo. However, factors such as the massive displacement in Syria and domestic war and regional powers' policy toward the war may be affecting those results.

Conclusion and Next Steps

The model results confirm existing theories about ethnic tensions. Kurdish identity, existing religious tension, and government hegemony all play a role in this ethnic conflict. However, the model is simple and general. Still, it is important to acknowledge that the purpose of building this model is to study a specific case study—a Kurdish conflict for independence—and it might apply to other conflicts with further consideration. To study other ethnic conflicts, modelers might consider economic factors as well, or they may try different scenarios. Future versions of this model should incorporate the effects of the ongoing Syrian displacement, adding Turkey to the case study, considering role of superpowers in the conflict, and using sensitivity analysis on the weighting of factors to understand how the weights affect the model outcomes.

Different groups might benefit from the result of this model: pro-Kurdish movements within the government that try to resolve the conflict, anti-Kurdish movements within the government, and Kurds themselves. Visually-based computational results provide the opportunity for Kurds and pro-government groups to study the results of this model and perhaps use it as a foundation for policy dialogue. This may provide Kurds and pro-government groups with methods to solve the religious tension among Kurds, and the emphasis on Kurdish nationalism might assist to alleviate this long-lasting conflict in the area. In contrast, this may help anti-government groups realize how a stable government is a crucial factor to secure border integrity and national security. Indeed, this model can help policymakers see the cities in which they might employ stronger control.

References

Arjomand, S. A. (1993). *The political dimensions of religion*: Suny Press.

Ashcroft, B., Griffiths, G., & Tiffin, H. (2013). *Post-colonial studies: The key concepts*: Routledge.

Bates, R. H., Epstein, D. L., Goldstone, J. A., Gurr, T. R., Harff, B., Kahl, C. H., ... Marshall, M. G. J. M., VA: Science Applications International Corporation. (2003). Political instability task force report: Phase IV findings.

Besançon, M. L. (2005). Relative resources: Inequality in ethnic wars, revolutions, and genocides. *42*(4), 393-415.

Billon, P. (2015). Oil, secession and the future of Iraqi federalism. *22*(1), 68-76.

Chughtai, A. (2019, 13 March). Syria's war: Who controls what? *Aljazeera*.

Davies, J. C. (1962). Toward a theory of revolution. 5-19.

Eisenstadt, S. N. (1993). Religion and the civilizational dimensions of politics. *The Political Dimensions of Religion*, 13-41.

Eriksen, T. H. (2002). *Ethnicity and nationalism: Anthropological perspectives*: Pluto Press.

Fox. (2002). Ethnic minorities and the clash of civilizations: A quantitative analysis of Huntington's thesis. *32*(3), 415-434.

Fox. (2004). The rise of religious nationalism and conflict: Ethnic conflict and revolutionary wars, 1945-2001. *41*(6), 715-731.

Fox, J. (2004). Is ethnoreligious conflict a contagious disease? *Studies in Conflict & Terrorism, 27*(2), 89-106.

Glavin, T. (2015). No friends but the mountains: The fate of the Kurds. *World Affairs*, 57-66.

Gurr, T. R. (1993). Why minorities rebel: A global analysis of communal mobilization and conflict since 1945. *14*(2), 161-201.

Hill, S., & Rothchild, D. J. (1986). The contagion of political conflict in Africa and the world. *30*(4), 716-735.

Humphreys, M. J. (2005). Natural resources, conflict, and conflict resolution: Uncovering the mechanisms. *49*(4), 508-537.

Huntington, S. P. (1993). The Clash of Civilizations? *Foreign Affairs*

Klingman, D. J. (1980). Temporal and spatial diffusion in the comparative analysis of social change. *74*(1), 123-137.

McGarry, J., & O'Leary, B. (1994). The political regulation of national and ethnic conflict. *47*, 94-94.

Nader, A., Hanauer, L., Allen, B., & Scotten, A. G. (2016). *Regional implications of an independent Kurdistan*. Retrieved from

Nagel, J. J. (1974). Inequality and discontent: a nonlinear hypothesis. *26*(4), 453-472.

Osaghae, E. E. (1998). Managing multiple minority problems in a divided society: The Nigerian experience. *36*(1), 1-24.

Rubin, M. (2007). Review of The Kurdish Nationalist Movement.

Rummel, R. J. (1997). Is collective violence correlated with social pluralism? , *34*(2), 163-175.

Russett, B. M., Oneal, J. R., & Cox, M. J. (2000). Clash of civilizations, or realism and liberalism déjà vu? Some evidence. *37*(5), 583-608.

Sadowski, Y. J. (1998). Ethnic conflict. 12-23.

Van Bruinessen, M. (1986). The Kurds between Iran and Iraq. (141), 14-27.

Yusoff, M. A., & Sarjoon, A. Ethnicity, Ethnic Minority and Self-Determination: An Examination of Conceptual Linkage.

System Structure of Agent-Based Model Responsible for Reproducing Business Cycles and the Effect of Tax Reduction on GDP

Shigeaki Ogibayashi
Chiba Institute of Technology
ogibayashi@ogi-lab.net

Kosei Takashima
Nagoya College of Child Welfare, Care Worker & Business
kosei.takashima.of@gmail.com

ABSTRACT

Validation is an important issue in the agent-based modelling (ABM) approach. It has been argued in the literature that deriving the necessary conditions for reproducing specific macro behavior is difficult due to the functional complexity of the models. However, based on our experience in ABM, we believe it is possible to define the necessary conditions for reproducing each macro behavior if we use the structure of the system to express the input conditions. Conducting a series of computer experiments to verify this idea, the present study analyzes business cycles and the effect of tax reductions on gross domestic product (GDP) as examples of fundamental macro behaviors of economic systems. The results indicate that the essential model structures for reproducing business cycles and the effects of tax reduction are the inclusions of credit creation for investment and factors relating to the inefficiency of the government's, household's, and firms' expenditures.

Keywords: agent-based modeling; model structure; business cycle; tax reduction; inefficiency of government expenditure; validity of model

Estructura del sistema del modelo basado en el agente responsable de reproducir los ciclos económicos y el efecto de la reducción de impuestos sobre el PIB

Resumen

La validación ha sido un tema importante en el enfoque de modelado basado en agentes (ABM). Se ha argumentado en la literatura que derivar las condiciones necesarias para reproducir un comportamiento macro específico es difícil debido a la complejidad funcional de los modelos. Sin embargo, según nuestra experiencia en ABM, creemos que es posible definir las condiciones necesarias para reproducir cada comportamiento macro si utilizamos la estructura del sistema para expresar las condiciones de entrada. Realizando una serie de experimentos informáticos para verificar esta idea, el presente estudio analiza los ciclos económicos y el efecto de las reducciones de impuestos sobre el producto interno bruto (PIB) como ejemplos de comportamientos macro fundamentales de los sistemas económicos. Los resultados indican que las estructuras modelo esenciales para reproducir los ciclos económicos y los efectos de la reducción de impuestos son las inclusiones de la creación de crédito para la inversión y los factores relacionados con la ineficiencia de los gastos del gobierno, los hogares y las empresas, respectivamente.

Palabras clave: modelado basado en agentes; estructura modelo; ciclo comercial; reducción de impuestos; ineficiencia del gasto público; validez del modelo

基于agent建模的系统架构：复制商业周期和减税对GDP产生的效果

摘要

有效性一直是基于agent的建模（ABM）方法中的重要议题。相关文献中曾探讨过：鉴于模型的功能复杂性，获取“复制特定宏观行为”的必要条件并不简单。然而，基于我们对ABM的研究经历，我们相信，如果使用系统架构来表达输入条件，那么“复制每种宏观行为”的必要条件是有可能被定义的。通过一系列计算机实验来验证该想法，本研究分析了商业周期、和减税对国内生产总值（GDP）产生的效果，将二者作为经济体系的重要宏观行为实例。研究结果表明，复制商业周期和减税效果，必需的模型架构包括投资信用产生、和分别与政府开支低效、家庭开支低效、企业开支低效有关的各因素。

关键词：基于agent建模；模型架构；商业周期；减税；低效政府开支；模型有效性

1. Introduction

Agent-based modeling (ABM) is a bottom-up modeling method in which we view artificial, computer-generated societies as laboratories where we attempt to grow specific social structures (Epstein & Axtell, 1996). The purpose of these models is to discover the fundamental local or micro-mechanisms that generate macroscopic social structures and collective behaviors (Epstein & Axtell, 1996). Although ABM is a promising methodology that can deal with heterogeneity, individual agents' bounded rationality, and non-equilibrium dynamics in social systems, validation still proves to be a significant issue. As pointed out in the literature (Ormerod & Rosewell, 2009), one common criticism by economists could be stated as follows, "you have presented one set of behavioral rules to explain your chosen phenomenon, but there must be many such sets which produce the same result, so how do you know yours is correct?" (p. 10). Some economists even go so far as to imply that it is excessively easy to construct an agent-based model that produces desired phenomena. As argued by Marks (2007), the problem behind this criticism is the functional complexity inherent in ABM. It has also been argued that macro behaviors may be insensitive to many micro variables; and, as a result, it would be difficult to derive the necessary conditions for the model to exhibit specific macro behaviors (Marks, 2007). The severity of this problem increases when the model is described with detail and realism, as this requires more variables and higher degrees of freedom (Marks, 2007). For this reason, the model should be as simple as possible, and even then, it would be difficult to achieve quantitative predictions.

When input conditions are expressed by specific values of micro variables or parameters, there is a great deal of freedom, as pointed out in the literature (Marks, 2007). However, it should also be noted that the freedom of input conditions decreases if they are expressed by the system structure of the model (i.e., model structure) (Ogibayashi & Takashima, 2014). Here, the model structure is defined as the set of the types of agents, their behavioral rules, and the relevant attributes variables. Consequently, it would be considered possible to specify the necessary conditions in the model structure to reproduce the specific macro behavior. This idea is consistent with the argument of Ormerod and Rosewell (2009), who pointed out that the current method used to build ABMs is a process of discovering the behavioral rules for agents that appear to be consistent with the phenomena we observe.

In this context, we believe that, although the model should be as simple as possible (based on the KISS Principle; Terano, 2008), it is also important to consider all of the factors required to reproduce the desired phenomena. That is, the model structure should be the same as, or similar to, the real system for the characteristics to emerge as they do in the real world. The factors essential for reproducing the desired characteristics of the system can be discovered by running a series of computer experiments in which only one constituent element of the model is changed at a time (Ogibayashi & Takashima, 2014).

Although many ABM research studies have focused on macroeconomic aspects, these studies have not fully clarified the structural factors necessary for their reproduction.

Motivated by this deficiency, the authors have constructed a simple, artificial economic model, consisting of consumers, three types of producers, a bank, and a government (some of which were reported in previous studies: e.g., Ogibayashi & Takashima, 2010 & 2014; Takashima, Kato, & Ogibayashi, 2014).

In the present study, some additional simulations are conducted to clarify the model structure necessary for reproducing business cycles and an increase in GDP caused by a tax reduction (which we take as examples of basic macro behaviors in a goods market). A series of simulation experiments are systematically conducted, changing the input conditions one by one, where the simulation program is constructed using C++. The study focuses on finding the model structure necessary to reproduce the above-mentioned macroeconomic phenomena.

2. The Model

2.1 Outline of the Model

The agent-based model of the artificial economic system in the present study includes consumers, producers, a bank, and a government as autonomous decision-making agents. The type of agents and their behavioral rules are shown in Table 1, which are changed depending on the experimental levels. Consumers are divided into three types of agents: workers as the base type, executives who are included or not in the model in the analysis of the effect of corporate tax reduction and public workers when the government is taken into account in the study of the effect of tax reduction. Producers are divided into three types of agents as shown in Table 1. Markets are also divided into three types: a goods market as the base type, which includes the markets for consumer goods and material goods, a stock market when it is taken into account in the analysis of business cycles and a labor market when it is taken into account in the study of the effect of tax reduction.

Each agent is heterogeneous in its state variables as well as in the other parameters included in their behavioral rules.

2.2 Sequence of Actions

The set of activities of each agent constitutes period-based units, where one period is assumed to correspond to one month in the real system. During each period, agents act according to the sequence of eight steps. At the end of the series of actions in each period, a GDP value is calculated based on an input-output table obtained by summing each agent's account data. The eight steps dictating the agents' actions are as follows:

1. Agents pay any unpaid tax from the previous period. After paying taxes, agents create a budget plan for consumption, paying wages, or public spending.

2. Raw material producers decide on the quantity and price of products to be produced, produce several types of raw materials, and supply these to the material goods market.

3. Retailers decide on the quantity and price of products to be produced, purchase raw materials in the material goods market, produce several types of consumer goods, and supply these products to the consumer goods market.

4. Consumers, retailers, raw material producers, and the government purchase products in the consumer goods market.

5. Each firm pays wages to employees and executive compensation to the executives while the government pays salaries to public workers.

6. Retailers and raw material producers consider expanding production capacity based on total sales in the previous periods, and, if necessary, they decide to invest in expansion by buying new equipment from the equipment manufacturer. When the labor market is taken into account in the model, employing a new worker is another alternative for them to expand production capacity, which is to be chosen depending on the financial merit.

7. When the model includes a stock market, consumers buy or sell stocks aiming to increase their financial assets.

8. Each agent settles its accounts using the double-entry bookkeeping method. They calculate their income and profit for the current term and then determine the amount of tax to be paid based on these figures.

Table 1. *Outline of Agents and Their Behavioral Rules*

Agent	Type	Output to be supplied	Product type to purchase	Outline of behavioral rules
Consumer	Worker	The labor force for firms	Consumer goods	Consumers work and obtain the wage from the producer, bank, or government, pay tax, and purchase consumer goods. A part of the income will be deposited in the bank account as per the Keynesian consumption function. Buying consumer goods is performed according to the utility that each consumer uniquely holds. Consumers transact in the stock market, aiming to increase their assets when the model includes the stock market.
	Executive	Management for firms		
	Public workers	The labor force for government		
Enterprise				Enterprises employ consumers, get profits from operating activities, and pay wages and tax.
Producer				Producers supply and sell products in the goods market.
	Retailer	Consumption goods	Consumer goods, Materials, Equipment	Retailers and raw material makers decide both the quantity and price of each class of product to be produced based on the number of goods in stock. If necessary, they invest in equipment based on the demand to expand production capacity.
	Raw material maker	Material goods	Consumer goods, Equipment	
	Equipment maker	Equipment	-	
Bank	Bank	The fund for producers' investment	-	The bank keeps the surplus money of other agents in their respective bank accounts and lends money to firms for investment.
Government	Government	Redistribution of wealth	Consumer goods	The government collects tax from other agents, pays wages to public workers and spends the remaining money on public expenditure.

2.3 Outline of Agent's Decision-Making Rules

2.3.1 Behavioral rules of consumers

Consumers create a budget for consumption E_b^t. This budget is calculated by adding after-tax income $I^t(1-r_{i\_tax})$, which represents the Keynesian consumption function (Keynes, 1936), to the money withdrawn from the deposit described as their bank deposit $\boldsymbol{D^t}$ multiplied by a withdrawal ratio $\boldsymbol{r_{wd}}$ at each fiscal period $\boldsymbol{t}$. The formula for the budget is shown in Equation (1). Here, $\boldsymbol{r_{i\_tax}}$ is the income tax rate, $\boldsymbol{a}$ is the consumer's autonomous consumption, and $\boldsymbol{b}$ is the marginal propensity to consume as per the Keynesian consumption function. The withdrawal ratio $\boldsymbol{r_{wd}}$ is selected randomly for each agent during each period.

$$E_b^t=a+bI^t(1-r_{i\_tax})+r_{wd}^tD^t \quad (1)$$

When purchasing products in the consumer market, consumers select goods based on their utility and affordability (as determined by the utility function for each class of products and the agent's budget constraint, respectively). Moreover, when a stock market is included in the model as an experimental level to analyze the reproducibility of business cycles, consumers buy or sell stocks aiming to increase their financial assets. Takashima et al. (2014) described consumers' action rules in the stock market in detail.

2.3.2 Behavioral rules of producers

The retailers and raw material producers both decide the quantity and price of their product at the beginning of each period. The price of each product is increased or decreased depending on the number of goods they held in stock at the end of previous period. The quantity to be produced is decided in such a way that the probability of being out of stock must be less than 5%; this is estimated based on total sales from the last ten periods.

The production capacity $\boldsymbol{Y}$ is defined by the Cobb-Douglas function (as shown in Equation (2)), where $\boldsymbol{K}$ is the number of units of capital equipment, $\boldsymbol{L}$ is the number of employees, and α is assumed to be 0.25. Besides, $\boldsymbol{A}$ is a bounded proportionality constant representing the total factor productivity that is randomly assigned being assumed to be unique to each producer $\boldsymbol{i}$.

$$Y_i(K,L)=A_iK^{\alpha}L^{1-\alpha} \quad (2)$$

Retailers and raw material producers initially have one unit of equipment and a specified number of employees. They will invest to increase their production capacity when their products produced at maximum production capacity continued to be sold out during a specified number of periods. When the model includes the labor market as an experimental level, they have two choices for performing investment: buying a piece of equipment from the equipment manufacturer or employing a new worker from the labor market, depending on the financial merit.

When investing in equipment, they may finance the funds by either borrowing from the bank, issuing new shares in the stock market, using their internal funds, or using some combination thereof. The funds financed by the bank are repaid with interest in equal-sized payments each period for a constant number of consecutive periods. An upper limit of the number of loans is placed on total investment so that, during the repayment period, additional financing will be limited. The equipment manufacturer produces equipment following the requirements of retailers and raw material producers as long as it is within their capacity. In the present study, the price of equipment is assumed to be constant. The decision-making rules for investment and financing were described previously (Takashima et al., 2014).

One executive and several workers are initially assigned to each of the producer agents. The producers pay wages to workers and wages plus executive compensation to the executive in each period. The executive compensation comprises a salary, a bonus, and long-term incentives. Wages comprise a fixed salary and a bonus, which are randomly assigned to each employee between a lower and an upper limit. The bonus is assumed to be paid only when the producer's profit is positive.

2.3.3 Behavioral rules of the bank

The bank lends money in the form of long-term loans to producers (in line with their demands for investment), charging a 3% interest rate. The bank also lends money to producers in the form of short-term loans so that they may meet their requirements when their working capital to pay fixed wages and or purchase raw materials becomes sufficiently depleted. In the present study, the bank is initially given a massive quantity of funds so that there is no limitation on lending to producers, except in the case where the firm applying for a loan has already borrowed funds being during the repayment period, and the number of loans has already reached the upper limit. This limitation of borrowing especially restricts the investment when the upper limit of the number of loans is assumed to be one, which is the case of the base model.

2.3.4 Behavioral rules of government

The government collects corporate and income taxes, pays wages to public employees, and uses the surplus funds for public expenditure, as dictated by their expenditure policy. Public employees' salaries are calculated in each fiscal period so that they are equal to the average income of private employees.

Concerning expenditure policies, the study tests market purchasing, subsidies for firms, and combinations thereof. Market purchasing is an extreme form of efficient public expenditure in which the government directly purchases goods at the market price. This policy corresponds to the government placing job orders with firms at the market price in an entirely competitive situation. The subsidy for firms is an extreme form of inefficient public expenditure in which the government distributes funds to producers, without any limitations on their use. In this case, most of the funds distributed could be transferred to the bank account without being used in the market. This policy corresponds to the government placing job orders at a value far above the market price or paying money for jobs that have no economic value. The ratio of the expenditure for the subsidy for firms to the total spending is defined as the inefficiency of government expenditure.

3. Simulation Conditions

The simulation conditions as experimental levels are divided into two categories, as shown in Table 2: analyses of the reproducibility of periodic changes in GDP (i.e., business cycles) and the positive effects of tax reductions on GDP.

In the former experiment, producers' decision-making processes regarding investment in equipment and the means of financing said equipment are changed as input conditions to find the necessary model structure for reproducing periodic change in GDP (i.e., a business cycle). The changes in consumers' wages and the amount of money spent on investing in equipment are also analyzed. The criteria of the producers' decision-making on investment as experimental levels include the case based on demand, the case without investment, the case with random investment at a fixed interval, and the criterion based on internal rate of return. In the case based on internal rate of return, the producers decide to invest when the internal rate of return is expected to be greater than the interest rate, which is assumed to be constant. This criterion on investment corresponds to the case of decision-making based on the marginal efficiency of capital proposed by Keynes (1936). Here, the internal rate of return is calculated using the expected value of the investment's marginal productivity, the price of the product, and the operating ratio of the equipment. The life of the equipment is assumed to be 60, and the price of the equipment is assumed to be $\boldsymbol{EP^{t+1}=EP^{t}(1+0.1(O^{t}/Y))}$, where $\boldsymbol{EP^{t}}$ is the price of the equipment in period $\boldsymbol{t}$, $\boldsymbol{O^{t}}$ is the number of equipment orders received in period $\boldsymbol{t}$, and $\boldsymbol{Y}$ is the production capacity of the equipment manufacturer. The means of financing the funds for buying one unit of equipment as experimental levels include the case with bank financing, the case with internal funds, the case with the issuance of stock, and the combination of them. In the base model, funds for investment are assumed to be financed from the bank in half and internal funds in half.

Thus, the factors relating to the model structure changed in the former experiment are decision-making rules on investment and financing rules for investment, including the experimental levels of four and three, respectively.

In the latter experiment, government and executives are added to the base model as additional agents and consumers are divided into the public and private workers and executives. Paying tax is added to the base model as additional behavioral rules for consumers who pay income tax and for firms who pay corporate tax. Paying executive compensation is also added as an additional behavioral rule for firms. The firms' decision-making on investment is assumed to be based on demand, and the necessary funds are assumed to be financed from the bank in half and internal funds in half. The upper limit of the number of loans is also changed from one to three as an experimental level to clarify the influence of the mitigation of credit rationing on the positive effect of corporate tax reduction on GDP. The behavioral rules of government are also added to the base model, which are characterized by the inefficiency of government expenditure, as described in the previous section. The inefficiency of government expenditure is changed between 0% and 100%, with 10% intervals.

In this study, the influence of the inclusion of a labor market is also analyzed as one of the experimental levels because it is well known that corporate tax reduction results in reducing unemployment in the real system (Sakuma, Masujima, Maeda, Fukawa, & Iwamoto, 2011), which could contribute the emergence of the positive influence of corporate tax reduction. In the model taking into account the existence of labor market, it is additionally assumed that the firm can decide either to invest in equipment or to employ a new worker depending on the financial merit when it needs to expand the production capacity. In the latter case, the firm puts a help-wanted advertisement in the labor market to employ a new worker. On the other hand, if a firm goes bankrupt, the workers in the firm become out of work, applying for a new job in the labor market, while getting unemployment benefits from the government.

The parameter values changed to analyze the influence of the factors mentioned above on GDP are the followings. For the analysis of the income tax rate, income tax rate is varied between 10 and 30%, with a 5% interval, corporate tax rate is assumed to be 20%, executive compensation is changed between 0 and 0.5, and the withdrawal ratio is varied between 0 and the maximum value, which is assumed to be 0.2, 0.5, or 0.8. Changing the withdrawal ratio corresponds to altering the levels of the marginal propensity to consume, as given in Equation (1). For the analysis of corporate tax reduction, the corporate tax rate is changed between 10% and 30%, with a 5% interval, the income tax rate is assumed to be 20%, executive compensation is changed to 0.75, 0.85, and 0.95, and the withdrawal ratio is changed between 0 and 0.5. The inefficiency of government expenditure is varied between 0% and 100%, with a 10% interval for both analyses.

Thus, the factors relating to the model structure changed in the latter experiment are the inefficiency of government expenditure, the inclusion of executive compensation, the use of internal funds for investment, the upper limit of the number of loans (i.e., mitigation of credit rationing), and the inclusion of labor market.

Table 2. *Simulation Conditions for the Experiment in Which Factors Relating to the Model Structure Are Changed As Input Conditions*

		Structure of basic model	Analysis of reproducing the periodic change of GDP			Analysis of reproducing the influence of tax reduction
			Analysis of investment rules	Analysis of financing rules	Analysis of MEC model	
Agent	Government	Without	Without			With
	Executives	Without	Without			With/Without
	Others	With	With			With
Rules of producers	The decision-making rule of equipment investment	Based on demand	No investment / Fixed interval	Based on demand	Based on an internal rate of return	Based on demand
	The rule of financing	Loan and internal funds	Loan	Using internal funds/issuance of stock	Using internal funds	Loan and internal funds
	The rule of executive compensation	Without	Without			With/without
	The deletion of equipment	Without	Without		With	Without
	The price of equipment	Fixed	Fixed		Variable	Fixed
	The upper limit on the number of loans	One	One		Unlimited	One/three
Rules of consumers	The rule of deposit withdrawal	With	With			With/without
Rules of government	Taxation	Without	Without			With
	Inefficiency of government expenditure	Without	Without			With
Market	Goods market	With	With			With
	Stock market	Without	Without	Without	Without	Without
	Labor market	Without	Without			With/without

Those factors relating to the model structure (such as the type of agents, their behavioral rules including relevant attributes variables) are systematically changed one by one in the simulation to elucidate their effect on the tendency of the emergence of business cycles, positive influence of the reductions in income tax rate, and corporate tax rate on GDP.

4. Simulation Results

4.1 The Necessary Model Structure for Reproducing Business Cycles

Figures 1(a), 1(b), and 2 show the simulated results under the base model condition, in which it is assumed that investment decision-making is conducted based on demand, and the necessary funds for investment are financed from the bank with fixed repayment periods in half and internal funds in half. Here, it is confirmed that the inclusion of internal funds is not essential because similar results are obtained in the case with bank financing only. Figures 1(a) and 1(b) show that the cyclical changes in GDP, which incorporate the synchronized movements in the average price of consumption goods and average consumer income, are reproduced showing the emergence of business cycles. Moreover, the level of aggregate funds for investment is high during the period of a booming economy where GDP is increasing (see Figure 1(a)). An increase in investment also results in an increase in the level of workers' wages at equipment makers during the same period of a booming economy, which induces the following increase in the level of workers' salaries at retailers, as shown in Figure 2.

From these results, the business cycle mechanism reproduced by the base model is as follows. In the beginning periods of the booming stage, some firms with strong sales decide to invest in equipment, causing an increase in the wage levels of workers at equipment makers, which induces an increase in demand, wages, and other firms' investment at the aggregate level. After the majority of producers have made their investments, the total

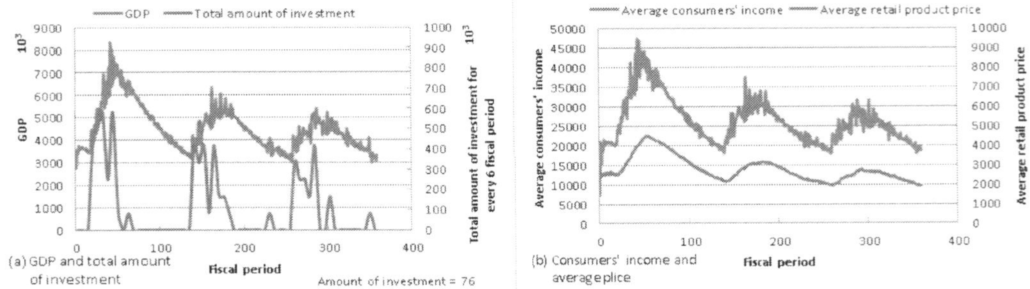

Figure 1. Change in GDP and total amount of investment (Panel a) and average consumer income and average consumer price over time (Panel b) under the conditions of the base model (bank financing and investment decision-making on the basis of demand).

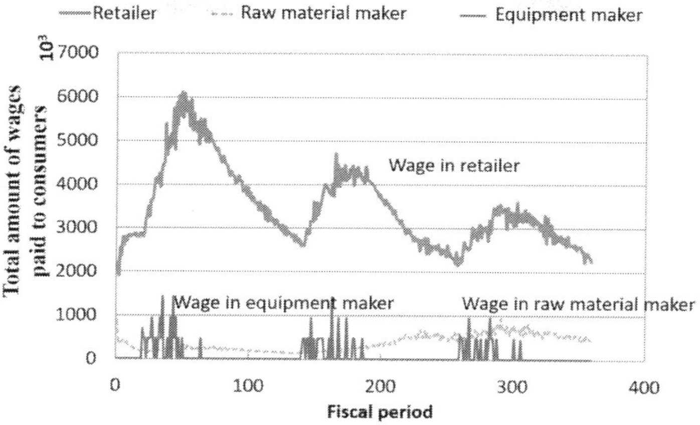

Figure 2. Change over time in consumer's wage over time under the condition of the base model (bank financing and investment decision-making on the basis of demand).

amount of repayment per period becomes more significant than the total amount of borrowing because of credit rationing. This flow of funds from the market to the bank induces a decrease in total sales, workers' wages, and investments, thus resulting in a recession. The details of this flow of funds were described previously (Ogibayashi & Takashima, 2010).

When we assume that producers either do not invest (i.e., there is no debt) or conduct investment randomly, with no regard to total sales, then there is no periodic change in GDP (as shown in Figure 3). Therefore, we can conclude that the model must incorporate endogenous decision-making about capital investment based on demand to reproduce business cycles.

Financing from the bank (i.e., the existence of loans) is another essential condition for reproducing business cycles. When investment is financed by the issuance of new shares in the stock market without borrowing from the bank, periodic changes in GDP (i.e., business cycles) do not emerge, as shown in Figure 3 (see the case involving financing by the issuance of stock in Figure 3). The absence of business cycles in the case of financing by the issuance of stock is because there is almost no specific restriction for conducting additional investment with respect to funding.

When only internal funds finance investment, GDP shows slight cyclical variations, as shown in Figure 4(a). This variation in GDP incorporates cyclical fluctuations in the average price of products (i.e., consumer price) and consumers' income, as shown in Figure 4(b), indicating that the variation in GDP shows a kind of business cycle that is caused by the requirement for the time interval for firms to raise funds for additional investment. However, financing by internal funds is not considered a major cause of business cycles, because the amplitudes of the

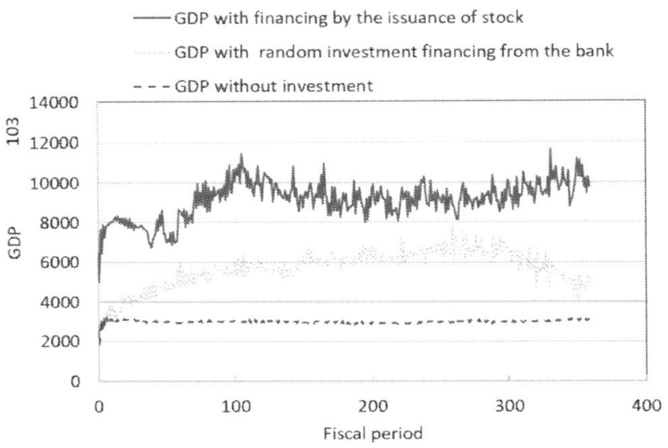

Figure 3. Changes in GDP over time in the cases without investment, with random investment financed from the bank, and with demand-based investment financed by the issuance of stock.

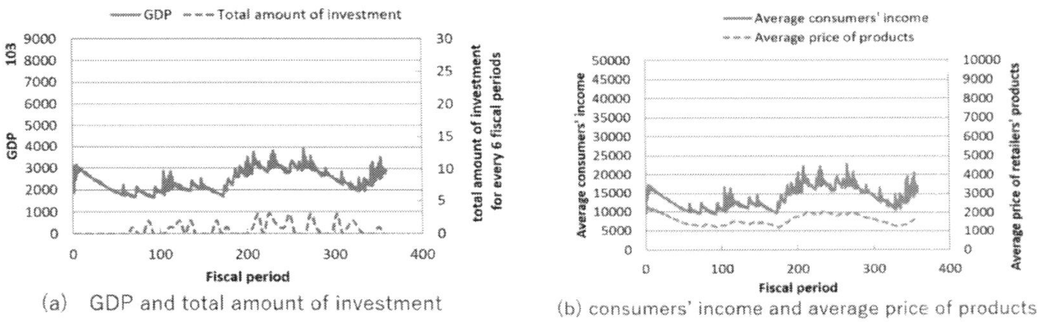

Figure 4. Changes over time in GDP and the total amount of investment (Panel a) and average consumers' income and the average price of retailers' products (Panel b) in the case with demand-based investment financed only by internal funds.

variations in GDP and in consumers' income and price are very small and the period correspondence between GDP and the amount of investment is not clear compared to those in the case with bank financing.

Therefore, in an agent-based model in which producers' production and pricing activities and consumers' buying and working activities are already included, it is concluded that the essential conditions for reproducing business cycles would be the inclusion of bank financing and demand-based investment decision-making in the model structure.

On the other hand, Keynes (1936) proposed that the marginal efficiency of capital (MEC) is the primary determinant of the business cycle. This, in turn, implies that the internal rate of return is the essential factor underlying business cycles. Following this reasoning, an additional experiment was conducted in which producers decide to invest when the internal rate of return is expected to be greater than the current interest rate and the funds for investment are assumed to be financed by internal funds only (i.e., without bank financing). Calculated chronological change in GDP and average price of products indicates that the cyclical variations, namely business cycles, do not emerge under this experimental condition, as shown in Figure 5. Not that the price of equipment as well as internal rate of return also do not show cyclical variations, as shown in Figure 6. The primary reason for this is that there is little to no change in the aggregate capacity of supply. Decreases in production capacity suffered by some producers due to the scrapping of equipment are balanced out by the surpluses of others. As such, without bank financing, variation in production capacity due to the scrapping of or investment in equipment cannot, by itself, influence the price of the retail product or the expected return. Therefore, marginal efficiency of capital is not considered a major factor for generating business cycles when there is any degree of surplus in the aggregate production capacity.

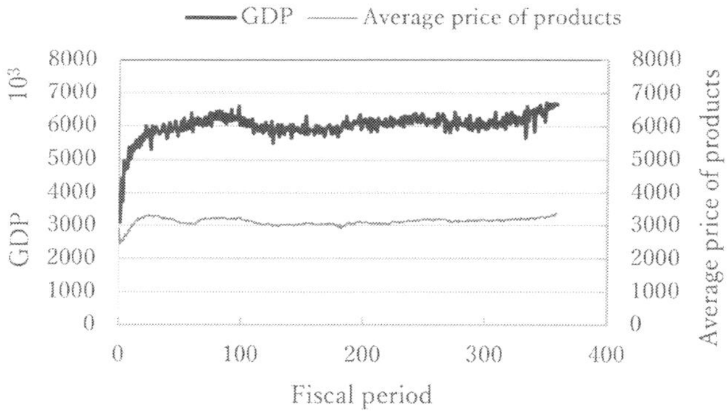

Figure 5. Changes over time in GDP and the average price of products in the case with financing by internal funds only, where investment is judged based on the internal rate of return.

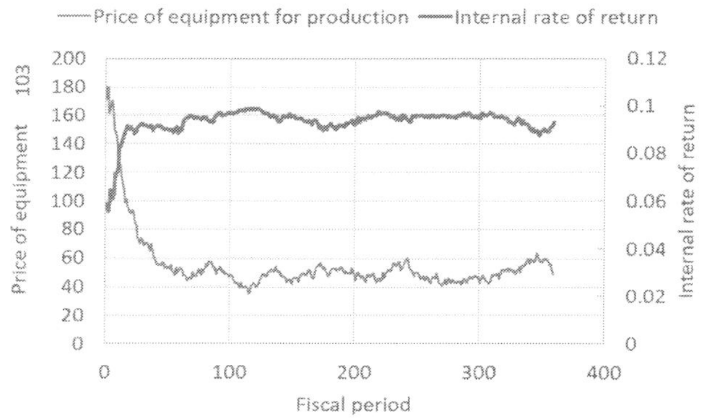

Figure 6. Changes in the price of equipment and internal rate of return over time.

4.2 The Necessary Model Structure for Reproducing the Influence of a Reduction in Income and Corporate Taxes on GDP

The calculated relationship between the income tax rate and GDP is shown in Figure 7(a). Note that the negative correlation between the income tax rate and GDP is only reproduced when some inefficiency exists in government expenditure. Note also that the critical inefficiency level at which the correlation changes from positive to negative decreases when the substantial marginal rate of consumption of consumers, which is dependent on the withdrawal ratio on bank deposits and the existence of executives, increases. This result indicates that the negative correlation between the income tax rate and GDP is more likely to occur when the inefficiency in government expenditure is large enough even if the rate of consumption of consumers is small enough.

On the contrary, if government expenditure is 100% efficient, GDP increases with an increase in tax rate as shown in Figure 7(a). As the efficiency (i.e., 1-inefficiency) of government expenditure corresponds to the government's marginal propensity to consume, the reason for this tendency is as follows. If the efficiency in government expenditure is larger than the consumers' marginal propensity to consume, some consumers' money to be deposited in the bank will be transferred to the government by taxation and then consumed in the market, leading to an increase in GDP with an increased tax rate.

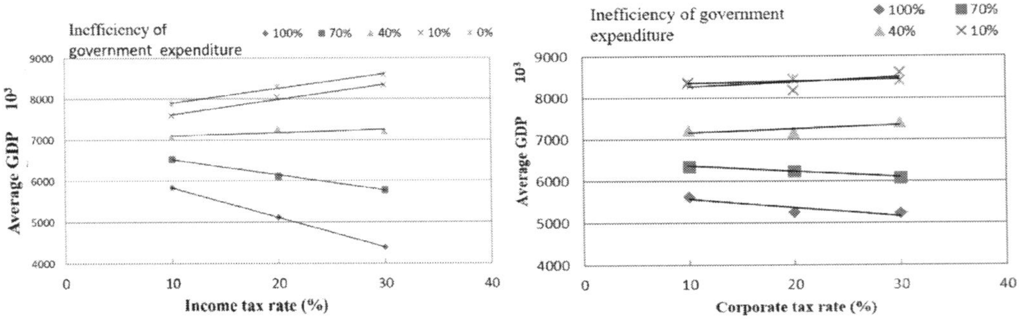

(a) Relationship between GDP and Income tax rate (b) Relationship between GDP and corporate tax rate

Figure 7. Influence of inefficiency of government expenditure on the relationship between GDP and income tax rate (Panel a) and corporate tax rate (Panel b). In the latter case, executive compensation, the use of internal funds for investment, and the mitigation of credit rationing are taken into account.

Thus, it is concluded that a necessary condition for the model to reproduce the positive effect of income-tax reduction on GDP is that some inefficiency exists in government expenditure. Moreover, the underline mechanism of the positive effect of tax reduction is as follows. When the substantial marginal propensity to consume of the government is smaller than that of consumers, some consumers' money to be transferred to the government by taxation is consumed in the market due to the income tax reduction, thus leading to an increase in GDP with a decreased tax rate.

In the case of corporate tax, the inefficiency of government expenditure is also a necessary factor to reproduce the negative correlation between the corporate tax rate and GDP (i.e., positive effect of corporate tax reduction on GDP) as shown in Figure 7(b). However, some additional factors are required in the model to reproduce the positive effect of corporate tax reduction.

These include executive compensation, the use of internal funds for investment, and an increase in the upper limit of the number of loans (i.e., mitigation of credit rationing). Figures 8(a) and 8(b) show the effect of executive compensation, the use of internal funds for investment, and bank financing on the relationship between corporate tax rate and GDP. Here, the upper limit of the number of loans is assumed to be 3 and the inefficiency of government expenditure is assumed to be 0.3. Figure 8 shows that the negative relationship between corporate tax and GDP occurs only when executive compensation, the use of internal funds for investment, and the inefficiency of government expenditures are included in the model. An increase in the upper limit of the number of loans (i.e., mitigation of credit rationing) is another necessary condition to reproduce the positive effect of tax reduction.

Figure 9 shows the influence of the upper limit of the number of loans on the relationships between corporate tax rate and GDP (see Figure 9(a)) and the number of investments (see Figure 9(b)) when both executive compensation and financing using internal funds are included in the model and the inefficiency of government expenditure is assumed to be 0.3. Note that negative relationships between the corporate tax rate and GDP and the number of investments are only reproduced when the upper limit of the number of loans is 3 (i.e., mitigation of credit rationing is applied).

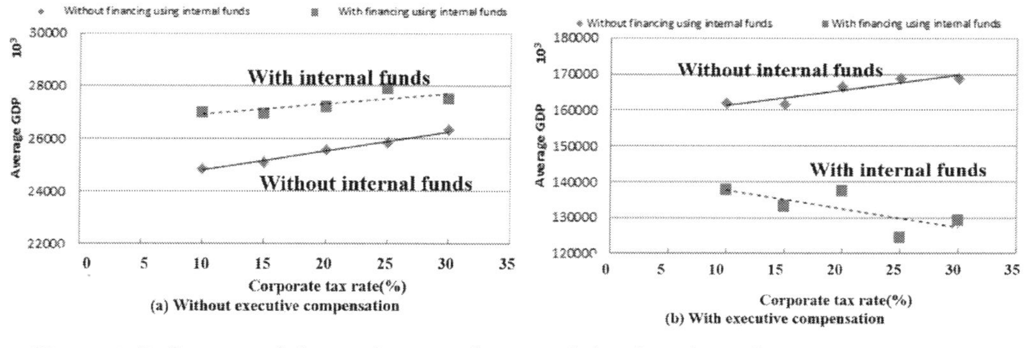

Figure 8. Influence of the inclusion of internal funds rule and executive compensation rule on the relationship between the GDP and corporate tax rate, where assumed inefficiency of government expenditure is 0.3, and the upper limit of the number of loans is 3.

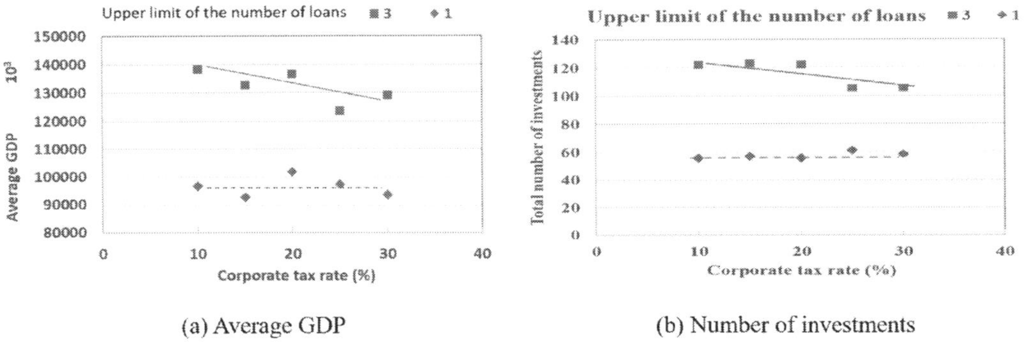

Figure 9. Influence of the upper limit of the number of loans on the relationships between corporate tax rate and GDP (Panel a) and total number of investment (Panel b).

In this study, the influence of the labor market is also analyzed. However, as shown in Figure 10, the positive effect of corporate tax reduction is reproduced without depending on the inclusion of the labor market, if the four factors mentioned above are already included in the model. Thus, we conclude that inclusion of the labor market is not a required condition for reproducing the positive influence of corporate tax reduction.

In sum, it is concluded that four factors—the inefficiency of government expenditure, executive compensation, the use of internal funds for investment, and an increase in the upper limit of the number of loans (i.e., mitigation of credit rationing)—must be included in the model to reproduce the negative correlation between the corporate tax rate and GDP. If any one of these factors is not included, the positive effect of corporate tax reduction cannot be reproduced. In other words, among the 16 possible combinations that include or exclude each of these four factors, only one case in which all four factors are included successfully reproduced the positive effect of corporate tax reduction. Although we considered before the experiment that unemployment levels could affect the influence of tax reduction, the results show that the negative correlation between GDP and the corporate tax rate is consistently reproduced regardless of the existence of the labor market if the four factors mentioned above are included in the model, as shown in Figure 10, indicating that the inclusion of the labor market in the model is not an indispensable condition for reproducing the negative correlation.

Now, let us consider the reason why these four factors are necessary to reproduce the positive influence of corporate tax reduction. It is noted that two of the four factors, namely, the use of internal funds for investment and the mitigation of credit rationing are the factors that promote a firm's investment, which makes the firm's surplus money increased by the corporate tax reduction consumed in the market without being deposited in the bank. Executive compensation is another factor that promotes the firm's surplus money

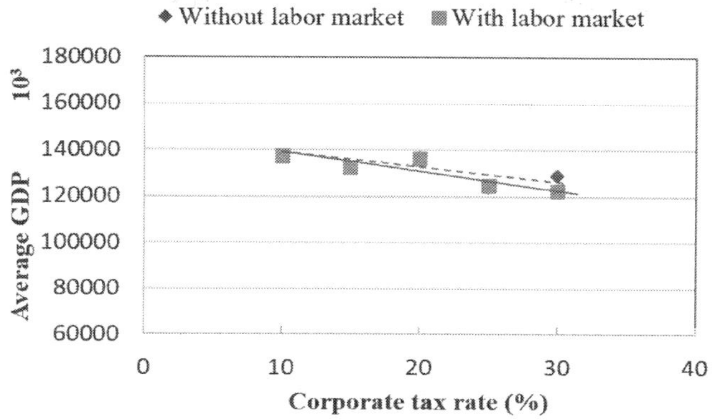

Figure 10. Influence of the labor market on the relationship between corporate tax rate and GDP, under the condition that includes all four factors, namely, government inefficiency, executive compensation, the use of internal funds, and the mitigation of credit rationing (i.e., the upper limit of the number of loans is assumed to be 3).

flowing out to the market. Funds that flow out from the bank to the market increase someone's income, increasing consumption, thus increasing GDP. The substantial marginal propensity to consume by the private sector is the ratio of the funds flowing out to the market (e.g., in the form of firms' investments as well as executives' consumptions) to the total amount of firms' surplus funds increased by the tax reduction.

The efficiency of government expenditure, on the other hand, is considered to be a substantial marginal propensity to consume by the public sector.

Therefore, the positive effect of corporate tax reduction is realized when the substantial marginal propensity to consume by the private sector (including both firms and consumers) is greater than that of the public sector. In addition, the four factors mentioned above are collectively required to reproduce the positive effect of corporate tax reduction, because the marginal propensity to consume in the private sector could be larger than that in the public sector only when all of four factors exist in both the model system and the real system.

This finding suggests the following:

First, when input conditions of the ABM model are expressed by the model structure, it is possible to discover which conditions in the system structure are necessary to reproduce specific macro behavior, using a series of systematic computer experiments. By considering why those factors are required to reproduce the phenomenon, we can gain a better understanding of the underlying mechanisms of the social phenomenon.

Second, corporate tax reduction increases GDP only when the government's effective marginal propensity to consume (expressed by the degree of efficiency [i.e., 1-inefficiency] of government expenditure) is smaller than that of the aggregate private sector. Namely, corporate tax reductions increase GDP when producers' surplus money (increased by the tax reduction) can be spent effectively in the market, in the form of firms' investment and/or consumption by executives and workers.

Third, inefficiency of government expenditure weakens the economy. In the model, the degree of inefficiency is defined as the ratio of firm subsidies to the total amount of public expenditure. In the actual system, the inefficiencies might be caused by many factors, such as public orders with higher-than-market prices, subsidies to firms in the industry, or rent-seeking behavior (Tollison & Congleton, 1995).

5. Discussions: The Validity of the Model in ABM

As described in the introduction, the validity of the ABM has been widely criticized. For example, Marks (2007) claimed that, because of the functional complexity of an ABM system, one could not assume that the factors that successfully reproduce the desired macro phenomena are necessary conditions.

On the contrary, the results of this study indicate that the necessary conditions exist for reproducing both business cycles and GDP reactions to tax reductions. The necessary conditions are the sets of factors that characterize the model structure, which can be elucidated by running a series of computer experiments where each of the factors is changed one at a time. These factors are indispensable for the model to reproduce the desired phenomenon as shown by the fact that the phenomenon does not emerge in the artificial society if any one of these factors is not included in the model in ABM. A typical example is the condition for reproducing the positive effect of corporate tax reduction. As the present research study revealed, four factors are required to reproduce the phenomenon because, among 16 possible combinations involving these four factors, only one case results in the emergence of the phenomenon, namely, the case in which all four factors are included in the model.

Moreover, by considering why such factors are required to reproduce each phenomenon, as described earlier in this paper, we can gain a better understanding of the causal mechanisms of these social phenomena. The reason for this is discussed below.

A system is a set of interacting objects and is defined as a proper relation on sets (Mesarovâic & Takahara, 1989). In the case of social systems, objects that are responsible for the emergence of social phenomenon are autonomous decision-makers (i.e., agents, such as individuals and organizations), because any social phenomenon is considered to emerge from agents' actions and their interactions. The set of the factors characterizing the agents' actions and their interactions is the system structure, which is defined as a set of categories of agents, their behavioral rules and relevant attributes variables. The behavioral rules and relevant attributes may include environmental factors of the system as well as factors relating to non-human entities, such as markets. Note also that the numerical values of variables are not crucial for the qualitative reproducibility of the social phenomenon, because the emergence of the macro phenomenon is insensitive to the numerical values of the variables.

Therefore, because ABM is a bottom-up modeling method, the macro phenomena that emerge in the model system will be similar to those of the real-world system if the system structure of the model defined as described above is similar to that of the real system. This principle holds true because, for any social phenomenon, there must be a causal mechanism where system structure is an input and the phenomenon is the output. In other words, if the factors that characterize the system structure of the model are different from those of the actual system, then the macro phenomena in question will not be reproduced, even qualitatively, in the model.

Therefore, in case of 100% bottom-up model in ABM, we can conclude that the system structure of the model and the causality of any phenomenon in the model are the same as or similar to those of the real system if the phenomenon in question is qualitatively reproduced in the model. Moreover, this causal relationship between the system structure and the phenomenon can be elucidated by running a series of computer experiments, in which one factor relating to the system structure is systematically changed one by one, while other factors are kept constant.

In the present study, the facts that we could specify the conditions of the model necessary to reproduce business cycles and the positive effects of tax reductions, and that we could reason about the underlying mechanisms of the phenomena, are offered as evidence of the validity of the model in ABM, following the preceding principle.

Note also that the model structure that can reproduce the desired macro phenomena might not be unique because there might be multiple causes for each of the phenomena. However, this does not undermine the validity of the model mentioned above, because if different system structures cause the same phenomenon in the model, it is considered so even in the real system. In any cases, we can gain a better understanding of the causal mechanisms of the social phenomena by piling up the knowledge on the indispensable system structure for each of the macro phenomena.

6. Conclusion

The necessary conditions of the model structure for reproducing business cycles and the positive effects of tax reductions are analyzed using an agent-based model, which includes producers' activities of production, pricing and investment, consumers' buying and working activities, and the government's activities of taxation and expenditure. As a result, the following findings were obtained.

1. The factors necessary to reproduce business cycles are the inclusion of bank financing (i.e., credit creation) and producers' demand-based investment decision-making.

2. The only factor required to reproduce the positive effect of income tax reduction is inefficient government expenditure. Factors required to reproduce the positive effect of corporate tax reduction include inefficient government expenditure, executive compensation, the use of internal funds for investment, and the mitigation of credit rationing.

3. Based on these findings, this study proposed causal mechanisms of business cycles and the positive effect of tax reduction. Business cycles emerge because overborrowing from the bank promotes an economy that is followed by excessive repayment due to credit rationing that worsens the economy. Positive effect of tax reduction emerges when substantial marginal propensity to consume at private sector is larger than that at public sector.

4. This study proposed new perspectives on the validity of ABM based on these findings, the essence of which is the following. In case of 100% bottom-up model in ABM, necessary conditions for qualitatively reproducing each of the macro phenomena can be identified if the input conditions of the model are expressed by the model structure defined by the set of the categories of agents, their behavioral rules, and relevant attributes variables. We can elucidate the necessary factors in the model structure by running a series of systematic computer experiments in which elements are changed one by one at a time with other factors kept constant. By considering the reason why such factors are required to reproduce the phenomenon, it is possible to gain a better understanding of the causal mechanism of the phenomenon.

References

Epstein, J. M., & Axtell, R. (1996). *Growing artificial societies: Social science from the bottom up*. Washington, DC: Brookings Institution Press.

Keynes, J. M. (1936). *The general theory of employment, interest, and money.* London, England: Macmillan.

Marks, R. E. (2007). Validating simulation models: A general framework and four applied examples. *Computational Economics, 30*(3), 265-290.

Mesarovâic, M. D., & Takahara, Y. (1989). *Abstract systems theory*. New York, NY: Springer-Verlag.

Sakuma, T., Masujima, M., Maeda, S., Fukawa, K., & Iwamoto, K. (2011). *The ESRI short-run macroeconometric model of the Japanese economy: Basic structure, multipliers, and economic policy analyses (2011 version)* (no. 259, pp. 41-44). Tokyo, Japan: Economic and Social Research Institute, Cabinet Office.

Ogibayashi, S., & Takashima, K. (2010). Multi-agent simulation of fund circulation in an artificial economic system involving self-adjusted mechanism of price, production and investment. *ICIC Express Letters, 4*(3B), 885-892.

Ogibayashi, S., & Takashima, K. (2014). Influence of the corporation tax rate on GDP in an agent-based artificial economic system. In S. Chen, T. Terano, R. Yamamoto, & C-C. Tai (Eds.), *Advances in computational social science* (pp. 157-173). Tokyo, Japan: Springer Japan.

Ormerod, P., & Rosewell, B. (2009). Verification and validation of agent-based models in the social sciences. In F. Squazzoni (Ed.), *Epistemological aspects of computer simulation in the social sciences* (pp. 130-140). Berlin, Germany: Springer.

Takashima, K., Kato, K., & Ogibayashi, S. (2014). Analysis of the influence of firm's financing strategies for investment on GDP in an agent-based economic system. *Information (Japan), 17*(6), 2583–2603.

Terano, T. (2008). Beyond the KISS principle for agent-based social simulation. *Journal of Socio-informatics, 1*(1), 175-187.

Tollison, R. D., & Congleton, R. D. (Eds.). (1995). *The economic analysis of rent seeking*. Cheltenham, England: Edward Elgar.

The Effects of Immigration on the U.S. Economy

Jovana Morales-Tilgren
M.A. Public Policy, Claremont Graduate University
Jovana.Morales-Martinez@cgu.edu

Yuan-Yuan Lee
PhD Student (Computational Analytics & World Politics), Claremont Graduate University
Yuan-Yuan.Lee@cgu.edu

Ryan Cummins
PhD Student (Public Policy), Claremont Graduate University
Ryan.Cummins@cgu.edu

ABSTRACT

Immigration is continuously circulating at the forefront of discussion and debate in the United States and North America. Advocates share the position that robust immigration into the United States enriches the country and continues the foundational traditions of the nation. Opponents argue that any increase in immigration is a threat to employment opportunities for U.S. citizens and presents a financial drain on the economy. This paper examines the impact of immigration in the United States based on its economic effect and shows that immigration has a positive economic effect overall on native U.S. individuals. The research question for the purpose of this paper is: How do foreign-born individuals and foreign direct investment (FDI) impact the U.S. economy?

Keywords: foreign direct investment (FDI); immigration; time-series; panel data; economy; endogenous growth theory

Efectos de la inmigración en la economía de EE. UU.

Resumen

La inmigración ha sido continuamente un tema que circula en la vanguardia de la discusión y el debate en los Estados Unidos y América del Norte. Los defensores comparten la posición de que la inmigración robusta a los Estados Unidos enriquece al país y continúa las tradiciones fundamentales de la nación. Los opositores argumentan que a medida que aumenta la inmigración, es una amenaza para las oportunidades de empleo para los ciudadanos estadounidenses y presenta una fuga financiera en la economía. Este documento examina el impacto de la inmigración en los Estados Unidos en función de su efecto económico y mostrará que la inmigración tiene un efecto económico positivo en general en las personas nativas de los Estados Unidos. La pregunta de investigación para el propósito de este documento es: ¿Cómo afectan los individuos nacidos en el extranjero y la Inversión Extranjera Directa (IED) a la economía de los Estados Unidos?

Palabras clave: Inversión Extranjera Directa (IED); inmigración; series temporales; datos de panel; economía; Teoría del Crecimiento Endógeno

移民对美国经济产生的影响

摘要

移民一直是美国和北美地区围绕在探讨和辩论中心的话题。倡导者认为，强劲的移民潮涌入美国将使其更为富有并延续该国的基本传统。反对者主张，随着移民数量的上涨，美国公民就业面临威胁，同时将对经济造成财力消耗。本文基于移民的经济效果，检验了移民对美国造成的影响，同时表明，移民整体上对美国本土公民产生了积极的经济效果。本文的研究问题是：外国出生的个人和外国直接投资（FDI）如何影响美国经济？

关键词：外国直接投资（FDI）；移民；时间序列；面板数据；经济；内生增长理论

Introduction

Leading up to the U.S. presidential election in 2016, Republican candidate Donald Trump made immigration one of the central issues to his campaign. Whether it was the construction of a wall along the United States-Mexico border or a moratorium on H-1B visas, the message conveyed from candidate Trump was clear in its intent to reduce the number of immigrants entering the United States (de Brauw, 2017). Previous research has indicated that a comprehensive reform of current immigration laws, as opposed to imposing wholesale restrictions on immigration, would increase wages across the U.S. economy (Hinojosa-Ojeda, 2012). The election of Donald Trump was a localized result of rising far right political parties in national elections around the world that espouse anti-immigrant rhetoric (Gebremedhin & Mavisakalyan, 2013). The increase in ethnocentric thinking poses a threat not only to human rights, but also to economic integration between nations (Andrews, Leblang, & Pandya, 2018).

Research Design

Much of the literature has stated that immigration is a driving force behind economic growth in the United States. This paper contributes to the preceding research in several aspects and provides two different methods of analyzing the effects of immigration on the U.S. economy. The first method employed analyzes the impact of immigration on the U.S. economy at the national level and the second analyzes the impact at the state level. Based on past theories, two hypotheses were generated. First, we consider the impact that foreign-born individuals have on the U.S. economy. With the constant turmoil and rhetoric of the Trump administration, we seek to verify whether foreign-born individuals are, in fact, stealing jobs from American citizens, lowering wages for the poorest workers, and how the cutback of legal immigration of high skilled workers is affecting the U.S. economy (Schwartz & Lohr, 2018). Therefore, policies aligned with reducing immigration may be detrimental to the United States, which leads to the first hypothesis.

Hypothesis 1: Foreign-born individuals impact the U.S. economy.

Not only is immigration a strong component of the U.S. economy, but so too is foreign direct investment (FDI). Adam S. Posen, from the Peterson Institute for International Economics, has conducted studies on the effect of President Trump's policies towards trade and immigration. According to Posen (2018), "the falloff [of FDI inflows] is a result of a general decline in the United States' attractiveness as a place to make long-term business commitments." This leads to the second hypothesis.

Hypothesis 2: FDI impacts the U.S. economy.

Methods

An ordinary least squares (OLS) regression was conducted and after testing for heteroscedasticity since we would use Feasible Generalized Least Square (FGLS) to fix heteroscedasticity issue. FGLS is modeling proceeds which is estimated by OLS estimator, and the residuals are used to build a consistent estimator of the errors covariance matrix. When the errors follow a time series process, generally needs some theoretical assumptions on this process to ensure that a consistent estimator is available. As noted in the literature review, immigration may be endogenous to economic growth, as the amount of immigration and migration depends on the increase of regional economic growth and vice versa. Therefore, we use the Two-Stage Least Squares Regression Analysis (2SLS) to rectify for the endogeneity by using instrumental variable. We try to test our hypothesis if we have endogenous variables, variables that are influenced by other variables in the model. In other words, we would use it to account for unexpected behavior between variables. Using an instrumental variable to identify the possible or potential correlation allows you to see the true correlation between the explanatory variable and the response variable. We then utilize a vector autoregressive model to address the autocorrelation; the data are from 1961-2016, representing 55 years.

Data description. The variables used to measure the effects of immigration on the U.S. economy are shown in Table 1 (see Appendix A). Gross domestic product (GDP) growth rate was utilized as the first dependent variable, as this is a measurement of the U.S. economy. The second dependent variable is the unemployment rate, to determine whether immigration has an impact on the unemployment rate in the United States, another measurement of the U.S. economy. Consumer price index (CPI), the third dependent variable, measures the consumption of all individuals in the United States; this is an important measurement of the U.S. economy because, if CPI increases, there is a positive impact. The final dependent variable is the urbanization index. Studies have shown that as the urban population increases, it signifies a growing economy; hence, it is the fourth measurement of the U.S. economy.

The key independent variables in this study are FDI and lawful permanent resident population as these are measurements of the immigration population. The FDI and lawful permanent resident population were transformed using log to establish a more substantive comparison between variables. Key independent variables were interacted with other independent variables to analyze the impact they have on the dependent variables.

There are four models to test the effects that immigration has on the GDP growth rate, unemployment rate, CPI, and urbanization index. The dependent variables are measurements used to test the hypotheses. The model specification can be seen in Appendix A.

First, an OLS regression was run on all four models. As expected, there is heteroskedasticity and multicollinearity, as shown in Appendix A. Robust standard errors and FGLS were utilized to rectify this and a weight was added to each observation. Table 3 in Appendix A shows results with standardized coefficients.

The coefficients are standardized for the independent variables to compare the effects they have on the dependent variables. This is important because the independent variables have different measurements and it is difficult to see the impact without standardizing the coefficients. For GDP growth rate, we can see that the lawful permanent resident population has the biggest impact on GDP growth rate. One standard deviation change in the lawful permanent resident population results in beta value 2.11 standard deviations change in GDP growth rate. For the unemployment rate, we can see that the logged variable of the lawful permanent resident population has the biggest impact on unemployment rate. One standard deviation change in logged the lawful permanent resident population results in beta value 7.86 standard deviations change in unemployment rate. For CPI, we can see that the median family income has the biggest impact on CPI. One standard deviation change in median family income results in beta value 0.98 standard deviations change in CPI. For the urban index, we can see that median family income also has the biggest impact on the dependent variable urban index. One standard deviation change in median family income results in beta value 1.25 standard deviations change in urban index.

Overall, the number of lawful permanent residents, FDI, and median family income has an impact on the dependent variables. This is important because it validates our assumption that immigration has an impact on the U.S. economy. However, because there is endogeneity between economic growth and immigration, we must consider this and correct for it.

Vector autoregressive model. The data are at the national level in scope and on a timeline from 1961 to 2016 across the United States. With time series data, four different models were created (see Appendix A, Model Specification for Vector Autoregressive Model). Again, the search is to identify the effects of immigration on the U.S. economy. However, due to time lags, we do not want to ignore values affected by those same values in the past. This is a problem of autocorrelation, which we test for. Due to autocorrelation, we must difference the variables to produce a stationary process. Once the variables were stationary, we ran the Dickey-Fuller Test for stationary. This process was repeated for the four models until every model was stationary.

The results for the effect of immigration on the U.S. economy can be seen in Figure 1. In Figure 1, the first highlighted graph shows us that at five periods, FDI begins to impact GDP; there is a slight decrease at 9.5 periods. The second highlighted graph shows that at two periods, FDI causes an increase in the top marginal tax rate, followed by some periods of fluctuation, and finally a bigger increase at nine periods. The third highlighted graph shows that at two periods, FDI causes a decrease in the poverty rate, followed

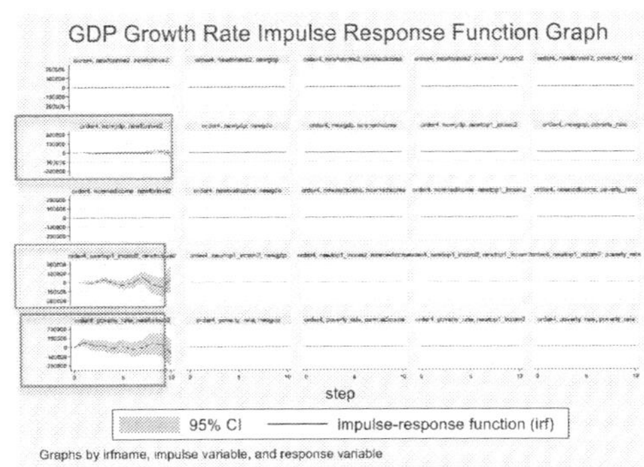

Figure 1. Effects of FDI on GDP growth rate, top marginal tax rate, and poverty rate

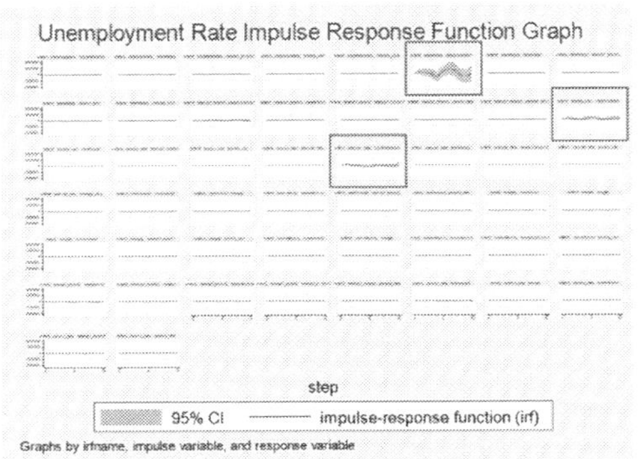

*Figure 2. Effects of interaction term, LPR population*recession, on LPR in log form, poverty rate,*

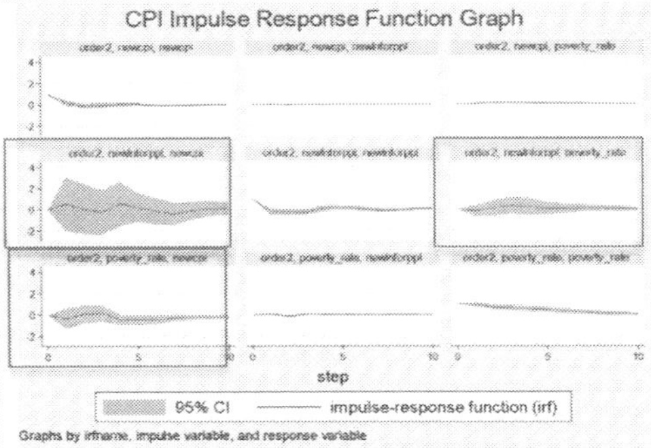

Figure 3a. Effects of CPI and poverty rate on lawful permanent residents in log form poverty and poverty rate

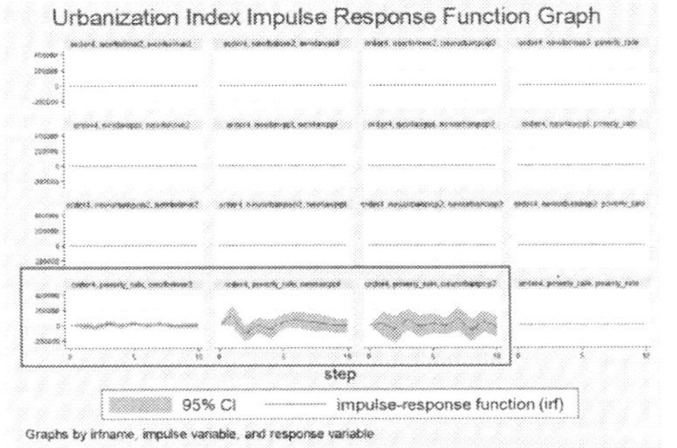

Figure 3b. Effects of CPI and poverty rate on lawful permanent residents in log form poverty and poverty rate

by an increase at three periods, a higher increase at seven periods, and a larger decrease at eight periods.

This reveals that FDI has a positive impact on the U.S. economy by increasing GDP growth rate, increasing the top marginal tax rate, and decreasing the poverty rate. This indicates that current and future administrations should take this into consideration when creating policies that restrict immigration to the United States or complicate relations with foreign countries. This study shows the impact that immigration has on the U.S. economy.

Figure 2 shows the results for the effects of immigration on unemployment rate. The first highlighted graph shows that at two periods, the interaction term of lawful permanent residents and recession starts to impact the log form of lawful permanent residents, with an increase at five periods, followed by a decrease at 6.5 periods and an increase at nine periods. The second highlighted graph shows that at two periods, the interaction term of lawful permanent residents and recession starts to impact the poverty rate; there is negligible increase or decrease. The third highlighted graph shows that at two periods, the interaction term of lawful permanent residents and recession begins to impact the unemployment rate. There are slight increases and decreases, but none of significance. The first graph shows the most impact, which reaffirms the previous research regarding the impact of recessions on the inflow and outflow of immigration.

Figure 3a provides the results of the impact of immigration on CPI. The first highlighted graph on the left side in Figure 3a shows that at two periods, CPI starts impacting the interaction term of lawful permanent residents. This is a significant impact. At three periods, it begins to increase, followed by a slight decrease, leading to an increase at six periods. At 10 periods, it appears to plateau. The second highlighted graph on the right side shows that at two periods, there is a slight increase in the log form of lawful permanent residents, followed by a slight decrease then a plateau. The third highlighted graph shows a substantial decrease and increase between zero and four periods, but it ultimately plateaus as well. This suggests that CPI and poverty rate are endogenous and that there is a causal relationship between CPI and lawful permanent residents; this again supports the literature on the endogeneity between immigration and economic growth.

Figure 3b shows the results of the effects of immigration on the urbanization index. The first highlighted graph shows that at two periods, there is an impact of FDI on the poverty rate. There is a slight increase and decrease and an apparent plateau at 10 periods. The second highlighted graph is more significant. At one period, we see a sharp increase, followed by a sharp decrease at two periods, increase at five periods, and a slow decrease at six periods. The third highlighted graph also shows a shock to the urbanization index at two periods, which causes an increase in the poverty rate. There is a continued decrease and increase throughout each period.

This shows that urbanization has a pronounced impact on poverty rate; more so than FDI, which again supports the research that, as immigrants move to a city, poverty rates increase. FDI and lawful permanent residents have an impact, but not that great, which supports the hypothesis that FDI and lawful permanent residents have a positive effect on the U.S. economy.

The time series analysis provides some evidence that foreign-born individuals (lawful permanent residents) have a positive impact on the U.S. economy; it further adds to the literature that immigration is an important part of the United States via the economy. It also provides evidence that FDI has an impact on the U.S. economy. We have seen that FDI increases the top marginal tax rate and decreases the poverty rate.

Now we want to look at a more systematic approach to the effects of immigration on the U.S. economy by analyzing the results from cross-sectional and time series data. We look at immigration and the U.S. economy by state, from 2010 to 2017.

Forecast Model Performance

Two different methods were used for the predictions. First, ARIMA was used to determine how the dependent variables are impacted by the immigration variables. Another method used is empirical forecast intervals to reveal how the GDP growth rate and unemployment trend will change in the next 15 years (2017-2031). Moreover, in Figure 4, we can see that the GDP growth rate is above zero and more stable without changing significantly. In Figure 5, the prediction trend of the unemployment rate is between 4% and 6%, with slight increases. In the other words, when the GDP growth rate declines, unemployment may increase.

Furthermore, in Figure 6, CPI shows an increasing trend for the next 15 years. CPI is one of the important indicators for marketing and economic and government monetary policy. When CPI is more stable, the employment rate is higher and GDP grows. However, a rapid increase in the CPI causes inflation and economic instability. In Figure 7, we can see that the urbanization index is below zero, which means the urban population may not be able to spread more extensively to other metropolitan areas.

Empirical Forecast Intervals

Lee and Scholtes's (2014) empirical prediction intervals were constructed based on the distribu-

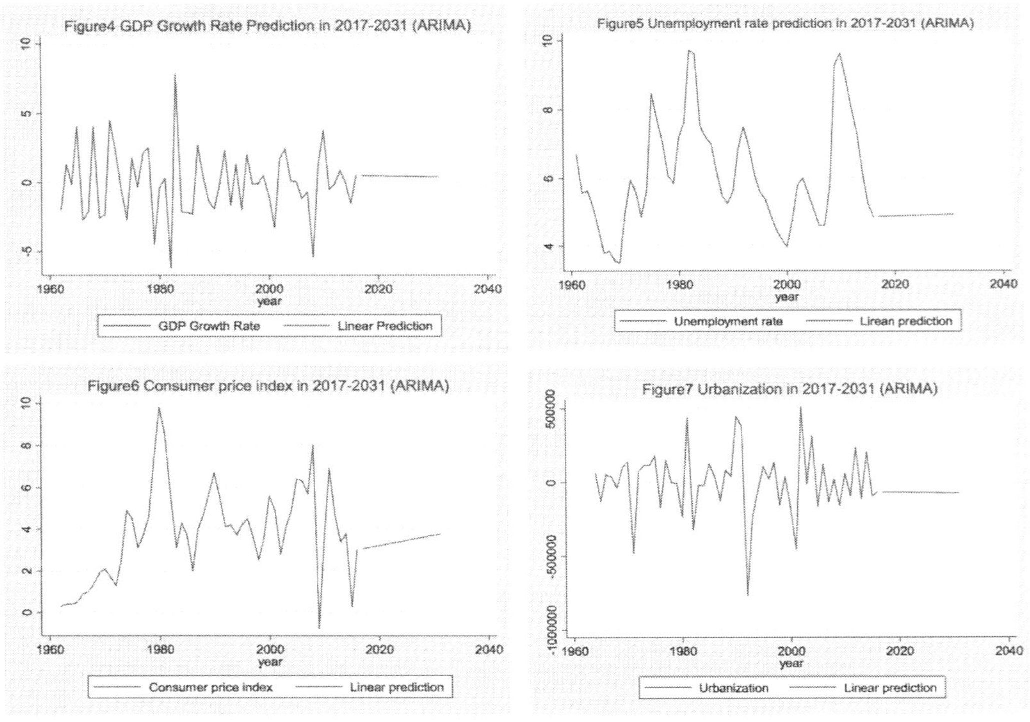

Figures 4-7. ARMIA forecast predictions.

tion of previous out-of-sample forecast errors. Given historical data, a sample of such forecast errors is generated by successively applying a chosen point forecasting model to a sequence of fixed windows of past observations and recording the associated deviations of model predictions from actual observations out-of-sample. The suitable quantiles of the distribution of these forecast errors are then used together with the point forecast made by the selected model to construct an empirical prediction interval (Lee & Scholtes, 2014, p. 217). Vector autoregressive models of GDP growth rate and unemployment rate were used to see overall prediction for 2017-2031. Additionally, we employ detrending for the dependent variables, which removes a trend from the time series. Considering the removal of an aspect from the data, it may lead to some distortion.

First, in the GDP growth rate prediction, we consider FDI, lawful permanent residents, corporate profits, poverty rate, median family income, urban population growth rate, education, and top 1% income share. In Figure 8, the GDP growth rate is linear, increasing above zero from 2017 to 2031. Also, the results in Figure 4 could be compared to identify the trend of GDP growth rate in stable predictions above zero. Hence, we posit that FDI and immigrants could have a positive impact on the GDP growth rate overall.

Second, for the unemployment rate prediction, we consider FDI, lawful permanent residents, corporate profits, poverty rate, median family income, urban population growth rate, education, top 1% income share, FDI interaction with the president's party, poverty rate interaction with the president's party, and lawful permanent residents' interaction with recession year. Figure 9 shows that the prediction is linear and slowly increasing over 15 years with prediction values between 4% and 6%. Comparing Figure 5 in ARIMA, the unemployment rate would be stable between 4% and 6%. Moreover, in the empirical forecast intervals model, other variables would be considered to have an influence on unemployment. For example, when a recession occurs, it may impact job opportunities and cause the unemployment rate to increase. On the other hand, the political party in power also impacts foreign investment through policy choices. Earlier, the positive impact that FDI has on unemployment was discussed; when FDI decreases it may cause the unemployment rate to increase. Overall, we assume unemployment would slowly increase between 4% and 6%.

Policy Implications

Figure 10a shows that FDI exists in relationship with GDP growth rate and urbanization. However, FDI has a negative impact on the GDP growth rate. When there is a change in FDI of $1 million dollars, it is associated with a 2.37e-06 decrease in the GDP growth rate. This indicates that FDI has a slightly negative impact. We can see in Figure 10b that in a recession year, FDI is less compared to a non-recession year. Also, we can assume that econom-

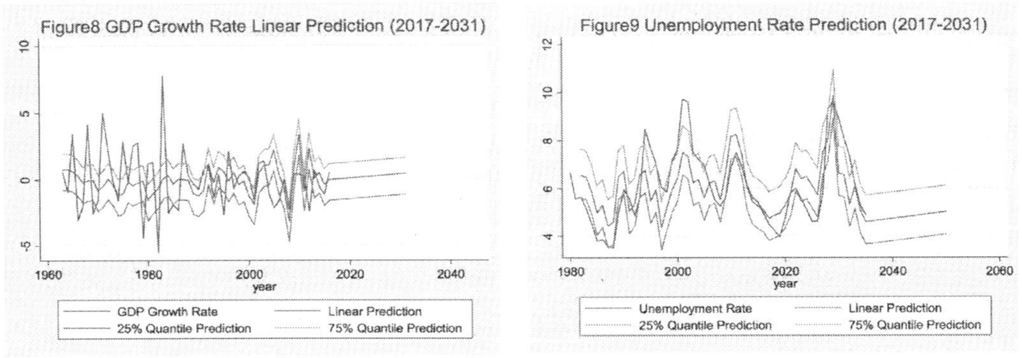

Figures 8-9. Empirical forecasts.

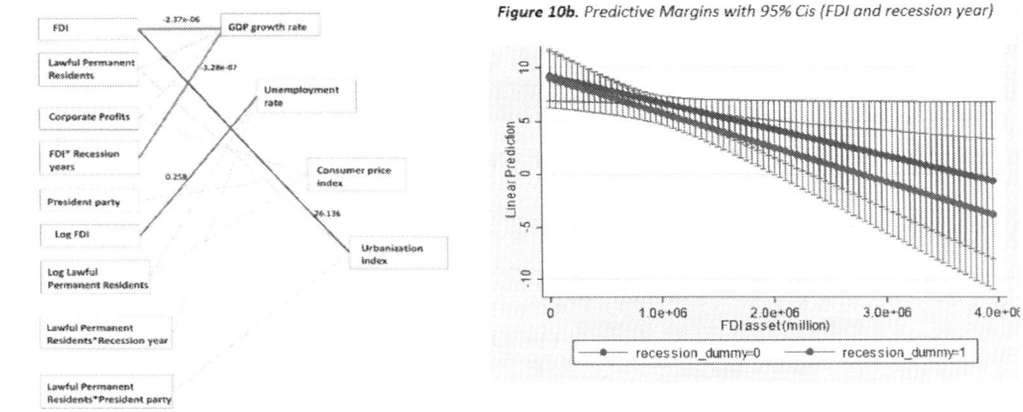

Figure 10a. *The relationship between FDI and dependent variables*

Figure 10b. *Predictive Margins with 95% Cis (FDI and recession year)*

Figure 10. FDI, dependent variables, and recession.

ic recession affects the intention of foreign investment, particularly in recession years, which have a larger impact on FDI. Therefore, we can determine that when a recession takes place within a year, FDI declines more than in a non-recession year.

Moreover, urbanization is a global phenomenon crossing developed and economically developing countries. It not only leads to a higher density population in metropolitan areas, it also means more economic and political activity. It can be seen in Figure 10a that FDI has a positive effect on urbanization. When FDI increases by $1 million dollars, it is associated with a 26.136% increase in urbanization. We can determine that FDI has a positive effect, improving urbanization in cities.

Furthermore, we can see in Figure 10a that FDI has a positive impact on the unemployment rate. When FDI increases by 1%, it is associated with a decrease in the unemployment rate of 0.258%. As Peri (2012) stated, as addi-

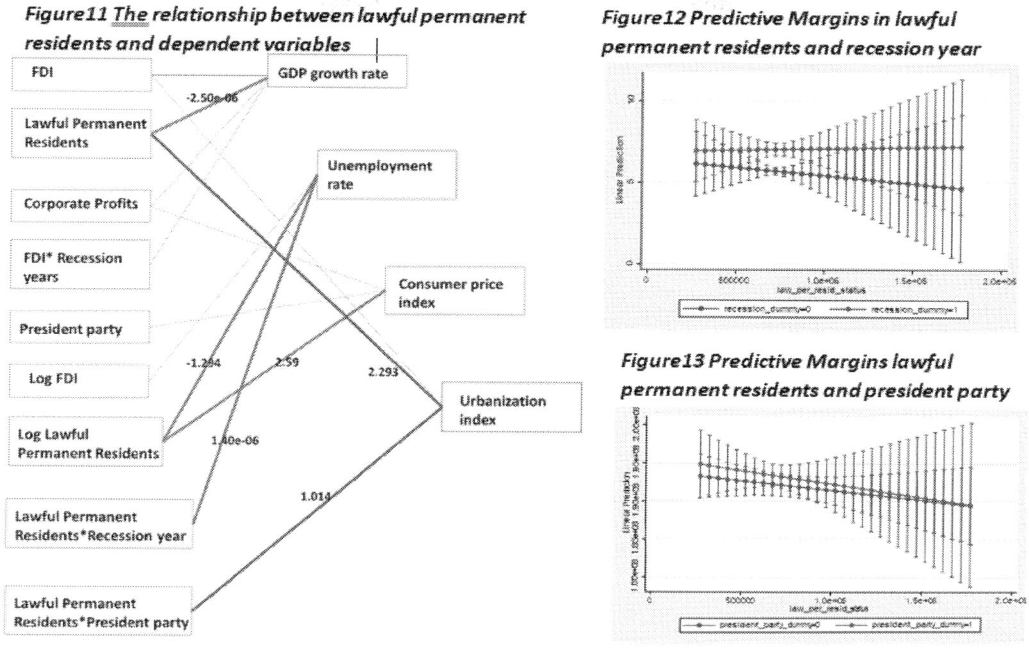

Figure 11. Lawful permanent residents, dependent variables, and recession year.

tional workers become available, capital increases and investment occurs, which promotes expansion and innovation. Therefore, encouraging foreign investment may motivate international enterprises to increase investment, which would in turn improve GDP and may increase job opportunities.

We can see in Figure 11 that immigrants have a negative impact on the GDP growth rate when there is a change of one unit, which is associated with a 2.350e-06 GDP growth rate decline. This indicates that immigrants slightly affect the U.S. economy; however, there are other factors that could affect GDP growth rate that correlate to immigration. Additionally, immigration numbers negatively impact the unemployment rate when immigrants change by 1%. This is associated with unemployment rate increasing 1.294%. Also, as seen in Figure 12, in a recession year, immigrants have a larger impact than in a non-recession year; particularly when the immigration number is larger.

Furthermore, immigrants have a positive impact on CPI. In Figure 11, we can see that when immigration changes 1%, it is associated with an increase in CPI of 2.59%. This indicates that the immigration number has a positive impact on consumption, which is significant, as CPI is an important indicator of the U.S. economy. The ability for consumption may denote economic performance and that economic growth is on the rise and individuals are more willing to spend money. Therefore, immigrants have a positive impact on economic performance in the United States.

Immigrants not only have a positive impact economically, but they also positively affect urbanization in the United States. Figure 11 shows that when there is a one-unit change in immigration, it is associated with a 2.293% increase in urbanization. In California, there are significant concentrations of immigrant populations and current economic indicators show California is one of the top three state economies in the United States. Moreover, Figure 13 shows that presidential party influences immigrants and urbanization. During Democratic Party control, there is a larger impact on immigration numbers. However, when immigration numbers are larger, the impact of the president's party is only slightly different.

Corporate profit is another important indicator of the U.S. economy, which provides insight into corporate financial health. We can see in Figure 14 that corporate profit positively impacts the GDP growth rate and CPI. When there is a change in corporate profit of $1 billion dollars, it is associated with a change in the GDP growth rate of 0.0009%. Moreover, when the corporate profit change is $1 billion dollars, it is associated with a 0.006 increase change in CPI. Corporate profit has a positive impact on both economic indicators, which is a source of retained earnings, providing much of the funding for capital investments that raise productive capacity. The estimates of profits and related measures may also be used to evaluate the effects on corporations with changes in policy or economic conditions. Hence, encouraging foreign investment may lead to an increase in corporate profit and potentially providing additional job opportunities, which, ultimately, has a positive influence on the U.S. economy.

Conclusions

Based on this research and according to several variables, it can be determined that immigration has a positive economic effect in the United States. In addition to the positive effect of immigration, increases in ethnocentric policies have been shown to have a negative effect by decreasing the amount of FDI received at the state level. Endogeny occurs when, as the U.S. economy improves, the number of immigrants increases; the increase in immigrants who concentrate in the more economically robust areas of the United States leads to an increase in FDI, GDP, and wages. However, as immigration increases, there is a negative effect on the wages of native-born individuals without a high school diploma. Should U.S. policies toward immigration become increasingly restrictive, it could prove detrimental to the overall U.S. economy.

Throughout the literature regarding immigration, it is clear there is difficulty determining the accurate number of undocumented immigrants currently residing in the United States. As a result, it can lead to an inability to determine the direct economic effect on the U.S. economy from this population and, in some cases, difficult to differentiate any effects between the immigrant population and the undocumented population. This presents limitations to the research. In the interest of future research, a closer study of the economic impact at the state level, determining how directly a strong regional economy attracts immigrants, is warranted. Additionally, a study of the immigration policies on a state-by-state basis may prove beneficial in determining the scale of FDI received at the state level and its impact on the overall U.S. economy.

Appendix A

Table 1

Description of Variables for Time Series Model:

Description		Variables
GDP Growth Rate	DV 1	gdpgrow_rate
Unemployment Rate	DV 2	unemply_rate
CPI	DV 3	cpi
Percentage Urban Population	DV 4	urban_index
FDI (in millions)	IV	for_invest_asset_million
Lawful Permanent Resident	IV	law_per_resid_status
Corporate Profit (in billions)	IV	cop_profit
Top Marginal Tax Rate	IV	highest_tax
Median Income	IV	median_income
Poverty Rate	IV	poverty_rate
Urban Population Growth Rate Annual	IV	urban_pop_growth
FDI in Log Form	Logged IV	lnforin
Lawful Permanent Residents in Log Form	Logged IV	lnforppl
FDI*Corporate Profit	Interaction Term	newcopmoney
President Party (R=0, D=1)	Dummy Variable	president_party_dummy
FDI*President Party (Dummy Variable)	Interaction Term	formoneypresid
FDI*Recession (Dummy Variable)	Interaction Term	formoneyrecession
Lawful Permanent Resident*Recession (Dummy Variable)	Interaction Term	forpplrecession
Poverty Rate* Recession (Dummy Variable)	Interaction Term	povertyrecession
Poverty Rate*President Party (Dummy Variable)	Interaction Term	povertypresid
Lawful Permanent Residents* President Party (dummy)	Interaction Term	forpplpresid
Recession year (0=no recession 1=recession)	Dummy Variable	recession
Year 1961 - 2016	Time	year

OLS Model Specification:

Model 1: $GDP\_growth\_rate = \alpha + \beta_1 FDI + \beta_2 Lawful\_per\_resid + \beta_3 Corp\_profit + \beta_4 Highest\_tax + \beta_5 Median\_income + \beta_6 Poverty\_rate + \beta_7 FDI * Recession\_dummy + \varepsilon$

Model 2: $Unemployment\_rate = \alpha + \beta_1 LnFDI + \beta_2 LnLawful\_per\_resid + \beta_3 Corp\_profit + \beta_4 Highest\_tax + \beta_5 Median\_income + \beta_6 Poverty\_rate + \beta_7 Urban\_growth\_rate + \beta_8 FDI * Pres\_party\_dummy + \varepsilon$

Model 3: $CPI = \alpha + \beta_1 LnLawful\_per\_resid + \beta_2 Highest\_tax + \beta_3 Median\_income + \beta_4 Poverty\_rate + \beta_5 Urban\_growth\_rate + \beta_6\ Corp\_profit\ + \beta_6 Pres\_party\_dummy + \varepsilon$

Model 4: $Urban\_index = \alpha + \beta_1 FDI + \beta_2 Lawful\_per\_resid + \beta_3 Highest\_tax + \beta_4 Median\_income + \beta_5 Poverty\_rate + \beta_6 FDI * Corp\_profit + \beta_7\ Lawful\_per\_resid * Pres\_party\_dummy + \beta_8 Poverty\_rate * Recession\_dummy + \varepsilon$

Table 2

Models

Models	**VIF (Testing for Multicollinearity)**
Model 1: GDP Growth Rate	11.42
Model 2: Unemployment Rate	21.96
Model 3: CPI	7.34
Model 4: Urban Population Index	17.66

Table 3

FGLS Table with Standardized Coefficients

Independent Variables	Dependent Variables			
	gdp_growth_rate	unemployment_rate	cpi	urban_index
FDI	-1.283152			.1871046
Number of Lawful Permanent Residents	2.110127			.053659
Corporate Profit	.0595861	-.6675166	.2738657	
highest_tax	.197105	-.0432146	-.0710272	.01894
Poverty rate	-1.295799	-2.821911	.6813527	.6981347
FDI*Recession	-.0000135			
Median Family Income	-1.47696	-9.916798	.9813179	1.250497
Ln FDI		7.855243		
Ln Lawful Permanent Residents		-.9772898	.2474075	
Urban Population Growth Rate Annual		-.791744	.0388529	
FDI*President Party (Dummy Variable)		.3163946		
Poverty Rate*President Party (Dummy Variable)		-.3865165		
Lawful Permanent Resident*Recession (Dummy Variable)		.1971147		
President Party Dummy			.0126793	
FDI*Corporate Profit				-.0451541
Lawful Permanent Residents*President Party				.3174752
Poverty Rate* Recession (Dummy Variable)				-.0861477

Two-Stage Least Squares Regression Analysis (2SLS) Model Specification:

Model 1 : gdp_growth_rate
$= \alpha + \beta_1 top1\_income + \beta_2 edu\_bachgrad + \beta_3 FDI + \beta_4 Lawful\_perm\_resid$
$+ \beta_5 Corp\_profit + \beta_6 Poverty\_rate + \beta_7 FDI * Recession\_dummy$
$+ \beta_8 Median\_income$

Model 2 : $unemployment\_rate$
$= \alpha + \beta_1 top1\_income + \beta_2 edu\_bachgrad + \beta_3 LnFDI$
$+ \beta_4 LnLawful\_perm\_resid + \beta_5 Corp\_profit + \beta_6 Median\_income$
$+ \beta_7 Poverty\_rate + \beta_8 Urban\_growth\_rate + \beta_9 FDI * Pres\_party\_dummy$
$+ \beta_{10} Poverty\_rate * Pres\_party\_dummy + \varepsilon$

Model 3 : $cpi = \alpha + \beta_1 top1\_income + \beta_2 edu\_bachgrad + \beta_3 LnLawful\_perm\_resid$
$+ \beta_4 Corp\_profit + \beta_5 Median\_income + \beta_6 Poverty\_rate$
$+ \beta_7 Urban\_growth\_rate + \beta_8 Pres\_party\_dummy + \varepsilon$

Model 4 : $urban\_index$
$= \alpha + \beta_1 top1\_income + \beta_2 edu\_bachgrad + \beta_3 Lawful\_perm\_resid + \beta_4 FDI$
$+ \beta_5 Median\_income + \beta_6 Poverty\_rate + \beta_7 Urban\_growth\_rate + \beta_8 FDI$
$* Corp\_profit + \beta_8 Lawful\_perm\_resid * Pres\_party\_dummy$
$+ \beta_8 Poverty\_rate * Recession\_dummy + \varepsilon$

Table 4

2SLS, Results of 4 models

VARIABLES	(1) DV=gdpgrow_rate	(2) DV=unemply_rate	(3) DV=cpi	(4) DV=urban_pop
highest_tax	-0.0434	-0.219	-2.695***	-1.008e+06***
	(0.109)	(0.173)	(0.972)	(244,146)
lnforin		0.677		
		(1.328)		
lnforppl		-4.468*	-27.99	
		(2.561)	(19.83)	
cop_prof_billion	0.00103***	8.90e-05	0.0119***	
	(0.000372)	(0.000372)	(0.00312)	
median_family_incom	-0.000264	-0.000522**	0.00134	521.7
	(0.000266)	(0.000221)	(0.00227)	(727.4)
poverty_rate	-0.739**	-0.304	3.888	-498,205
	(0.358)	(0.439)	(4.113)	(1.127e+06)
urban_pop_growth_annual		-3.343**	-7.139	
		(1.507)	(9.343)	
formoneypresid		2.99e-07		
		(3.03e-07)		
povertypresid		0.0321		
		(0.0946)		
forpplrecession		2.32e-06**		
		(9.20e-07)		
for_invest_asset_million	-2.46e-06**			28.62***
	(1.20e-06)			(4.699)
law_per_resid_status	-3.00e-06			-15.86***
	(2.12e-06)			(5.886)
formoneyrecession	-7.82e-07*			
	(4.14e-07)			
president_party_dummy			12.30**	
			(6.032)	
newcopmoney				-0.000974**
				(0.000412)
forpplpresid				7.801***
				(2.875)
povertyrecession				311,493**
				(155,856)
Constant	37.29	108.8*	470.9	2.049e+08***
	(27.53)	(59.89)	(471.2)	(7.125e+07)
Observations	56	56	56	56
R-squared	0.616	0.043	0.949	0.975

Robust standard errors in parentheses
*** $p<0.01$, ** $p<0.05$, * $p<0.1$

Table 5

Seemingly Unrelated Regression Results

Seemingly unrelated regression

Equation	Obs	Parms	RMSE	"R-sq"	chi2	P
gdpgrow_rate	56	8	1.781226	0.6329	97.53	0.0000
unemply_rate	56	11	.6400463	0.8317	316.57	0.0000
cpi	56	8	4.780409	0.9953	12012.47	0.0000
urban_pop	56	9	3183281	0.9938	8991.15	0.0000

	Coef.	Std. Err.	z	P>|z|	[95% Conf.	Interval]
gdpgrow_rate						
for_invest_asse~n	-2.37e-06	9.80e-07	-2.41	0.016	-4.29e-06	-4.44e-07
law_per_resid_s~s	-2.50e-06	1.17e-06	-2.14	0.033	-4.79e-06	-2.08e-07
cop_prof_billion	.0009904	.0004008	2.47	0.013	.0002048	.0017759
poverty_rate	-.6989459	.3298877	-2.12	0.034	-1.345514	-.0523778
formoneyrecession	-3.28e-07	3.88e-07	-0.85	0.397	-1.09e-06	4.31e-07
median_family_i~m	-.0002172	.000236	-0.92	0.357	-.0006799	.0002454
top1_incom	-.0557129	.1211055	-0.46	0.645	-.2930753	.1816494
edu_bachgrad	.060689	.2299737	0.26	0.792	-.3900511	.5114291
_cons	30.84137	14.72715	2.09	0.036	1.976698	59.70605
unemply_rate						
lnforin	.258133	.6755822	0.38	0.702	-1.065984	1.58225
lnforppl	-1.293591	.5042821	-2.57	0.010	-2.281966	-.3052167
cop_prof_billion	-.0003527	.0000998	-3.54	0.000	-.0005482	-.0001572
median_family_i~m	-.0004583	.0000991	-4.63	0.000	-.0006525	-.0002641
poverty_rate	-.1230975	.1706837	-0.72	0.471	-.4576315	.2114364
formoneypresid	2.63e-07	1.67e-07	1.57	0.116	-6.49e-08	5.91e-07
povertypresid	-.0404546	.018153	-2.23	0.026	-.0760339	-.0048754
forpplrecession	1.40e-06	2.40e-07	5.82	0.000	9.28e-07	1.87e-06
top1_incom	-.0902184	.0410994	-2.20	0.028	-.1707716	-.0096651
edu_bachgrad	.6007966	.2186777	2.75	0.006	.1721963	1.029397
urban_pop_growt~l	-2.344766	.4986885	-4.70	0.000	-3.322177	-1.367354
_cons	44.44333	9.488415	4.68	0.000	25.84638	63.04029
cpi						
lnforppl	2.589987	3.478147	0.74	0.456	-4.227057	9.40703
cop_prof_billion	.0059209	.0006514	9.09	0.000	.0046442	.0071976
median_family_i~m	.0015128	.0007151	2.12	0.034	.0001114	.0029143
poverty_rate	4.022925	1.143849	3.52	0.000	1.781023	6.264827
president_party~y	.1284248	1.423402	0.09	0.928	-2.661391	2.918241
urban_pop_growt~l	5.636545	3.343563	1.69	0.092	-.9167178	12.18981
top1_incom	.245064	.2928866	0.84	0.403	-.3289831	.8191111
edu_bachgrad	6.146935	.7568444	8.12	0.000	4.663547	7.630322
_cons	-201.3229	70.28474	-2.86	0.004	-339.0784	-63.56731
urban_pop						
for_invest_asse~n	26.1363	2.60614	10.03	0.000	21.02836	31.24424
law_per_resid_s~s	-2.29324	2.187701	-1.05	0.295	-6.581056	1.994576
newcopmoney	-.0012478	.0002462	-5.07	0.000	-.0017304	-.0007653
forpplpresid	1.013677	1.33252	0.76	0.447	-1.598014	3.625367
povertyrecession	-59522.38	72537.8	-0.82	0.412	-201693.9	82649.1
median_family_i~m	340.5898	485.7101	0.70	0.483	-611.3844	1292.564
poverty_rate	-49383.54	664538.5	-0.07	0.941	-1351855	1253088
top1_incom	-381845.6	216433.4	-1.76	0.078	-806047.2	42356.04
edu_bachgrad	2944600	426074.4	6.91	0.000	2109509	3779690
_cons	1.07e+08	3.08e+07	3.47	0.001	4.64e+07	1.67e+08

Correlation matrix of residuals:

	gdpgrow_rate	unemply_rate	cpi	urban_pop
gdpgrow_rate	1.0000			
unemply_rate	0.1849	1.0000		
cpi	-0.4011	-0.3271	1.0000	
urban_pop	-0.2292	0.2496	0.0535	1.0000

Breusch-Pagan test of independence: chi2(6) = 23.503, Pr = 0.0006

Vector Autoregressive Model
Specification:

Model 1 :
$gdp\_growth\_rate_t = \alpha + \beta_1 top1\_income_t + \beta_2 edu\_bachgrad_t + \beta_3 FDI_t + \beta_4 Lawful\_perm\_resid_t + \beta_5 Corp\_profit_t + \beta_6 Poverty\_rate_t + \beta_7 Urban\_growth\_rate_t + \beta_8 Median\_income_t + \varepsilon_t$

Model 2: $unemployment\_rate_t = \alpha + \beta_1 top1\_income_t + \beta_2 edu\_bachgrad_t + \beta_3 LnFDI_t + \beta_4 LnLawful\_perm\_resid_t + \beta_5 Corp\_profit_t + \beta_6 Poverty\_rate_t + \beta_7 Urban\_growth\_rate_t + \beta_8 Median\_income_t + \beta_9 FDI * Pres\_party\_dummy_t + \beta_{10} Poverty\_rate * Pres\_party\_dummy_t + \beta_{11} Lawful\_perm\_resid * Recession\_dummy_t + \varepsilon_t$

Model 3 : $cpi_t = \alpha + \beta_1 top1\_income_t + \beta_2 edu\_bachgrad_t + \beta_3 LnLawful\_perm\_resid_t + \beta_4 Corp\_profit_t + \beta_5 Poverty\_rate_t + \beta_6 Urban\_growth\_rate_t + \beta_7 Median\_income_t + \beta_8 Pres\_party\_dummy_t + \varepsilon_t$

Model 4 : $urban\_index_t = \alpha + \beta_1 top1\_income_t + \beta_2 edu\_bachgrad_t + \beta_3 FDI_t + \beta_4 Lawful\_perm\_resid_t + \beta_5 FDI * Corp\_profit_t + \beta_6 Poverty\_rate_t + \beta_7 Median\_income_t + \beta_8 Lawful\_perm\_resid * Pres\_party\_dummy_t + \beta_9 Poverty\_rate * Recession\_dummy_t + \varepsilon_t$

Table 6

Description of Variables for Panel Data

Description		Variables
GDP Growth Rate	DV	gdp_growth_rate
Unemployment	DV	unemployment_rate
House Price Index	DV	hpi
Rate Foreign Population (%)	IV	foreign_born_pop
Poverty Rate	IV	poverty_rate
Median Income	IV	median_income
Bachelor's Degree or Higher	IV	total_edu
Foreign-Born Population (log form)	IV	lnforppl
Poverty Rate (log form)	IV	lnpovertyrate
Foreign-Born People*Bachelor's Degree or Higher	IV	ppledu
Foreign-Born People*Bachelor's Degree or Higher (log form)	IV	lnppledu
President Party	IV	pres_party_dummy

Model Specification:

Model 1: $gdp\_growth\_rate_{it}$
$$= \alpha_{it} + \beta_1 LnForeign\_born\_pop_{it} + \beta_2 Poverty\_rate_{it} + \beta_3 Median\_income_{it} + \beta_4 Total\_edu_{it} + \beta_5 Pres\_Party\_Dummy + \varepsilon_{it}$$

Model 2: $unemployment\_rate_{it}$
$$= \alpha_{it} + \beta_1 LnForeign\_born\_pop_{it} + \beta_2 Poverty\_rate_{it} + \beta_3 Median\_income_{it} + \beta_4 Total\_edu_{it} + \beta_5 Pres\_Party\_Dummy + \varepsilon_{it}$$

Model 3: hpi_{it}
$$= \alpha_{it} + \beta_1 LnForeign\_born\_pop_{it} + \beta_2 Poverty\_rate_{it} + \beta_3 Median\_income_{it} + \beta_4 Total\_edu_{it} + \beta_5 Pres\_Party\_Dummy_{it} + \varepsilon_{it}$$

Table 5

Hausman Test

Hausman Test		**FE/RE**
Model 1: GDP Growth Rate	Prob>chi2= 0.0008	FE
Model 2: Unemployment Rate	Prob>chi2=0.1996	RE
Model 3: Housing Price Index	Prob>chi2= 0.3962	RE

Table 6

Sensitivity Analysis for Fixed Effect and Random Effect Table

VARIABLES	Model 1 GDP Growth Rate	Model 2 Unemployment Rate	Model 3 HPI
foreign_born_pop	-0.000408		
	(0.000283)		
poverty_rate	-147.8**	-0.0200	-1.070***
	(59.41)	(0.142)	(0.315)
median_income	0.0171	-3.69e-05	0.000103
	(0.0128)	(3.12e-05)	(7.34e-05)
total_edu	47.20***	-0.205***	0.716***
	(10.19)	(0.0234)	(0.0577)
ppledu	2.10e-05***		9.39e-08***
	(4.31e-06)		(2.23e-08)
pres_party_dummy	-183.7	0.713	4.232
	(936.4)	(2.017)	(3.595)
lnforppl		-0.814*	-2.288**
		(0.442)	(0.963)
Constant	53,464***	27.90***	162.2***
	(1,210)	(6.600)	(13.43)
Observations	408	408	408
R-squared	0.303		
Number of id	51	51	51

Standard errors in parentheses
*** p<0.01, ** p<0.05, * p<0.1

References

Andrews, S., Leblang, D., & Pandya, S. S. (2018). Ethnocentrism reduced foreign direct investment. *The Journal of Politics, 80*(2), 697-700.

de Brauw, A. (2017). Does immigration reduce wages? *Cate Journal, 37*(3), 473-480.

Gebremedhin, T. A., & Mavisakalyan, A. (2013). Immigration and political instability. *Kyklos, 66*(3), 317-341.

Hinojosa-Ojeda, R. (2012). The economic benefits of comprehensive immigration reform. *Cato Journal, 32*(1), 175-199.

Lee, Y. S., & Scholtes, S. (2014). Empirical prediction intervals revisited. *International Journal of Forecasting, 30*(2), 217-234.

Peri, G. (2012). Immigration, labor markets, and productivity. *Cato Journal, 32*(1), 35-53.

Posen, A. S. (2018, July 24). The cost of Trump's economic nationalism: A loss of foreign investment in the United States. *Peterson Institute for International Economics.* Retrieved from https://piie.com/blogs/trade-investment-policy-watch/cost-trumps-economic-nationalism-loss-foreign-investment-united

Schwartz, N. D., & Lohr, S. (2018, September 2). Companies say Trump is hurting business by limiting legal immigration. *New York Times.* Retrieved from https://www.nytimes.com/2018/09/02/business/trump-legal-immigration-h1b-visas.html

The Validity of "Cheap, Fast, Good: Pick Any Two" in Evaluating Healthcare Systems

Lowell Wilson Ph.D.
Computational Social Science, George Mason University
Lwilso24@masonlive.gmu.edu

Abstract

Healthcare reform is attracting considerable attention worldwide, in large part due to improved technology and escalating costs. What is often absent from these discussions is a broad-based comparison of different systems using multiple measurements, or a broad explanation for their differences. This paper quantitatively compares healthcare systems based on their cost, speed, and quality, while utilizing an agent-based computer model to aid in understanding why differences may exist. One significant finding is that achieving an effective balance between cost, speed, and quality is difficult, and not common. Several countries performed well in two of the categories, but were deficient in the third. The other significant finding is that scale/size matter—as hard as it is to achieve a balance between all three attributes, it is significantly more difficult to do so in a larger market.

Keywords: Agent-based model; Cheap, Fast, Good; international healthcare systems

La Validez de "Barato, Rápido, Bueno: Elija Dos" En la Evaluación de los Sistemas de Salud

Resumen

La reforma sanitaria está atrayendo considerable atención en todo el mundo, en gran parte debido a la mejora de la tecnología y la escalada de costos. Lo que a menudo falta en estas discusiones es una comparación de base amplia de diferentes sistemas que utilizan múltiples mediciones, o una explicación amplia de sus diferencias. Este documento compara cuantitativamente los sistemas de atención médica en función de su costo, velocidad y calidad, mientras utiliza un modelo informático basado en agentes para ayudar a comprender por qué pueden existir diferencias. Un hallazgo significativo es que lograr un equilibrio efectivo entre costo, velocidad y calidad es difícil y no es común. Varios países obtuvieron buenos resultados en dos de las categorías, pero fueron deficientes en la tercera. El otro hallazgo significativo es que la escala / tamaño importa: por difícil que sea lograr un equilibrio entre los tres atributos, es significativamente más difícil hacerlo en un mercado más grande.

Palabras clave: modelo basado en agentes; Barato, rápido, bueno; sistemas internacionales de salud

评价医疗体系时“低收费、快捷、良好：任选其二”的合理性

摘要

医疗改革正从全球吸引大量关注，这在很大程度上是因为医疗技术的进步和不断上升的成本。相关医疗辩论中缺失的是，用多种衡量方法对不同体系进行广泛比较、或是对不同体系之间的差异进行广泛解释。本文基于医疗成本、速度和质量，从定量的角度比较了医疗体系，同时使用基于agent的计算建模来协助理解为何可能会存在差异。一项显著的研究发现表明，在医疗成本、速度、质量三者之间达到有效的平衡并不容易，也并不常见。几个国家在这三者中的其中两方面表现不错，但在剩余的那方面表现有所欠缺。另一个显著的研究发现则是，规模很重要，这一点与在上述三种属性间达到平衡同样困难，并且在更大的医疗市场中这一点的困难性更为显著。

关键词：基于Agent建模；低收费；快捷；良好；国际医疗体系

1. Introduction

A common aphorism is "cheap, fast, good: pick any two". The presumption is that services (or goods with a heavy service component, for instance in a restaurant) will, at best, only manage to achieve two of these measurements. Thus, something cheap and fast will not be very good, while something good and cheap will not be delivered fast, or something fast and good will not be cheap. As long as consumers and providers are aware of this apparent conflict between these three forces, it is not difficult for either to focus on the two characteristics each values most highly, and then pursue those.

This idea of cheap, fast, good as limiting factors is not restricted to any one field, but as an identified concept, it shows up most prominently in project management. Stafford (2012) applied it to Information Technology in a discussion on outsourcing, while Maiorino (2017) applied it to payroll systems. Downing (1997) extends the idea to an "iron triangle" in his discussion of the U.S. army's Cold War doctrine of tanks, where the focus was on firepower and armor, yet largely neglecting movement. In this context, it addresses a common problem, as tanks and other military vehicles need to balance offensive capability (firepower, number of bombs, etc.), defensive capability (armor, stealth, etc.), and movement (a balance of speed, range, and power). As with the concept of cheap, fast, and good, the idea is not to achieve all three, but to reach a level of balance between the three that corresponds to the desired role and mission. On a more quotidian level, there are numerous restaurants offering cheap food, served fast, but perhaps often at the expense of quality, as noted by Saunders, Saunders, and Middleton (2015). Health care systems are under similar constraints, as discussed by Beauchamp (2009), with the underlying reasoning that consumers, providers, legislators, and other involved parties should pick the two characteristics they desire, and aim to achieve those, with the understanding that this will bring at least some deficiency in the third area. With such a broad application, it is not surprising to see the quantity of health care research addressing various aspects of quality (e.g. Cylus & Papanicolas, 2015; Groenewegen, Kerssens, Sixma, van der Eijk, & Boerma, 2005; Valentine, Bonsel, & Murray, 2007), cost (e.g. Gelormino, Bambra, Spadea, Bellini, & Costa, 2011; Perkowski & Rodberg, 2016), and timeliness (e.g. Carroll, Horn, Soderfeldt, James, & Malmberg, 1995; Jaakkimainen et al, 2014; OECD/European Union, 2016; OECD, 2017a; Redaniel, Martin, Cawthorn, Wade, & Jeffreys, 2013; Viberga, Forsberga, Borowitz, & Moline, 2013). There are a few instances of quantitative research comparing multiple countries on two of these issues (e.g. Al-Jazaeri et al, 2017; Bucci et al, 2016; Hadad, Hadad, & Simon-Tuval, 2013; Rechel et al, 2016; Sawamura, Sano, & Nakanishi, 2015; Stephens, Ledlow, Sach, & Reagan, 2017; Tandon et al, 2000; Varabyova & Schreyögg, 2013; Varkevisser, van der Geest, & Schut, 2010; von Wyl & Beck, 2016; Weaver et al, 2010), but these are largely limited to either a small number of countries, they lack quantitative results that allow for consistent comparisons, or they focus on efficiency. Notable exceptions are the landmark 2018 GBD (Study on quality of healthcare across 195 countries (Anderson, Hussey, Frogner, & Waters, 2005; GBD 2016 Healthcare Access and Quality Collaborators, 2018), OECD (2017b), and Mossialos et al (2016). Multiple articles by Siciliani and various confreres (Hurst & Siciliani, 2003; Siciliani & Hurst, 2003; Siciliani & Verzullic, 2009; Siciliani, Moran, & Borowitz, 2013 & 2014) are also insightful, if restricted to OECD countries.

With the data available from these last sources, it is possible to draw a comparison between a number of countries to see how well they balance the various aspects of cheap, fast, and good; however, the result would be more instructive if placed in the larger context. That context can be achieved through use of a computer-driven agent-based model, which will serve to illustrate various challenges in a general marketplace where both consumers and providers interact with each other. The Methods section of this paper will discuss the computer model, and the technique used to compare various countries health care systems. Following that will be the Results section, followed by Discussion, and Conclusion.

2. Methods

The seminal work of Schelling (1969) with his social segregation model showed the power of agent-based models (ABM), while Rochlin, Sarnea, and Zussman (2013) discussed the value of simple agent-based models in providing insight to a large number of issues. The "Sugarscape" model by Epstein and Axtell (1996) addressed economic issues. Beyond repeatability, one key factor these models bring is the ability to observe how an environment changes over time, as agents act on it, and in some cases how the agents themselves survive or perish. This enables us to see how businesses and consumers are able to remain in the market, or are forced to exit it because of maladaptation. This model was built using NetLogo 6.0.4 (Wilensky 1999), and utilizes some of the inherent characteristics of NetLogo in driving interpretation of the model.

As can be noted in Figure 1, there are two parts of the model: Setup, and Operation. During the Setup phase, the operator chooses the number of both types of agents—Providers, and Consumers. These agents are then configured, and prepared for the Operation phase. One option for the Setup phase is the inclusion of *Balanced Providers*. These are providers who have a balance between cheap, fast, and good; where other providers are equally divided between *Fast & Good*, *Cheap & Good*, and *Cheap & Fast*. The Operation phase represents a single day, which then repeats. Each day, each consumer receives money and searchers for a provider.

The consumer compares providers based on whether or not the provider's values for cheap, fast, and good meet or exceed its own. If they do (and the consumer has sufficient money and

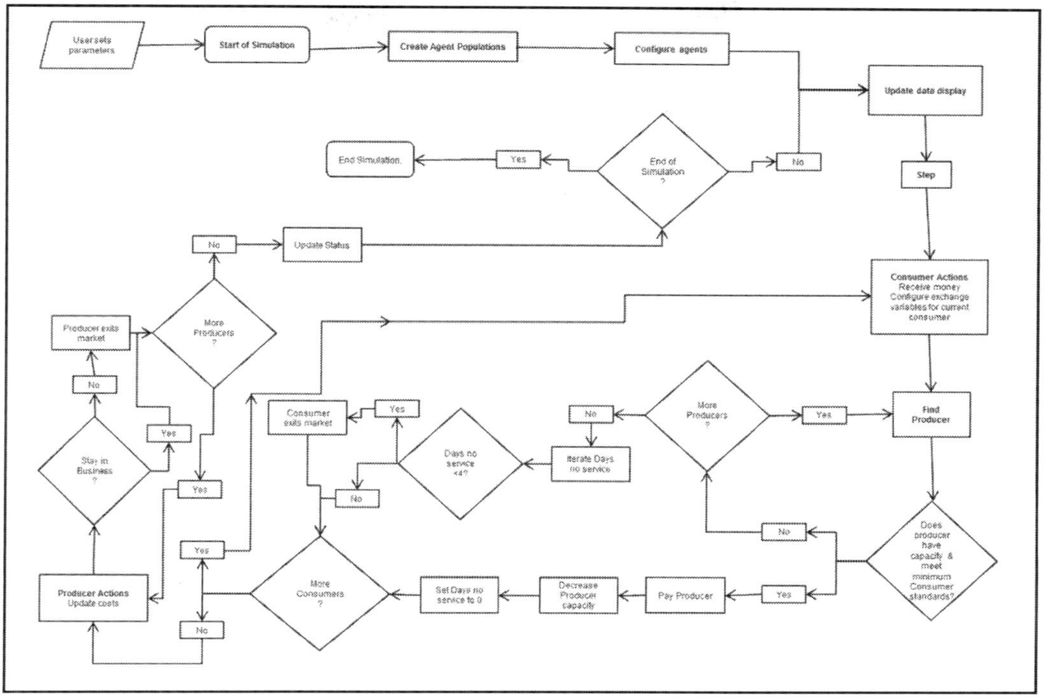

Figure 1. Model logic and interactions during a simulation.

the provider has sufficient capacity that day), then the consumer purchases the product. If not, then the consumer tries to find a suitable provider. If a consumer is unable to find a suitable provider for five consecutive days, the consumer exits the market. After all the consumers have had their chance to find a provider, each provider compares its costs and profit. At this point, if a provider is completely out of money, it leaves the marketplace. This concludes the daily cycle, which then repeats until the user notices that either consumers or providers are dropping out of the market, or that there is equilibrium between them. With the model operating as intended and free of bugs, it is at this point that the model can be said to be verified.

Although this paper is concerned with healthcare, the model is applicable and valid to any non-specific marketplace where consumers and providers interact and make decisions based on cheap, fast, and good, because it accurately describes these markets. While the value for "good" as relates to healthcare is taken from the GBD study (GBD 2016 Healthcare Access and Quality Collaborators, 2018), it would come down to the consumer's own preferences in a generic marketplace. For instance, in the case of food in a restaurant, "good" could mean "tastes good", "is healthy", "is ethically raised", "is spicy, like I like it", "is not spicy, like I like it", or any number of other meanings. The precise meaning of "good" is not of significance, only that the consumer has a means of evaluating it.

Just as the computer model compares consumers and providers based on cheap, fast, and good, we can also compare the health systems of multiple countries on the same basis. For this, each country is given a numeric score for each attribute; scores range from 0-10. The scores for quality (or good are taken from the GBD study (GBD 2016 Healthcare Access and Quality Collaborators, 2018); each country in this study is scored 0-100, so we merely divide by 10. The scores for cost (or cheap) are taken from Anderson et al (2005) and Mossialos et al (2016). The 0-10 score is done by taking the median of the given values, normalizing that as 5, and then dividing each country's cost by the median value.[1] For countries with data for both studies, their overall score is the average of the two. Scores for fast are done similarly to those for cheap, with the median value normalized to 5.[2] The data for these come from OECD (2017b), Mossialos et al (2016), and Contreras-Loya et al (2015). While these studies evaluate different procedures, and not all countries reported data in the same way, 0-10 scores were derived by averaging the scores for each where the data existed. This technique enabled a good comparison, and allowed for the addition of data on Mexico, using the same scores as the others.

With scores for each country, a comparison was made using triangles. Specifically, each value for cheap, fast, and good could be considered one side of the triangle; comparison of them was based on the relevant derived angles.[3] This allows for a comparison of all three values, and shows whether the healthcare system in each country is balanced, or if two attributes were emphasized at the expense of the third.

3. Results

The computer model was run 10 times for each of several different starting conditions. For the initial run conditions, the number of Providers varied, while the number of Consumers was held constant (at 1000); then, the percentage of Balanced Providers was varied (values for which were 0, 5, 10, 15, 20, and 25%). For each number of providers, the model was run until it appeared that an inflection point had been identified. The inflection point is where the ratio between Bankrupt Providers and Broke Consumers reversed itself. With a small number of Providers, more Consumers went broke than Providers went bankrupt. At some point, though, the market became oversaturated with Providers, and more Providers exited the market than Consumers. One challenge in working with a varying percent of *Balanced Providers* is that the total number of providers had to be significantly increased to accommodate one more. Thus, with *Balanced Providers* set to 5%, the first Balanced Provider could only be created when there were 20 providers, and the second one at 40 providers. This reduced the amount of precision that could be gained, but this became less

1 Just as with cost, some countries scored higher than 10 for speed; these scores were normalized in the same way.

2 Angles were determined using the Law of Cosines: $c^2 = a^2 + b^2 - 2ab * \text{cosine } C$

3 No triangle can have one side longer than the sum of the other two sides.

of a factor as the *Balanced Providers* percentage increased. A different challenge occurred with *Balanced Providers* at 15%; as this is not a number that evenly divides into 100, it may be noted that the total number of Providers does not directly match with the percentage one would expect with 100 consumers. In these cases, this must be accepted as an inevitable rounding error. After obtaining results for 1000 consumers, the model was run again, this time lowering the number of consumers to 800, 600, 400, and 200. In each case, the model was run until an inflection was reached, for the same number of balanced providers as with 1000 consumers. This was done to determine how big of a role scale played, as it had been observed that varying the number of balanced providers had a significant effect. With this in mind, the range for each the inflection point is shown in Table 1. In this table, two things become clear. One is that as the percent of *Balanced Providers* increases, the Inflection Point occurs at a higher ratio of Consumers to Providers, rising from a range of 6.30—6.41 with zero *Balanced Providers* to a range of 10.42—10.87 with 25% *Balanced Providers* for 1000 consumers. The second thing that becomes clear is that the inflection point generally trends lower for lower numbers of consumers. There are some exceptions, such as 25% *Balanced Providers* and 800 vs 600 Consumers, but these are rare. Note that Table 1 only shows the inflection points; it does not show the other runs above or below those points that helped narrow down the inflection points. Figures 3 and 4 show the upper and lower values of the inflection points, respectively. In these figures, the x-axis represents the percentage of *Balanced Providers* while the y-axis represents the ratio of Consumers to Providers.

Having noted that the inflection point increases with the increase in *Balanced Providers*, what does this actually mean? Among others, one thing this indicates is that having more, varied options for consumers fills a vacant niche, which makes the market more robust, and benefits all providers. The follow-on question then becomes the following: if a Cheap, Fast, Good provider can exist in a model, why do we say that it does not or cannot exist in

Table 1. Inflection Points, 200-1000 Consumers

Percent Balanced Providers	Inflection Point, 1000 Consumers	Inflection Point, 800 Consumers	Inflection Point, 600 Consumers	Inflection Point, 400 Consumers	Inflection Point, 200 Consumers
0	6.30 -- 6.41	6.30 -- 6.45	5.88 -- 6.06	5.80 -- 6.06	5.13 -- 5.55
5	7.14 -- 7.30	7.21 -- 7.34	7.23 -- 7.50	6.67 -- 7.02	5.71 -- 6.25
10	8.33 -- 8.70	8.0 -- 8.33	7.79 -- 8.11	8.0 -- 8.51	6.67 -- 7.41
15	9.09 -- 9.43	8.70 -- 8.99	8.82 -- 9.38	8.51 -- 9.30	7.41 -- 8.33
20	9.52 -- 9.80	9.64 -- 10.0	9.38 -- 10.0	8.89 -- 9.30	8.0 -- 9.09
25	10.42 -- 10.87	10.0 -- 10.53	10.0 -- 10.71	10.0 -- 11.111	8.33 -- 10

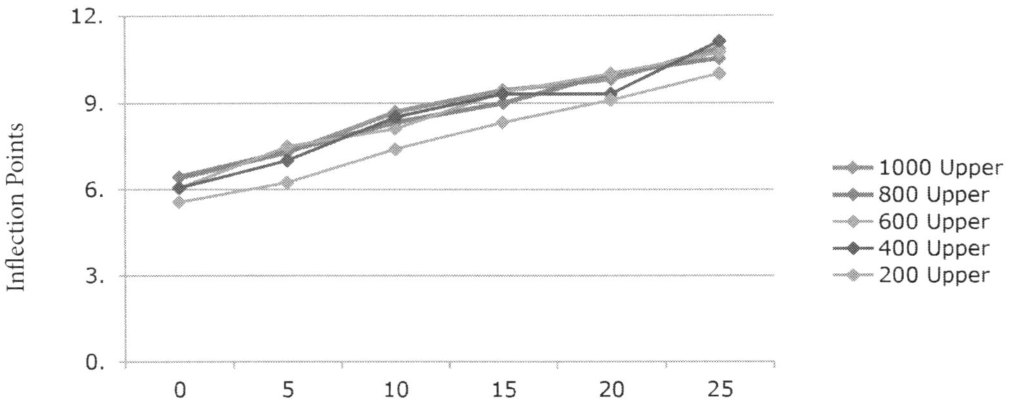

Figure 2. Upper values for inflection points, by percent balanced providers.

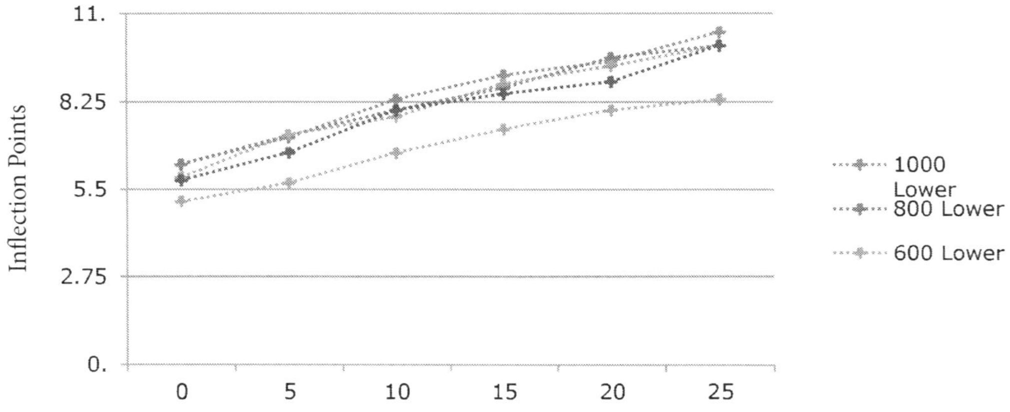

Figure 3. Lower values for inflection points, by percent balanced providers.

real life? Two major factors may explain this apparent exception. First, "good" is hard to define and measure. "Fast" can be quantified and measured, with tools ranging from a stopwatch to a calendar. "Cheap" can also be quantified and measured, using nothing more than a pocketbook. It may be noted that "cheap" and "fast" are relative terms, as what is cheap or fast to one person may not be so to another, but they can in fact be measured and compared in at least some degree. Contrariwise, as noted earlier, "good" cannot be so easily measured or consistently defined, even between a consumer and a provider.

The second factor that may help explain this contradiction is the idea of niches & specialization, and scale. During the development of this model and exploring the idea behind it, it has been noted that several restaurants managed to balance cheap, fast, and good; they may have been slightly more expensive and slower than a typical drive-thru (cheap & fast), but the quality was significantly higher. It should be noted that each one has a very limited menu, far narrower than most other restaurants. They have each specialized in a specific niche, and have managed to fill that role well (e.g., burritos, chicken sandwiches, two regional burger chains). These highly specialized restaurants thrive because they seem to have limited their menus by design, and then achieved that precarious balance between cheap, fast, and good. The fact that so few other restaurants can be cited as achieving this balance demonstrates the difficulty in doing so, especially on a large scale.

With a greater understanding of how cheap, fast, and good interact in the computer model, next is the examination of how they interact at a country level, in health care. Table 2 contains the scores for each OECD country. Population numbers were obtained from Wikipedia (2019) from the entry for each country. Of note, several countries (highlighted) only have scores for cheap or fast; this is because the missing attribute was not found in the sources used for the other countries, and a reasonable comparison could not be made.

With these scores in place, the next step was to draw a full comparison, as previously discussed. These results are found in Table 3. Of note, Iceland, Ireland, and Norway do not appear on this table; that is because, due to their low scores in two areas, the triangle for them would be undefined.[4] Of special note, several countries scored over 50 in 2 areas; these are highlighted in blue (Good & Fast), or purple (Cheap & Good). Notably, no country scored highly in all three areas, although Hungary and Israel both scored above 40 and below 90 for all three, demonstrating the closest balance of any.

5. Conclusion

Both the computer model and triangulation of health care systems successfully tackle some of the difficulties in achieving and maintaining a stable market while attempting to find a balance between cheap, fast, and good. Only a limited number of providers who deliberately fill a very narrow niche or on a smaller scale can apparently achieve this balance. Of the 9 countries who had balance in 2 attributes, only 2 (Germany, Italy) have populations exceeding 20 million, which illustrates the difficulties in scale in addressing cheap, fast, and good.

4 No triangle can have one side longer than the sum of the other two sides.

Table 2. OECD Countries Scores

COUNTRY	CHEAP	FAST	GOOD	POPULATION (millions)
Australia	4.902134	5.588273	9.6	25.4
[redacted]	4.939189		9.4	8.8
	4.359841		9.3	11.4
Canada	4.313617	6.14027	9.4	37.6
[redacted]		3.382276	7.8	17.6
	10.351		7.8	1,403
	9.807692		8.9	10.6
Denmark	4.425503	8.265364	9.2	5.8
[redacted]		1.821701	8.6	1.3
Finland	5.643335	5.983397	9.6	5.5
France	4.563457	6.775	9.2	67
Germany	4.21502	7.975	9.2	83
[redacted]	6.044653		9	10.7
Hungary	10.016	6.67953	8.2	9.8
Iceland	3.906306	2.275	9.7	0.36
Ireland	4.632446	4.171256	9.5	4.9
Israel	10	6.995435	8.5	9.0
Italy	5.062327	8.254577	9.5	60.5
[redacted]	5.645954		9.4	126.3
	10.1		9	51.4
	3.577488		9.6	0.602
Mexico	10.198	5.130196	6.6	126.6
Netherlands	4.249849	8.590999	9.6	17.3
New Zealand	5.847933	7.24898	9.2	4.9
Norway	3.587458	5.156566	9.7	5.3
Poland	10.168	2.104809	8.2	38.4
Portugal	6.442421	5.355607	8.6	10.3
[redacted]	7.749045		9	5.6
	10.157		8.3	5.4
		3.357892	9.1	2.1
Spain	6.661604	5.992037	9.2	46.9
Sweden	4.344402	7.616667	9.5	10.3
Switzerland	3.355797	8.066667	9.6	8.5
[redacted]	10.246		7.4	82
United Kingdom	5.856417	6.581909	9	67.5
United States	2.269454	6.85	8.9	327.2

Table 3. 19 Countries' Scores, Triangulated

COUNTRY	CHEAP (Score)	FAST (Score)	GOOD (Score)	GOOD (Angle)	FAST (Angle)	CHEAP (Angle)
Australia	4.90	5.59	9.60	132.34	25.49	22.18
Canada	4.31	6.14	9.40	127.23	31.34	21.43
[redacted]	4.43	8.27	9.20	[redacted]	[redacted]	28.72
Finland	5.64	5.98	9.60	111.28	35.50	33.21
France	4.56	6.78	9.20	106.84	44.82	28.34
[redacted]	4.22	7.98	9.20	[redacted]	[redacted]	27.23
[redacted]	10.02	6.68	8.20	[redacted]	41.54	[redacted]
[redacted]	10.00	7.00	8.50	[redacted]	43.50	[redacted]
[redacted]	5.06	8.25	9.50	[redacted]	[redacted]	32.17
Mexico	10.20	5.13	6.60	33.99	25.76	120.26
[redacted]	4.25	8.59	9.60	[redacted]	[redacted]	26.28
[redacted]	5.85	7.25	9.20	[redacted]	[redacted]	39.45
Poland	10.17	2.10	8.20	18.55	4.69	156.76
Portugal	6.44	5.36	8.60	93.13	38.45	48.42
Spain	6.66	5.99	9.20	93.13	40.57	46.30
[redacted]	4.34	7.62	9.50	[redacted]	[redacted]	26.61
[redacted]	3.36	8.07	9.60	[redacted]	[redacted]	19.53
United Kingdom	5.86	6.58	9.00	92.51	46.94	40.55
United States	2.27	6.85	8.90	150.79	22.06	7.15

References

Al-Jazaeri, A., Ghomraoui, F., Al-Muhanna, W., Saleem, A., Jokhadar, H., & Aljurf, T. (2017). The impact of healthcare privatization on access to surgical care: Cholecystectomy as a model. *World Journal of Surgery, 41*(2), 394–401. Retrieved from https://doi.org/10.1007/s00268-016-3739-z.

Anderson, G. F., Hussey, P.S., Frogner, B. K. & Waters, H. R. (2005). Health spending in the United States and the rest of the industrialized world. *Health Affairs, 24*(4), 903. Retrieved from https://doi.org/10.1377/hlthaff.24.4.903.

Beauchamp, G. R. (2009). QAACH, QAACH!—Quality, accessible, affordable health care. *Physician Executive Journal, 35*(4), 50-52.

Bucci, S., De Belvis, A. G., Marventano, S., De Leva, A.C., Tanzariello, M., Specchia, M. L., Ricciardi, W. & Franceschi, F. (2016). Emergency department crowding and hospital bed shortage:

Is lean a smart answer? A Systematic Review. *European Review for Medical and Pharmacological Sciences, 20*, 4209-4219.

Carroll, R. J., Horn, S. D., Soderfeldt, B., James, B. C. & Malmberg, L. (1995). International comparison of waiting times for selected cardiovascular procedures. *Journal of the American College of Cardiology, 25*(3), 557- 563.

Cylus, J. & Papanicolas, I. (2015). An analysis of perceived access to health care in Europe: How universal is universal coverage? *Health Policy.* 119: 1133–1144.

Downing, W. A. (1997). Firepower, attrition, maneuver--US Army operations doctrine: A challenge for the 1980s and beyond. *Military Review, 77*(1), 144-150

Epstein, J. M. & Axtell, R. (1996). *Growing artificial societies: Social science from the bottom up*. Cambridge, MA: Brookings/MIT Press.

GBD 2016 Healthcare Access and Quality Collaborators (2018). Measuring performance on the healthcare access and quality index for 195 countries and territories and selected subnational locations: A systematic analysis from the global burden of disease study 2016. *Lancet. 391*, 2236–2271.

Gelormino, E., Bambra, C., Spadea, T., Bellini, S., & Costa, G. (2011). The effects of health care reforms on health inequalities: A review and analysis of the European evidence base. *International Journal of Health Services. 41*(2) 209–230. Retrieved from https://doi.org/10.2190%2FHS.41.2.b.

Groenewegen, P. P., Kerssens, J. J., Sixma, H. J., van der Eijk, I., & Boerma, W. G. W. (2005). What is important in evaluating health care quality? An international comparison of user views. *BMC Health Services Research. 5*, 16-24. Retrieved from https://doi.org/10.1186/1472-6963-5-16.

Hadad, S., Hadad, Y. & Simon-Tuval, T. (2013). Determinants of healthcare system's efficiency in OECD countries. *European Journal of Health Economics, 14*, 253–265. Retrieved from https://doi.org/10.1007/s10198-011-0366-3.

Hurst, J. & Siciliani, L. (2003). Tackling excessive waiting times for elective surgery: A comparison of policies in twelve OECD countries. *OECD Health Working Papers*, No. 6. Retrieved from https://doi.org/10.1787/18152015.

Jaakkimainen, L., Tu, K., Barnsley, J., Salkeld, E., Lu, H. & Glazier, R. (2014). Waiting to see the specialist: Patient and provider characteristics of wait times from primary to specialty care. *BMC Family Practice, 15*, 16-28. Retrieved from https://doi.org/10.1186/1471-2296-15-16.

Maiorino, M. (2017, May 25). How do you want your HCM implementation? Good, fast or cheap? *Core HR, HRIS and Payroll Excellence Essentials.* Retrieved from https://www.hr.com/en/magazines/hris_payroll_excellence_essentials/may_2017_hris_payroll/how-do-you-want-your-hcm-implementation-good-fast-_j376sr6q.html.

Mossialos, E., Wenzl, M., Osborn, R. & Sarnak, D. (Eds.) (2016). 2015 international profiles of health care systems: Australia, Canada, China, Denmark, England, France, Germany, India, Israel, Italy, Japan, The Netherlands, New Zealand, Norway, Singapore, Sweden, Switzerland, and the United States. *The Commonwealth Fund.* Retrieved from https://www.google.com/url?sa=t&rct=j&q=&esrc=s&source=web&cd=1&ved=2ahUKEwj_1cmW77zkAhVqS98KHR8WAUcQFjAAegQIARAC&url=https%3A%2F%2Fwww.commonwealthfund.org%2Fsites%2Fdefault%2Ffiles%2Fdocuments%2F___media_files_publications_fund_report_2016_jan_1857_mossialos_intl_profiles_2015_v7.pdf&usg=AOvVaw3n0HFoS0r1KrJbuqy6oYkf.

OECD/European Union (2016). Waiting times for elective surgery. *Health at a Glance: Europe 2016: State of Health in the EU Cycle.* Retrieved from https://doi.org/10.1787/health_glance_eur-2016-61-en.

OECD (2017a). Waiting times for elective surgery, *Health at a Glance 2017: OECD Indicators.* Retrieved from https://doi.org/10.1787/health_glance-2017-28-en.

OCED (2017b). Health at a Glance 2017, *OECD Indicators (2017).* Retrieved from https://doi.org/10.1787/health_glance-2017-en.

Perkowski, P. & Rodberg, L. (2016). Cost sharing, health care expenditures, and utilization: An international comparison. *International Journal of Health Services. 46*(1) 106–123. Retrieved from https://doi.org/10.1177%2F0020731415615312.

Rechel, B., McKee, M., Haas, M., Marchildon, G.P. Bousquet, F., Blümele, M., ... Nolte, E. (2016). Public reporting on quality, waiting times and patient experience in 11 high-income countries. *Health Policy, 120,* 377–383. Retrieved from http://dx.doi.org/10.1016/j.healthpol.2016.02.008.

Redaniel, M. T., Martin, R. M., Cawthorn, S., Wade, J. & Jeffreys, M. (2013). The association of waiting times from diagnosis to surgery with survival in women with localised breast cancer in England. *British Journal of Cancer,* 109, 42–49.

Rochlin, I., Sarnea, D. & Zussman, G. (2013). Sequential multi-agent exploration for a common goal. *Web Intelligence and Agent Systems: An International Journal 11,* 221–244. DOI: 10.3233/WIA-130272.

Saunders, P., Saunders, A. & Middleton, J. (2015). Living in a 'fat swamp': exposure to Multiple sources of accessible, cheap, energy-dense fast foods in a deprived community. *British Journal of Nutrition, 113*(11), 1828–1834.

Sawamura, K., Sano, H., & Nakanishi, M. (2015). Japanese public long-term care insured: Preferences for future long-term care facilities, including relocation, waiting times, and individualized care. *JAMDA*, 16, 350.e9e350.e20. Retrieved from http://dx.doi.org/10.1016/j.jamda.2015.01.082.

Schelling, T. C. (1969). Models of segregation. *The American Economic Review*, 59(2), 488–493.

Siciliani, L., & Hurst, J. (2003). Explaining waiting times variations for elective surgery across OECD countries. *OECD Health Working Papers, No. 7*. Retrieved from http://dx.doi.org/10.1787/406746186162.

Siciliani, L., Moran, V., & Borowitz, M (2013). Measuring and comparing health care waiting times in OECD countries. *OECD Health Working Papers*, No. 67. Retrieved from http://dx.doi.org/10.1787/5k3w9t84b2kf-en.

Siciliani, L., Moran, V., & Borowitz, M. (2014). Measuring and comparing health care waiting times in OECD countries. *Health Policy, 118*, 292–303. Retrieved from http://dx.doi.org/10.1016/j.healthpol.2014.08.011.

Siciliani, L., & Verzullic, R. (2009). Waiting times and socioeconomic status among elderly Europeans: Evidence from SHARE. *Health Economics, 18*, 1295–1306.

Stafford, T. (2012). "Fast, Cheap or Good; Pick any Two". *Journal of Global Information Technology Management. 15*(3), 1-4.

Stephens, J. H., Ledlow, G. R., Sach, M.V. & Reagan, J. K. (2017). An Analysis of the Massachusetts Healthcare Law. *Hospital Topics*, 95(2), 32-39. Retrieved from http://dx.doi.org/10.01080/00185868.2017.1300473.

Tandon, A., Murray, C. J. L., Lauer, J.A., & Evans, D. B. (2000). Measuring overall health system performance for 191 countries. *World Health Organization GPE Discussion Paper Series*: No. 30, EIP/GPE/EQC.

Valentine, N. B., Bonsel, G.J ., & Murray, C. J. L. (2007). Measuring quality of health care from the user's perspective in 41 countries: Psychometric properties of who's questions on health systems responsiveness. *Quality of Life Research*, 16(7), 1107–1125.

Varabyova, Y. & Schreyögg, J. (2013). International comparisons of the technical efficiency of the hospital sector: Panel data analysis of OECD countries using parametric and non-parametric approaches. *Health Policy*, 112: 70– 79. Retrieved from http://dx.doi.org/10.1016/j.healthpol.2013.03.003.

Varkevisser, M., van der Geest, S. A. & Schut, F. T. (2010). Assessing hospital competition when prices don't matter to patients: The use of time-elasticities. *International Journal of Health Care Finance and Economics*, 10(1), 43–60.

Viberga, N., Forsberga, B. C., Borowitz, M., & Moline, R. (2013). International comparisons of waiting times in health care—limitations and prospects. *Health*

Policy, 112, 53–61. Retrieved from http://dx.doi.org/10.1016/j.healthpol.2013.06.013.

von Wyl, V. & Beck, K. (2016). Do insurers respond to risk adjustment? A long-term, nationwide analysis from Switzerland. *European Journal of Health Economics*, 17, 171–183.

Weaver, L., Donohue, E., Hedtke, B., Anderson, J., Martin, H., Wanduragala, D.,...Gille, C. (2010). Comparing health care systems: Can the United States learn from other countries? *Minnesota Medicine, 48,* 36-41.

Wikipedia (2019) List of countries and dependencies by population. Retrieved from https://en.wikipedia.org/wiki/List_of_countries_and_dependencies_by_population

Wilensky, U. (1999). NetLogo. *Center for Connected Learning and Computer-Based Modeling*, Northwestern University, Evanston, IL. Retrieved from http://ccl.northwestern.edu/netlogo/

Analyzing the Effectiveness of Anti-Child-Sex-Trafficking Policies Targeting Demand versus Supply Using Agent-Based Modeling

Khatera Alizada, Ph.D.
Post-Doctoral Research Fellow, Center for Mind and Culture
Corresponding author: khatera.alizada@gmail.com

Wesley J. Wildman, Ph.D.
Boston University and the Center for Mind and Culture
wwildman@bu.edu

Acknowledgements

We acknowledge funding support from the John Templeton Foundation. Laura Sabia, graduate researcher at the Center for Mind and Culture, assisted in creating diagrams and thinking through the model.

Abstract

The paper examines ways in which two law-enforcement strategies influenced the rate of child sex trafficking in King County in the state of Washington in the United States. These interventions were a) arresting and prosecuting minor victims of sex trafficking for prostitution charges and b) arresting and prosecuting buyers who purchase sex from minors. Using input data from King County, we built an agent-based simulation. The model simulates these two law-enforcement strategies in an artificial society and generates outputs in the form of the number of children trapped in commercial sex trafficking and the number of commercial sex transactions with children. Output data can be interpreted as a measure of policy effectiveness. We first describe the agent-based model: Commercial Sexual Exploitation of Children. We then evaluate the two law-enforcement strategies, calibrating the model using data from Seattle and the rest of King County. Our results show that targeting demand reduces child sex trafficking more effectively than targeting supply.

Keywords: agent-based model; policy analysis; child sex trafficking; King County

Analizando la efectividad de las políticas contra el tráfico sexual infantil dirigidas a la demanda versus la oferta utilizando modelos basados en agentes

Resumen

El documento examina las formas en que dos estrategias de aplicación de la ley influyeron en la tasa de tráfico sexual de niños en el condado de King, Washington en los Estados Unidos. Estas intervenciones fueron a) arrestar y enjuiciar a menores víctimas de tráfico sexual por cargos de prostitución, y b) arrestar y enjuiciar a compradores de sexo a menores. Utilizando datos de entrada del condado de King, creamos una simulación basada en agentes. El modelo simula estas dos estrategias de aplicación de la ley en una sociedad virtual y genera resultados en forma de la cantidad de niños atrapados en el tráfico sexual comercial y la cantidad de transacciones sexuales comerciales con niños. Los datos de salida pueden interpretarse como una medida de la efectividad de la política. Primero describimos el modelo basado en agentes: Explotación sexual comercial de niños. Luego evaluamos las dos estrategias de aplicación de la ley, calibrando el modelo utilizando datos de Seattle y el resto del condado de King. Nuestros resultados muestran que focalizar la demanda reduce el tráfico sexual infantil de manera más efectiva que focalizar la oferta.

Palabras clave: Modelo basado en agentes; análisis de políticas; tráfico sexual de niños; Condado de King

用基于agent建模分析“针对供求关系的反儿童性贩卖政策”的效果

摘要

两项执法策略从哪些途径影响了美国华盛顿州金县儿童性贩卖发生率，本文对此加以研究。这两项干预策略分别为a)逮捕涉及性贩卖的未成年人并就卖淫对其提起诉讼； b)逮捕并控告与未成年人进行性交易的买家。通过使用金县的输入数据，我们建立了一个基于agent的模拟建模。该模型在一个虚拟社会中模拟了这两项执法策略，并产生了以陷入商业性贩卖的儿童数量、和涉及儿童的商业性交易数量为形式的输出数据。输出数据能被诠释为一种对政策效果的衡量。我们首先将该模型描述为“商业性儿童性剥削”。我们随后评价了这两项执法策略，并使用从西雅图和金县其余地区的数据对模型进行了校准。研究结果显示，比起性供给，针对性需求的策略更能减少儿童性贩卖。

关键词：基于Agent建模；政策分析；儿童性贩卖；金县

Introduction

In October 2014, King County launched a policy program, Buyer Beware, designed to reduce the demand for purchase of commercial sex online (Satterberg, 2014). Its suggested policies shifted the prosecutorial focus from supply side (arresting prostituted people) to demand side (targeting buyers of commercial sex). Targeting demand through the Buyer Beware program can reduce prostitution by 20% within two years after its implementation (2015-2016) (Hopperstad, 2014). The Buyer Beware program is committed to running reverse-sting operations on a monthly or bi-monthly basis (Demand Abolition's CEASE Network Seattle). A reverse sting operation is when a police officer poses as a prostitute to arrest a buyer.

Around 300-500 children are commercially sexually exploited each year in King County (Briner, 2016). In 2015, Demand Abolition estimated that 60% to 80% of sex trades were facilitated by a third party (Gross, 2015). In Seattle, the cost of sex purchased online is \$125-\$150/30 minutes and \$175-\$200/hour. Pimps, who set quota ranges of \$500-\$800 for each girl, have two to three girls or women working on a daily basis in Seattle (Dank et al., 2014). There are 20,000–27,000 sex buyers in King County (Satterberg, 2014; Underwood, 2016). Even though a buyer might desire to engage in sex with adults only, they have no reliable way of verifying the age of those they solicit and many are children (under 18). According to a survey study of buyers of sex from adolescent girls in Georgia, 47% of buyers proceeded with their sex purchase even when they were given three cues that the prostituted person was underage (The Schapiro Group, 2010).

In 2009, before adopting the Buyer Beware program policies, 53 prostituted minors were charged for prostitution and 2 buyers were charged for buying sex from children. In 2015, 46 buyers were charged for buying sex from children and 0 children were charged for prostitution (Richey, 2018). Historically, over 90% of those arrested for prostitution in the United States are sellers and fewer than 10% are buyers (Demand Abolition's CEASE Network Boston). When comparing the effectiveness of supply-focused versus demand-focused intervention strategies, the empirical evidence suggests that demand-focused law enforcement is more effective in reducing commercial sexual exploitation of children. There is very little evidence that targeting supply yields more than a temporary suppression or displacement of prostitution (Hunt, 2013; Shively, Kliorys, Wheeler, & Hunt, 2012).

Related Work

The U.S. Department of Justice commissioned a national study examining the effectiveness of efforts to reduce prostitution and sex trafficking across the United States (US). This study found that the multifaceted nature of these intervention programs makes it hard to isolate the effect of a single component of the programs, such as a demand-suppression strategy. Some programs combine supply and demand intervention efforts so, when there is a positive change, it is hard to be certain which part of the strategy was more responsible for the measured outcome (Shively et al., 2012). For example, as a result of a comprehensive field experiment that included targeting demand through reverse-sting operations in Jersey City, New Jersey, prostitution declined by 75% (Weisburd et al., 2006). The study controlled for displacement effects, finding that the reduction in prostitution was not because of displacement effect to other areas. However, because of the comprehensive nature of the experiment, it was hard to identify the effect of targeting demand versus other elements of the program on the reduction of prostitution. Computational policy models can overcome these limitations.

Policy models permit experimentation in an artificial society, which has many advantages compared to extant methods. Existing methods are limited in their ability to break down how specific elements of the program, under what conditions and with what spatiotemporal dynamics at what cost worked or did not work because of the multifaceted nature of the program; we cannot change a single parameter and see the effect while keeping everything else equal (Gilbert, Ahrweiler, Barbrook-Johnson, Narasimhan, & Wilkinson, 2018). In addition, experimenting in the real-world policy domain is costly, time-consuming, and resource-intensive. Computational policy models can provide a deeper understanding of the policy domain.

Policy modeling has an important role to play in two areas of policy process: ex-ante policy design and appraisal and ex-post policy evaluation (Gilbert et al., 2018). Ex-ante policy design and appraisal refers to the assessment of the relative merits of competing policies in meeting policy objectives, leading to better policy design. Ex-post policy evaluation examines whether a policy meets its objectives and determines how a policy might be working, for whom, or where. Policy models can be used to examine several policy possibilities to find out which has the most robust or most sustainable or most affordable outcome. A policy model is used to experiment with alternative policy options and assumptions about the system in which it is intervening by changing parameters and rules in the models and comparing their outcomes. This is valuable because it saves the time and cost associated with having to run experiments or pilots in the real-world policy domain.

Policy modeling allows for testing alternatives and can be used as counterfactuals in place of experiment. For example, it is possible to run a simulation with a target policy implemented and not implemented and then compare the outcome of the two simulations. A policy model can be a powerful tool to engage and inform stakeholders about policies and their implications by involving them in the modeling process or by using the model to experiment with different scenarios and assumptions, comparing outcomes (Gilbert et al., 2018). Several types of computational models simulate social change over time. One technique that can overcome the limitations of experiments in the real-world policy domain is agent-based modeling (ABM).

An ABM consists of many artificially intelligent (AI) entities interacting in a virtual environment. A model of this kind draws on scientific data of several kinds. Data is used to guide the design of the AI agents' cognition, emotion, and behavior. Data is critical to the design of agent interactions and is essential for evaluating the accuracy and realism of emergent social phenomena arising from agent interactions. When there is a good match between model and data both at the low level of agent characteristics and interactions and at the high level of emergent social phenomena, we gain confidence in the model design and its validity for use in the evaluation of real-world policy options.

We are unaware of any previous agent-based models examining the effectiveness of child sex trafficking policies. However, ABMs have been used in related crime fields, such as drug trafficking and burglary, which is an indication of the widening role of modeling and simulation in guiding at least some kinds of policy discussion. For example, Dray, Mazerolle, Perez, and Ritter (2008) used an ABM to examine the effect of three policing strategies on the street-level drug market. Their findings showed that the responding-to-problems policing strategy is the most effective law-enforcement strategy in disrupting the street-level drug market. Malleson, Heppenstal, and See (2010) simulated the occurrence of burglary in light of individuals' decision rules. The results expanded understanding of the domain and helped develop effective crime-prevention policies.

Using an ABM, we built a proof-of-concept model targeted at a single policy option: arresting and prosecuting victims of child sex trafficking versus arresting and prosecuting buyers of trafficked children (Commercial Sexual Exploitation of Children; CSEC). CSEC demonstrates the usefulness of computational modeling and simulation in this domain by examining how the two policy approaches impact child sex trafficking. The standards in the Overview, Design Concepts, and Details protocol (ODD) guide documentation of the model and simulation (Grimm et al., 2010).

The Model: Overview, Design Concepts, and Details (ODD)

Overview

Purpose. This ABM examines the ways in which two law-enforcement strategies influence child sex trafficking in King County, Washington. These interventions are a) targeting supply by arresting and prosecuting child victims of sex trafficking and b) targeting demand by arresting and prosecuting buyers who purchase sex from children. The model simulates these two law-enforcement strategies in an artificial society and generates outputs in the form of the number of children trapped in commercial sex trafficking and the number of commercial sex transactions with children. Output data can be interpreted as a measure of policy effectiveness. An associated goal is to demonstrate the effectiveness of computational modeling and simulation for analyzing policy proposals in this domain.

Entities, state variables, and scales. CSEC entities are prostituted persons (children), buyers (johns), suppliers or pimps (traffickers), and the law-enforcement officials who combat trafficking of children (police).

Children are characterized by two state variables: *act* and *desired sale*. The variable *act* represents the number of commercial sex transactions. At initialization, *act* has a value of zero, which means zero commercial sex transactions, and then it increments each time an individual interacts with a buyer. The value of *desired sale* is based on the quota set by pimps in Seattle. With each commercial sex transaction, the value of *desired sale* updates. Each child's objective is to fulfill the *desired sale* during the period of a simulation run.

Each buyer is assigned two state variables: *purchase* and *purchase threshold*. The *purchase* variable increments each time a buyer makes a purchase. The purchase threshold variable is the number of times a buyer wants to purchase sex in a year and is initialized using Monto and Milrod's (2013, p. 802) survey data of buyers. This dataset presents the number of times buyers had sex with a prostitute during the previous year.

In the Buyer Beware program, the police in King County committed to running monthly or bimonthly sting operations (Demand Abolition's CEASE Network Seattle). The number of police departments plays no role in model dynamics. Depending on the policy in place, in sting operations police randomly arrest buyers or children. According to Farley et al. (2011), 100% of interviewed sex buyers reported that they would be deterred if they were sentenced to a one-month jail term. Therefore, the model assumes that once purchasers are arrested, they are deterred from going back to purchasing commercial sex for the duration of the simulation period of one year. Similarly, children who get arrested will not be prostituted after they get arrested. In other words, we assume that the recidivism rate of arrested buyers and arrested children is zero within the simulation period, which is one year.

On average, every pimp in Seattle controls three girls (Dank et al., 2014). However, the number of traffickers plays no role in model dynamics, so all girls are treated as being controlled by a single trafficker. At each time step, if supply is lower than demand, that trafficker recruits one person to meet the demand.

Process overview and scheduling. According to his purchase threshold, each buyer randomly interacts with one prostituted child, who has a *desired sale* greater than 0. As a result of this interaction, the state variables, *purchase threshold*, *desired sale*, *act*, and *purchase* are updated. The values of *purchase threshold* and *desired sale* decrease. The values of *act*, which counts commercial sex transactions, and *purchase*, which captures the number of purchases, increment. Every time-step when supply is lower than demand, the trafficker will recruit a prostituted person to increase the supply. Supply is the sum of desired *sale* of prostituted children. Demand is the sum of *purchase threshold* of buyers.

Design Concepts

In the simulation, each time step represents one week and the simulation stops when one year is completed, at step 52. The entities are randomly located on a grid. Different colors of buyers represent their purchase threshold. Yellow represents buyers with a purchase threshold of zero. Brown represents buyers with a purchase threshold of once a year. Blue represents buyers with a purchase threshold of less than one time a month. Grey represents buyers with a purchase threshold of twice a week. White represents buyers with a purchase threshold of three times a week. The buyers' color changes to green after getting arrested. Prostituted children are displayed in red. Children's color changes to orange after getting arrested.

Basic principles. This model applies the economic principle of demand and supply to child sex trafficking. The demand-supply framework has not been previously applied to an agent-based model of child sex trafficking.

Emergence. There is variability in the number of purchases each buyer can make. The number of purchases and the demand for commercial sex emerge from interaction between buyers and sellers.

Sensing. Buyers know whether the variable *desired sale* is above zero. They purchase sex from a prostituted child having a *desired sale* of greater than zero.

Interaction. Buyers and prostituted children interact if the buyers did not reach their *purchase threshold* and if the prostituted children have a *desired sale* of greater than zero.

Stochasticity. The interaction between buyers and prostituted persons is a stochastic process because interaction partners are chosen randomly.

Observation. Two plots are used for

observation: a line plot with the number of prostituted children over time and a line plot that shows the number of purchases in each time step.

Details

Initialization. To manage computational load during the simulation, we created a 1:10 scale representation of the population.

Children. Approximately 300-500 children are commercially sexually exploited each year in King County (Briner, 2016). Assuming 380 sexually exploited children, the simulation is initialized with 38 children, with the variable *act* (the number of commercial sex transactions) set to 0. Each child has an initial *desired sale* of 1456, which is based on the *daily sale* quota set by the pimp in Seattle. The cost of online sex purchase is \$125-\$150/30 minutes and \$175-\$200/hour and pimps set quota ranges \$500-\$800 for each girl on a daily basis in Seattle (Dank et al., 2014). Based on the quota set by the pimps in Seattle, the commercial sex transaction is assumed to be four per day, with a price of \$200 per customer.

Buyers. There are 20,000-27,000 sex buyers in King County (Satterberg, 2014; Underwood, 2016). According to another study, 47% of buyers proceeded with their sex purchase even when they were given cues that the prostituted person was underage (The Schapiro Group, 2010). We assume that 47% (12,690 individuals) of (27,000) buyers in King County proceed with their purchase of sex even when they are given cues that the seller is underage. Thus, each CSEC run is initialized with 1,269 buyers randomly located on the grid. Each buyer's *purchase* variable is initialized at zero and increments each time the buyer makes a purchase. Purchase thresholds for buyers are based on Monto and Milrod's (2013, p. 802) survey data of buyers. This data presents the number of times that buyers purchased sex with a prostitute during the previous year. Buyers marked yellow have a purchase threshold of 0. Buyers marked brown have a purchase threshold of 1. Buyers marked blue have a purchase threshold of 10. Buyers marked grey have a purchase threshold of 104 (twice per week). Buyers marked white have a purchase threshold of 156 (three times per week).

Police. One police department is located on the grid. In reality, there are many police departments, sometimes with different policies and sting arrangements. However, the number of police departments plays no role in model dynamics, so there is no need for more than one.

Traffickers. One trafficker is located randomly on the grid. In reality, there are typically many traffickers controlling a small number of children each. However, the number of traffickers plays no role in model dynamics, so there is no need for more than one.

Input Data. The model execution allows for simulations with two intervention options: a) targeting demand (arresting and prosecuting buyers) and b) targeting supply (arresting and prosecuting prostituted persons, including children). CSEC can be run for a year in which King County law enforcement targeted supply (2009) and a year in which King County law enforcement targeted demand (2015). The results of the two runs are compared to assess the impact of these contrasting policies on the frequency of child sex trafficking.

According to records from the King County Prosecuting Attorney's Office (Richey, 2018), in 2015, 46 buyers were arrested and charged for buying sex from children, and 0 children were arrested and charged for prostitution. By contrast, in 2009, 2 buyers were arrested and charged for trying to purchase sex from a child and 53 children were arrested and charged for prostitution.

Using the King County data, in 2009, when law enforcement targeted supply, at every time step the police arrested one prostituted child and the police arrested one buyer at time step 1 and another at time step 30. In 2015, when law enforcement targeted demand, police arrested no prostituted children, but arrested four buyers after every 5-time step, reflecting monthly reverse-sting operations.

Submodels. The following table lists all model parameters.

Table 1. Parameter Descriptions

Parameter	Description
Number-recruited-children	Number of prostituted minors
Number-johns	Number of buyers
Number-cops	Number of police departments
Number-traffickers	Number of traffickers
Arrest-johns	Number of buyers being arrested
Saved-children	Number of arrested children

Commercial sex transaction: purchase. In each time step, based on the purchase threshold for each buyer, some buyers randomly choose one prostituted child to interact with. As a result of this interaction, the state variables—*purchase threshold, desired sale, act*, and *purchase*—get updated.

The number of purchases ranges between 0 and 3 purchases per week. The highest number of buyers (66.3%) makes 1 purchase every 5 weeks. The second highest number of buyers (24.7%) makes 2 purchases per week. Approximately 5.4% of buyers make one purchase during the simulation period and 2.2% of buyers make 3 purchases every week.

If purchase threshold = 10 → buy-target1→ buy sex from a prostituted child with desired sale > 0 at every 5 steps → set purchase + 1, purchase threshold – 1, desired sale – 1, act + 1

If purchase threshold = 104 → buy-target2 → buy sex from a prostituted child with desired sale > 0 -→ set purchase + 2, purchase threshold – 2, desired sale

Table 2. Annual Commercial Sex Transactions

Frequency of commercial sex in previous year	Percent of buyers
No times	1.4
One time	5.4
Less than once per month	66.3
Once or twice per week	24.7
More than 3 times per week	2.2

Table 3. Weekly Commercial Sex Transactions

Number of commercial sex purchase	Percent of buyers	Buyers annual purchase threshold
1/52 time steps	5.4	1 (brown)
1/ 5 time steps	66.3	10 (blue)
0/52 time steps	1.4	0 (yellow)
2/time step	24.7	104 (grey)
3/time step	2.2	156 (white)

– 2, act + 2

If purchase threshold = 156 → buy-target3 → buy sex from a prostituted child with desired sale > 0 -→ set purchase + 3, purchase threshold – 3, desired sale – 3, act + 3

If purchase threshold = 1→ buy-target4 → buy sex from a prostituted child with desired sale > 0 at step 1 -→ set purchase + 1, purchase threshold – 1, desired sale – 1, act + 1

Recruiting prostituted minors. At every time step when supply is lower than the demand, the trafficker will recruit one prostituted child to meet the demand.

Desired sale (1456) = 4 sales per day * 7days per week * 52 weeks per year

Supply = sum of the desired sale variables of all prostituted children

Demand = sum of the purchase threshold variables of all buyers

If supply < demand → recruit 1 prostituted person with desired sale 1456 – (28 * time step)

Model Execution Results

CSEC replicates the King County policy experiment by simulating the pre-change policy situation in 2009 and the post-change policy situation in 2015. Comparing the outputs of the two intervention strategies illustrates that intervention focused on targeting demand is more effective than

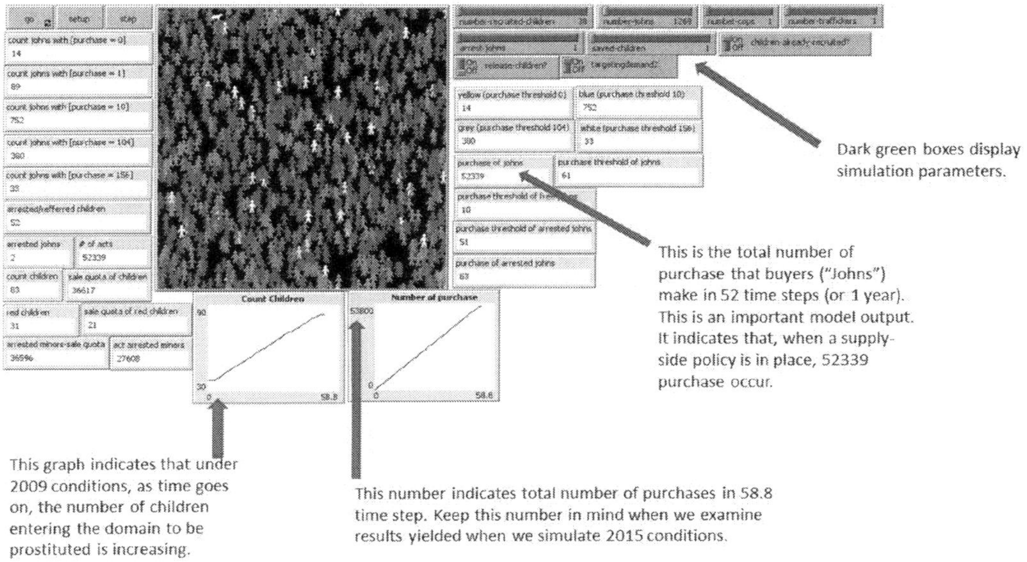

Figure 1. Pre-change policy situation (2009).

intervention focused on targeting supply in terms of reducing the number of trafficked children forced into the commercial sex industry. This finding aligns with existing literature, which shows very little empirical evidence for the effectiveness of targeting supply in commercial sexual exploitation (Shively et al., 2012).

Figure 1 is the simulation grid for the pre-change policy situation (2009).

The simulation grid for the post-change policy situation (2015) has a few differences, as the following annotated screen capture shows (Figure 2).

Figure 3 depicts the percentage difference between purchases in 2009 and purchases in 2015 over the one-year period of the simulation, with 52 one-week time-steps. A positive percentage number indicates that the 2009 number is higher by that percentage than the 2015 number. At the beginning of the year, there is not much difference, but the difference grows, producing an end-of-year situation in which there are 1.5% fewer purchases in 2015 than in 2009, with a 3.5% decrease in the number of buyers in 2015. Since the simulation runs reflected the policy change from supply-side arrests to demand-side arrests, and since these models are causal and not merely correlational (as statistical models are), *we know that the change occurs because of the policy shift*.

We can also use the number of prostituted minors over the course of one year to evaluate the policy change (Figure 4). The blue line tracks 2009 conditions (with a supply-side focused law-enforcement policy). The orange line tracks the relatively stable number of prostituted minors in the model over time under 2015 conditions (with a demand-side focused policy).

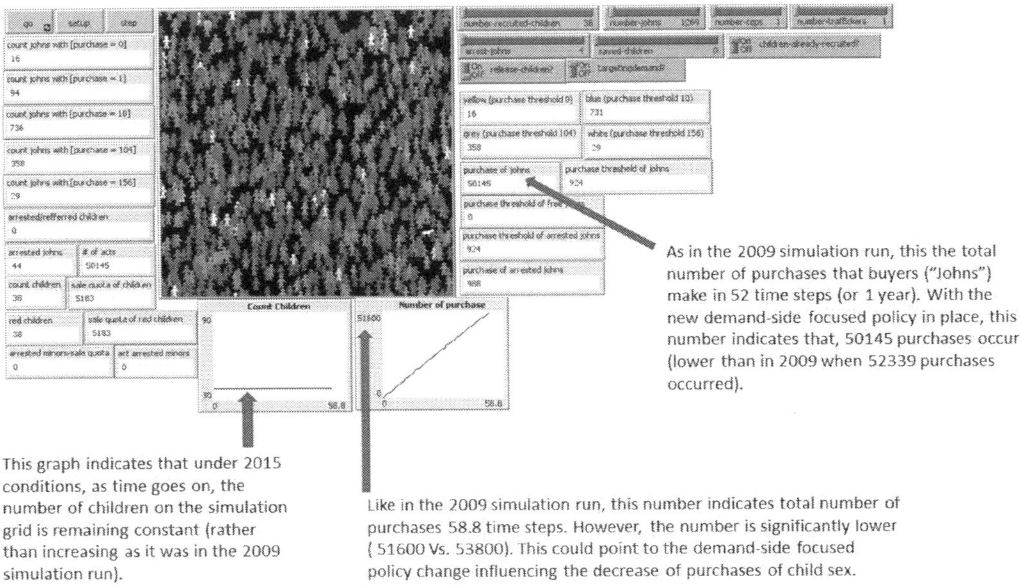

Figure 2. Post-change policy situation (2015).

Figure 3. Commercial sex purchase.

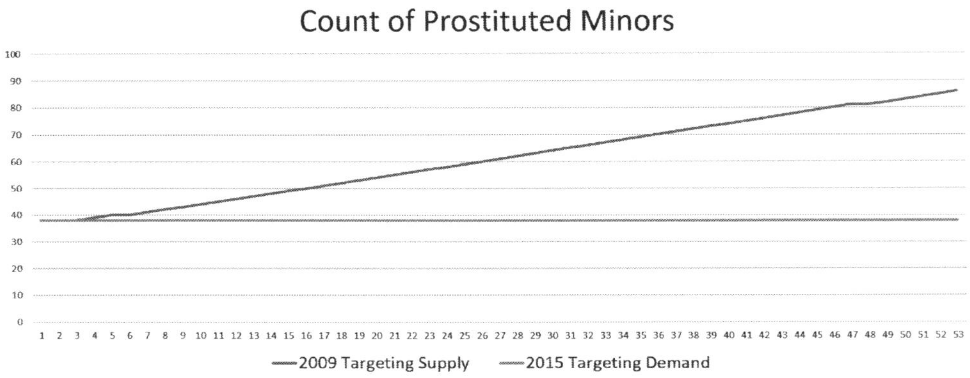

Figure 4. Count of prostituted minors.

Our results show that targeting buyers and protecting victims has a more significant impact on overall reduction of commercial sexual exploitation of minors in King County, matching the results of their policy experiment.

Conclusion: High-Tech Tool Can Improve Policy Discussions

Computational models are becoming vital for public policy processes (development, implementation, and evaluation). These models allow policy professionals to experiment with policy options in a virtual world before spending money and political capital on real-world policy change. Experimenting in a real-world policy domain is costly, time-consuming, and requires more resources. Computational models can teach us about the policy domain without impacting any real-world situations where they could prove risky.

Virtually evaluating policies has other advantages relative to extant methods. Traditional approaches have often been unable to indicate how, why, where, for whom, at what cost, and under which conditions policies are effective. But computational models give us detailed clues about what causes what. For instance, we can change one policy assumption at a time to determine the sensitivity of effects to that assumption.

Policy models can be used to investigate counterfactuals in lieu of real-world experimentation. For example, in our model, the simulation is run twice, once while implementing the new policy and once without implementing it. The outcomes of the two simulation runs are compared to evaluate effectiveness of the policy shift.

Policy modeling is a powerful tool for engaging and informing stakeholders and the public. Successful policy modeling requires intensive collaboration among stakeholders: modelers, clients, data-suppliers, law enforcement, government, and NGOs. These new tools are valuable adjuncts to the accrued wisdom of policy professionals and stakeholders. They do not replace policy expertise. Far from it: computer models are impossible without stakeholder expertise. But these tools augment policy expertise in a vital way, generating a new kind of policy debate.

References

Briner, L. (2016). Sexual exploitation of trafficking and youth. *U.S. Department of Health and Human Services.* Retrieved from http://kingcounty.gov/~/media/depts/executive/performance-strategy-budget/documents/pdf/RLSJC/2016/2016-01-28-Sexual-Exploitation-and-Trafficking-of-Youth-Presentation.ashx?la=en

Dank, M., Khan, B., Downey, P. M., Kotonias, C., Mayer D., Owens C., ... Yu, L. (2014). Estimating the size and structure of the underground commercial sex economy in eight major U.S. cities. *The Urban Institute.* Retrieved from https://www.urban.

org/research/publication/estimating-size-and-structure-underground-commercial-sex-economy-eight-major-us-cities/view/full_report.

Demand Abolition Boston. The illegal commercial sex industry in Boston. *Demand Abolition's CEASE Network.* Retrieved from https://www.ceasenetwork.org/boston/

Demand Abolition Seattle. Cities empowered against sexual exploitation. *Demand Abolition's CEASE Network.* https://www.ceasenetwork.org/seattle/.

Dray, A., Mazerolle, L., Perez, P., & Ritter, A. (2008). Policing Australia's 'heroin drought': Using an agent-based model to simulate alternative outcomes. *Journal of Experimental Criminology*, *4*(3), 267-287.

Farley, M., Schuckman E., Golding, M. J., Houser, K., Jarrett, L., Qualliotine, P., & Decker, M. (2011, July 15). Comparing sex buyers with men who don't buy sex: You can have a good time with the servitude VS. You're supporting a system of degradation. Paper presented at *Psychologists for Social Responsibility Annual Meeting*, Boston, MA.

Gilbert, N., Ahrweiler, P., Barbrook-Johnson, P., Narasimhan, K. P., & Wilkinson, H. G. (2018). Computational modelling of public policy: Reflections on practice. *Journal of Artificial Societies and Social Simulation*, *21*(1), 1-14. Retrieved from http://jasss.soc.surrey.ac.uk/21/1/14.html

Grimm, V., Berger, G. U., DeAngelis, D. L., Polhill, J. G., Giske, J., & Railsback, S. F. (2010). The ODD protocol: A review and first update. *Ecological Modelling*, *221*, 2760-2768.

Gross, S. J. (2015, February 12). Boston joins campaign against sex trafficking. *The Daily Free Press.* Retrieved from https://dailyfreepress.com/blog/2015/02/12/boston-joins-campaign-against-sex-trafficking-2/

Hopperstad, J. (2014, October 15). Buyer beware: King County going after men who buy sex. *Q13 Fox News.* Retrieved from http://q13fox.com/2014/10/15/buyer-beware-king-county-going-after-men-who-buy-sex/

Hunt, S. (2013, September 28). Deconstructing demand: The driving force of sex trafficking. *Demand Abolition.* Retrieved from https://www.demandabolition.org/news/deconstructing-demand-driving-force-sex-trafficking

Malleson N., Heppenstal, A., & See, L. (2010). Crime reduction through simulation: An agent-based model of burglary. *Computers, Environment and Urban Systems*, 34, 236-250.

Monto, M. A., & Milrod, C. (2013). Ordinary or peculiar men? Comparing the customers of prostitutes with a nationally representative sample of men. *International Journey of Offender Therapy and Comparative Criminology*, *58*(7), 802-820. doi:10.1177/0306624X13480487

Richey, V. (2018). *KCPAO data.* King

County Senior Deputy Prosecuting Attorney, Special Assault Unit. King County Prosecuting Attorney's Office.

Satterberg, D. (2014, October 16). Local jurisdictions join together to launch new approach to reduce demand for prostitution. *King County Prosecuting Attorney.* Retrieved from http://www.kingcounty.gov/depts/prosecutor/news-media-center/news/2014/october/prostitution.aspx

The Schapiro Group. (2010). Men who buy sex with adolescent girls: A scientific research study. *YouthSpark.* Retrieved from http://youth-spark.org/wp-content/uploads/2016/07/TSG-Complete-Demand-Study.pdf

Shively, M., Kliorys, K., Wheeler, K., & Hunt, D. (2012). A national overview of prostitution and sex trafficking demand reduction efforts, final report. *The National Institute of Justice.* Retrieved from https://www.ncjrs.gov/pdffiles1/nij/grants/238796.pdf

Underwood, T. (2016, July 19). Seattle busts 200 buyers; could collect up to $275K for sex trade victims. *Demand Abolition.* Retrieved from https://www.demandabolition.org/news/seattle-busts-200-buyers-collect-275k-sex-trade-victims-seattle-police-departments-vice-high-risk-victims-unit-launched-first-kind-sting-july-11-arrest/

Weisburd, D., Wyckoff, L. A., Ready, J., Eck, J. E., Hinkle, J. C., & Gajewski, F. (2006). Does crime just move around the corner? A controlled study of special displacement and diffusion of crime control benefits. *Criminology, 44*(3), 549-591.

Planning for Social Environments: Social Capital in the Context of Critical Realism and the Dynamics of Complex Systems

Milton J. Friesen
School of Planning (Faculty of Environment), University of Waterloo
m2friese@uwaterloo.ca

Abstract

Measuring phenomena as intricate and difficult as those arising from human interactions at neighborhood scales requires careful methodological and conceptual framing. A strategy that balances directive progress with permissive exploration is needed. Critical realism provides a philosophical framework within which to situate qualified knowledge development arising from complex systems insight. In turn, network science provides a vital set of mathematical and analytical tools and strategies that are directly applicable to social capital phenomena. Around and through this open approach to exploration, novel methodologies, such as the relationship between social capital and spatial use in urban areas, can be considered for their potential to assist urban planners and policymakers in understanding and evaluating the social impact of past, present, and future plans as a means of increasing the sophistication and effectiveness of strategies and evaluations.

Keywords: critical realism; complex adaptive systems; network science; social capital; computational models; urban planning

Planificación para entornos sociales: capital social en el contexto del realismo crítico y la dinámica de los sistemas complejos

Resumen

La medición de fenómenos tan complejos y difíciles como los que surgen de las interacciones humanas a escala de vecindario requiere un marco conceptual y metodológico cuidadoso. Se necesita una estrategia que equilibre el progreso directivo con la exploración permisiva. El realismo crítico proporciona un marco filosófico dentro del cual ubicar el desarrollo de conocimiento calificado que surge de la comprensión de sistemas complejos. A su vez, la ciencia de redes proporciona un conjunto vital de herramientas y estrategias matemáticas y analíticas que son directamente aplicables a los fenómenos del capital social. En torno a este enfoque abierto de exploración, se pueden considerar metodologías novedosas, como la relación entre el capital social y el uso espacial en las zonas urbanas, por su potencial para ayudar a los planificadores urbanos y a los responsables políticos a comprender y evaluar el impacto social del pasado, presente y futuro. planes como un medio para aumentar la sofisticación y efectividad de las estrategias y evaluaciones.

Palabras clave: realismo crítico; sistemas adaptativos complejos; ciencia de redes; capital social; modelos computacionales; planificación urbana

社会环境规划：批判性现实主义和复杂系统动态背景下的社会资本

摘要

衡量复杂和困难的现象，比如由邻里互动引起的现象，需要在方法论和概念上进行仔细建构。需要一个能在指令进展和许可探究之间求取平衡的策略。批判性现实主义提供一个哲学框架，在这个框架内能建立一个合格的、源于复杂系统见解的知识发展。反过来，网络科学提供一组重要的数学分析工具和策略，它们能直接应用于社会资本现象。通过这一开放探究方法，新奇的方法论—例如城市地区的社会资本和空间使用之间的关系—能被纳入考量范围，因为其作为一种增加策略和评价的复杂性和有效性的方法，有潜力协助城市规划者和决策者理解并评价过去、现在、未来计划所产生的社会影响。

关键词：批判现实主义；复杂适应系统；网络科；社会资本；计算模型，城市规划

1. Planning and the Measurement of Social Capital

Social capital as a subject of formal research is relatively new, although the phenomena of social structures clearly is not (Aristotle, 2012; Tocqueville, 2001). Amid significant and wide-ranging academic interest in social capital (Friesen, 2018b), agreement on measurement and consensus on the scope of what is included in social capital remain elusive. This need not be a significant worry as science has always proceeded from partial understanding, competing theories, and unclear boundaries (Brody, 1970; Chomsky, 1996; Serres, 1995). There are dozens of varying definitions of social capital (see Appendix 1 for a representative list of definitions and authors) but for this paper, the term *social capital* is intended to refer to the density and quality of human relational networks, both formal and informal. Social capital is a phenomena whose effect is significant (Coleman, 1988; Kawachi, Kennedy, Lochner, & ProthrowStith, 1997; Ostrom & Ahn, 2003), despite the difficulty of consistent definition and agreed-to measurement. Latent constructs, such as social capital (Sekar & Rai, 2018), are gateways for insight about our understanding of the social infrastructure of urban communities at the scale of neighborhoods is particularly important for planners and policymakers. This local scale is related to a significant number of phenomena that are vital to well-being such as mental health, longevity, educational achievement, economic performance, and belonging (Bethune, 2014; Dunkelman, 2014; Pinker, 2014).

1.1. Issues of Scale in Social Capital Measurement

National and regional social trends become visible through instruments like the General Social Survey (GSS), allowing us to learn about how people spend their time, how they perceive their neighbors, what they think of the organizations in their communities, and so on. While this scale of analysis is of some use to planners, it is much less valuable in the context of community level design and decision-making. This is particularly true for social capital, where local conditions are key drivers of the relational ecology of citizens at these scales (Bechard & Marchand, 2006). The GSS instrument does not provide this resolution.

Neighborhood-level social capital measurement requires a data collection approach that is sufficiently economical for deployment across cities at neighborhood levels. Saturation surveys (outside of a census) are generally not feasible given cost and complexity, but the increasing ubiquity of mobile devices that collect geographic positioning systems (GPS) data means ever-larger data sets are at least potentially available for emerging data analysis approaches (Cohen, 2011; Pentland, 2014). For example, it would be expensive to collect a representative sampling at neighborhood levels for an entire city with the additional burden of mapping the social networks of participants. Participant surveys, though common as a form of data generation and in addition to their cost, continue to face the problems that are inherent with respondent-driven instruments (Bernard, Killworth, Kronenfeld, & Sailer, 1984). Despite the difficulties and expense, this approach to gathering data is an important facet of social capital research to date (Edwards, 2004; Lochner, Kawachi, & Kennedy, 1999). Novel methodologies that grow out synthetic approaches could lead to more effective and reliable measures. These methodologies include behavioral data collection using machine learning with large datasets harvested from ubiquitous sources, such as smart phones or devices in the environment, to infer socio-spatial relational ties (Crandall et al., 2010; Eagle, 2005). Understanding and making effective use of these emerging data science methods is an important task for current social capital research in planning and policy contexts.

1.2. Social Capital Elements

Research in social capital requires strategies that can respond to the complex and overlapping social phenomena of relationship networks, including the qualities of those relationships, such as the degree of trust present. The lack of agreement on definitions (Friesen, 2013a) suggests that social capital research may still be early in its development (Kuhn, 1962) or too complex to define in simple ways. Core elements, however, can be discerned across the range of definitions. A review of existing scholarship reveals that trust and social ties are key elements across definitional differences (Carpiano & Fitterer, 2014; Chow & Chan, 2008; Richey, 2007; Veenstra, 2002). The range of phenomena that contribute to social capital (Dugundji, Scott, Carrasco, & Paez, 2012; Kwan, 2007; J. R. Logan, 2012; van der Gaag, 2002) suggests a need to establish a framework suitable for capturing common elements, while allowing room for variation. The approach must be clear and coherent enough for use at community levels, where policy impacts on social infrastructure need to be understood.

We know lower levels of trust lead to increased relational fragmentation, social isolation, and decreased levels of social capital (Bethune, 2014). Social fragmentation can increase pressure on municipal resources through increased litigation, greater involvement by police or municipal enforcement in disputes, low voter turnout and volunteering, and low levels of informal interaction, with consequent increased health service demands (Browning, Feinberg, & Dietz, 2004; McDoom, 2014). Recent work in Holland points to increased social capital as an effective means of lowering the costs of public health service while improving positive results for patients with Parkinson's disease (Tod et al., 2016).

1.3. Framework for Social Capital Measurement

A Government of Canada expert report that reviewed social capital from a policy perspective considered measurement approaches at the *macro* (structural including national-regional, such as the General Social Survey), *meso* (local communities, neighborhoods, Census Tracts), and *micro* levels (individuals or immediate networks of individuals) (Franke, 2005). Findings reveal that more time and effort have been invested in designing and carrying out either *macro* level international and national research programs (Chung, Choi, & Lee, 2014; Garcia, Martinez, & Radoselovics, 2008; Gesthuizen, van der Meer, & Scheepers, 2009; van Oorschot & Arts, 2005) or highly contextual *micro* level ethnographic or site-specific research projects, where behavior of a specific group, type of individual, or social unit is examined (Boneham & Sixsmith, 2006; McPherson, Smith-Lovin, & Brashears, 2006).The *meso* scale, which is particularly relevant to planners, represents an important research and policy opportunity. The meso level of social structure is strategic for improving research and policy tools that planners can use in developing strategies for city building that more fully integrate social implications in decision-making and resource allocation processes, including a much better understanding of the social impact of decisions.

1.4. Social Capital and other Social Phenomena

Complex phenomena with unclear or highly diverse causal mechanisms may feature significant clusters of interacting systems and causal dynamics that cannot be understood in isolation from each other (Alexander, 2001; Gunderson & Holling, 2002). Where this is the case (e.g., human health and environmental conditions) scientists can often gain insight into the higher order phenomenon by understanding the dynamics of subsystems of phenomena (Stanley, 2007). Early social capital research and theory explored key causal factors, such as trust and cultural norms (Bourdieu, 2008; Coleman, 1988; Paldam, 2000). Untangling the complex nature of these causal factors in neighborhood social phenomena is ongoing (Chung et al., 2014) and reflects long traditions of deliberations that concern planning theory and complex phenomena (Jacobs, 1959; Lindblom, 1959; Simon, 1962; Weaver, 1948). Research progress will be difficult given these realities.

Progress in social capital research may, as a result of these challenges, require significant timeframes (Ostrom & Ahn, 2003) and a fuller consideration of the nature of the problems encountered. The proposed approach to a research framework has been designed with an awareness of these dynamics, including the ways in which they involve the contested relationship between natural and social sciences (Gadamer, 1960; H. Putnam, 1988; Rorty, 1998), challenges regarding the efficacy of theory in guiding research (Kuhn, 1970; G. Thomas, 1997), and the degree of confidence we can have in research results, particularly social science results, as true (or complete) representations of reality (Derman, 2011; Rorty, 1979).

2. Structuring Social Capital Research

The idea of an open and exploratory approach to research is complimented in the field of architecture by the concept of an armature (Hu, 2014; Kojima, 2014). An armature is a structure that acts as a point of focus for something to develop rather than acting as an external constraint fencing something in. Armatures are commonly used in sculpture, in model building in stop motion film, and in architectural design processes. A lattice or framework that vines can grow on, sometimes referred to as a *thyrsus*, is another example of an armature (Baudelaire, 1981, pp. 72-73). From an urban vantage point, a road can act like an armature along which vendors, gas stations, parks, and other structures develop over time. By contrast, a formal suburban master plan develops out of a fully proscribed set of pre-formed terms where dynamics about the future are assumed (Allmendinger, 2009; Fainstein & Campbell, 2011; Fischler, 2000). The nature of social capital lends itself to a directed, but open, approach where new insight is gained from new data sets designed to explore the complex phenomena involved. I employ a carefully structured research strategy with sufficient flexibility to allow for novelty and discovery on the way (Alexander, 2003a; Westley, Zimmerman, & Patton, 2006; Wheatley, 2006).

2.1. A Strategy for Extending Social Capital Research

The armature approach is reflected in the structure of this paper. Movement from left to right (Figure 1) reflects a framework that scales from meta-philosophical considerations to particular phenomena that can be investigated empirically. This simplified logic supports an approach to social capital research methods and strategies that advance explanation without succumbing to either totalizing claims or reductive traps (Abbott, 2009; Kuhn, 1970).

Critical Realism >>> Complexity Science >>> Networks >>> Social Capital >>> Spatial Data

Figure 1: Conceptual armature from broad to specific.

Within this analytic structure, critical realism forms a meta-theoretical framework within which complex systems and behaviors are both expected and partially understood. Network analysis provides a formalized means of understanding those complex systems which are driven by both the structure (topology) and process (dynamics) of various elements and components (including nested systems of systems) (Albert & Barabási, 2001; Cohen & Havlin, 2010): in this case, social interactions in space and time comprise the social infrastructure of cities (Friesen, 2013b). Following this logic, each of the elements of the proposed armature is examined more closely below.

3. Critical Realism

CRITICAL REALISM >>> **COMPLEXITY SCIENCE** >>> **NETWORKS** >>> **SOCIAL CAPITAL** >>> **SPATIAL DATA**

Figure 2

Critical realism holds promise as a primary framework for orientation in this challenging space and can improve social capital theory and shape further research. The particularities of critical realism are oriented around four key general concepts and commitments within which we can extend our understanding of social capital: regularity in scientific knowledge, historical knowledge, human agency, and emergence.

3.1. Scientific Knowledge

First, for knowledge to be generated, shared, and built on, some degree of *regularity in scientific knowledge* is required. It is possible and common for knowledge gained through research to be shared with and understood by other people given that reality exists apart from our mental interactions with it (Mir & Watson, 2001, p. 1170). In this regard, science may be thought of as a cultural practice with rules and practices that guide how that knowledge is generated, evaluated, shared, and disputed (Kuhn, 1962). The subject of inquiry is the world around us at all scales, including individual and collective expressions of human society. The approaches to different subjects vary widely but even the most isolated forms of inquiry reflect a dependence on pre-existing knowledge, culture, instruments, and theories (R. K. Logan, 2007). Critical realism asks "what must be true about reality for scientific experiments to be intelligible" (Steinmetz, 1998, p. 176).

Critical realism affirms this characteristic of scientific knowledge, but qualifies the over-reach of naturalism by arguing that neither reductivism (explanation of primary elements constitutes a full description) nor scientism (only what qualifies as scientific knowledge is valid knowledge) is adequate (H. Putnam, 1988). Advancing research about social capital for meso-level urban settings requires ongoing commitments to a meaningful synthesis of a wide range of research approaches and removal of artificial barriers between fields of inquiry (Bhaskar, 1978; Scheffer et al., 2015). The deep causal complexity of social capital factors requires a commitment to disciplined but provisional conclusions that traverse narrow disciplinary boundaries (Fairfield, 2003; Feyerabend, 1970; Gadamer, 1960; Taylor, 2004).

The regularity of scientific knowledge permits us to accumulate understanding beyond the intellectual and temporal limits of individual human beings—what we know can be passed on, added to, refined or changed within cultural and formal structures. Traditional scientists have believed, at various points, that in principle this process could be totalizing and exhaustive and would lead to complete knowledge of the world and ourselves. This encyclopedic aspiration was seen in, for example, statements of some late 19th century scientists who believed that all that was left for science to discover in their time was decimal places and details (Badash, 1972). Scientific knowledge, like other forms of knowledge, is always partial and can shift significantly with new discoveries, such as has occurred in experiments on entanglement in quantum physics (Varnava et al., 2016). Our most sophisticated and intensive efforts to explore, experiment, and formalize knowledge have led to a realization that what we know, in both degree and kind, is very partial indeed, even in the most formalized fields of science. Significant causal complexity and the deep interrelatedness of all phenomena suggest that there are in-principle limits, not something that will be remedied by better research or more sophisticated computation. Even where causal assumptions are made or patterns are noted, the nonlinear nature of interacting dynamics results in a temporal reality that is never free of contingencies (Steinmetz, 1998; Taleb, 2010). This is something which planning and policy have increasingly recognized as a permanent feature of the dynamic theatres they operate within (Allmendinger, 2009, pp. 18-23), including in the evaluation of complex phenomena, such as social infrastructure.

3.2. Historical Knowledge

Second, *historical knowledge*, including social patterns that we can perceive through statistical data, direct experience, and cultural knowledge, has always been used to guide decisions about the future. From a critical realist perspective, cognitive abilities, such as reason, logic, deduction, induction, and related analytic devices, enable us to synthesize information and improve our judgment. However, historical knowledge, however complete, cannot lead us to predictive certainty (Reed & Harvey, 1992, p. 357). Prediction premised on causal, linear processes has yielded important knowledge, but much of the world around us—both social and natural—is not linear. Deep contingencies give rise to interconnections of nonlinear interacting systems at all scales and critical realism insists that in any setting (natural, social, or otherwise), there are "constellations of causal factors" (Steinmetz, 1998, p. 172). Highly controlled laboratory settings provide the most significant degree of prediction, generating critical knowledge of how causal-mechanical interactions operate, but these settings also have limits (Feyerabend, 1970).

3.3. Human Agency

Third, critical realism recognizes that one of the logical consequences of partial knowledge (historical and future) is that *human agency*—the ability to act independently of external constraints—is limited. Our expectations about what may be gained in studying social capital phenomena must consider that knowledge gained is always incomplete. Two events or conclusions that appear the same could have different causes. Single causal mechanisms, given the nature of reality, are in principle impossible

(Alexander, 2003b; Steinmetz, 1998). Our experience suggests that individual humans have a degree of choice—what to wear or what to eat on a given day—but that choice is more limited than we might initially think. While we may choose to eat whatever we want, our location, resources, biological limits, and many other factors narrow what appears to be an open choice down to a very narrow range: e.g., we may not walk to Australia however much we will it. Having limits is not equivalent, however, to an acceptance of determinism. Although we may exercise options within limits, we do have an ability to act on the phenomena and systems around us and to understand them to some degree. Progress in research, including social phenomena, is therefore possible and meaningful, and knowledge leading to action can be developed, examined, modified, and pursued further. Determinism is an important compliment to agency (Caro, Sandoval-Hernandez, & Luedtke, 2014). The structures—natural, social, cultural—out of which the natural world, human life, and consciousness arise are in many instances highly regularized. We expect to find our apples beneath, not above, the trees. We very usefully speak of laws, principles, constants, and other causal terms. In the human sphere, our first language has a strong influence on how we see the world. —Our thought patterns and perception are shaped by the distinctive analytic features of a given human language (Gilson, 1988). That shaping occurs in us long before we are conscious of its effects such that, while we may try and consciously reject it, we can never uninstall the linguistic frameworks we grew up in or fully undo its effect on us (Chomsky, 1996; Martinich, 1996). Language requires individuals—without them there is no language, as evidenced by extinct languages, and there is no language if there is only one individual—verbal communication is a function of collective process in development, use, and modification (Kripke, 1996). A language broken into pieces for analysis is no longer human language, however useful such a reductive process may be for other purposes (Gilson, 1988). Social phenomena (and language represents a cluster of social phenomena) can be partially understood through pre-existing capabilities (Chomsky, 1996) but only functioning wholes can provide robust explanation

Critical realism recognizes and holds in creative tensions the demands of both agency and determinism from the individual human to our wider societies and social structures, recognizing that society exists as something that profoundly structures who we are but also as something that we can study, learn about, and act on: "Society may thus be conceived as an articulated ensemble of such relatively independent and enduring structures; that is, as a complex totality subject to change both in its components and their interrelations" (Bhaskar, 1978, p. 13).

3.4. Emergence

Fourth, critical realism allows for *emergence*. One of the important results of the tensions of agency and determinism is that law-like functions at one level can give rise to novel phenomena at higher orders: what is commonly referred to as *emergence* (Friesen, 2018a). Emergence in a critical realist context is "the relationship between two [structural levels of reality] such that one arises diachronically (or perhaps synchronically) out of the other but is capable of reacting back on the lower level and is causally irreducible to it" (Steinmetz, 1998, p. 173). The implication is that even where we may find law-like behavior by looking at isolated lower order interactions (e.g., the conservation of energy in the atomic structure of hydrogen), the explanation provided by that law does not encompass all aspects of behavior that occurs at higher orders.

Emergence complicates our efforts to sort out direct causal arrows (Richardson, Snowden, & Allen, 2006). Current scholarship reveals an important role for emergence in scientific investigation:

> After a long hiatus, emergence is finding new usefulness and recent scholarship suggests that generative atomism is one common philosophical version of emergence and includes: a. Facts about fundamental kinds of entities; b. Facts about permanent properties of these fundamental entities; c. Facts about transitory properties the fundamental entities can have; d. Facts about the laws that govern the distribution of the entities and the nature of their properties. (paraphrase of longer explanation, Humphreys, 2016, pp. 11-12).

Physical descriptions of parts, wholes, and laws do not mean that social interactions are excluded from the insights of emergence. It is possible to consider that the generative nature of social interactions arises from individual humans as the basic elements and their thought processes as a capability of those elements. The relations among parts, elements, people, natural entities, and everything else around us is deeply complex at a causal level. Critical realism seeks to understand how law-like behavior on the one hand is related to less understood or unexpected causal effects on the other. At the meso level of social structural analyses, such as investigations of social capital at neighborhood levels, these patterns and regularities amid potentially wide variations are a persistent challenge.

4. Complexity Science

CRITICAL REALISM >>> COMPLEXITY SCIENCE >>> NETWORKS >>> SOCIAL CAPITAL >>> SPATIAL DATA

Figure 3

The critical realist framework suggests what may be known and how it may be known at a general level. Complexity science is directly concerned with the causally difficult phenomena we experience and of which we are a part. This includes the social systems and structures that arise from and shape human interactions at all scales, including meso-level neighborhood contexts in urban settings.

4.1. Cities as Complex Systems

When Jane Jacobs wrote "The Death and Life of Great American Cities" in the early 1960s, complexity science as we know it today was still in its infancy. Cybernetics had been around since the 1940s when Norbert Weiner began to explore what comprised the various dynamics of purposeful systems (Moray, 1963). Jacobs (1959) identified an important 1958 review essay on scientific progress and complexity by Warren Weaver that signaled growing awareness of complex systems consequences generally and what such thinking might mean in the context of cities and their functions. Lindblom (1959), writing a year or so ahead of Jacobs, reached similar conclusions about the limits of administrative planning, in principle—despite desires and efforts, accounting for and projecting all variables into the future as a way of controlling outcomes was simply not possible. Cities are not machines, Jacobs (1959) argued, because they are characterized by non-linear processes implying irreducibility. Like natural systems of energy and motion, social structures and human systems seem to hold order and chaos in tension, reflecting both predictability and novelty (Byrne, 1998; Lewin, 1999; Simon, 1962; Waldrop, 1993).

Understanding these dynamics is an important feature of our efforts to understand social structures generally and social capital measurement in particular. There are several key features that are particularly relevant. Whether or not complex systems are deterministic (Goldspink, 1999), they are certainly not linear (Feigenbaum, 1983). As discovered by Lorenz while running data on weather prediction models, even where the environment is a computer operating system running algorithms, very slight variations of initial conditions can yield remarkably different outcomes (Lorenz, 1963). In lab experiments and other attempts to create closed systems, this sensitivity to initial conditions can be problematic, since a failure to control even a small variable affecting a phenomenon (e.g., the number of decimal places used) can lead to unexpected or erroneous outcomes. In quasi-closed systems, like networks of sensors or operating systems, these unwanted nudges make prediction (and troubleshooting) difficult. This sensitivity is operative even in the case of a simple push button switch that will "bounce" and be randomly open or closed owing to micro-states if a limit strategy is not coded into the software or built into the electronic circuits (Margolis, 2012). In open systems, like societies and other human social structures, the avenues for sensitivity are numerous indeed and formal repeatability is not possible. Given the sensitivity of systems to these inputs, the deep complexity and non-linearity of an open system appears to make predictability impossible in principle:

> Almost every event in social life is produced by rare but consequential shocks and jumps; all the while almost everything studied about social life focuses on the 'normal,' particularly with 'bell curve' methods of inference that tell you close to nothing. Why? Because the bell curve ignores large deviations, cannot handle them, yet makes us confident that we have tamed uncertainty. Its nickname in this book is GIF, Great Intellectual Fraud. (Taleb, 2010, p. xxiv)

This is an important caution that must be taken seriously wherever statistical analyses assume normal distributions.

4.2. Social Feedback

Another characteristic of complex systems is feedback. Feedback in systems refers to the characteristic of a system to recursively make use of its own outputs as new inputs. When feedback amplifies existing signals, it is referred to as positive (regardless of whether it is desired—e.g., feedback in a sound system is very irritating, but is considered to be formally positive, given that it amplifies a given system signal). Negative feedback, on the other hand, mutes a system's given direction or process. Feedback of this sort is not characteristic of linear systems, but is common in social systems at all scales (Simon, 1962). An example of this can be found in research on innovation in organizations where corporate processes designed to promote high margin products internally will "kill off" innovative new products that fail to meet that margin, even if those new products could, over time, dramatically outperform existing products (Christensen, 2011; Christensen, Baumann, Ruggles, & Sadtler, 2006). The built-in logic of corporate processes constitutes a feedback mechanism that "mutes" anything that does not fit the mechanism's logic. Universities and other common types of organizations, such as municipal bureaucracies, function in a similar way (Blais, 2010; Christensen & Eyring, 2011). Living systems typically interact with both higher order and lower order systems, thus incurring a degree of novelty and a means by which even small changes within or adjacent to one system are fed back into that system, generating high sensitivity to initial conditions, as noted above (Batty, 2012; Buchanan, 2000).

In social systems, such as those that constitute the conditions for social capital formation and function, agents within the network of the system can and do change and influence it from within. When a higher order system influences the sub-systems that form it or with which it interacts, it is referred to as "supervenience" (Murphy, 1997, pp. 22-23). The above noted example of corporate processes generating feedback loops optimized for one type of product profit margin at the expense of another is an example of supervenience: formal company policy or embedded policy in the form of corporate culture rewards certain types of agent (employee) behavior and punishes divergent behavior. Top-down causation is a means by which the characteristics of a larger system constrain the range of motion or the function space of a smaller or lower order system of interactions.

From a social systems vantage point, individuals are constrained by various expressions of the group as seen in rules, formal laws, cultural norms, and expectations. Norms are the result of countless preceding individual decisions and interactions, foundational mechanisms that lead to cultural practice. These collective properties supervene on individuals and limit their range of options (Trofimova, 2000). From a network perspective, the topology of larger structures plays a significant role in determining the range of motion possible for the lower order systems (Sekara, Stopczynski, & Lehmann, 2016). Emergence, as described earlier, is an important feature of complex systems (Kim, 1999). Complex systems are comprised of networks. Entities or actors plus the relations between them lead to phenomena, such as social capital. Social capital is not possible where there are only individuals with no connections at all:

> [A]fter three hundred years of dissecting everything into molecules and atoms and nuclei and quarks, [scientists] finally seemed to be turning the process inside out. Instead of looking for the simplest pieces possible, they were starting to look at how those pieces go together into complex wholes. (Waldrop, 1993, p. 16)

Complex systems are the result of dynamic interactions among elements. The tightly coupled nature of these systems means that at given times, any variation within the network of relations can cause a cascading set of influences to occur in all the connected sub- and super-systems. When a system becomes linked in this way, it is said to be at a critical state: any perturbance can lead the system toward a chaotic state before moving to a new state of equilibrium. This can be seen experimentally in, for example, the phase change of water and mathematically through computer-enabled iterations of simple equations with tunable variables (May, 1976). These dynamics enable the various orders of interacting systems to adapt to both internal and external signals, to receive feedback not only in a loop, but as novel information or influence from the environment (external variables). Historical reflections on social systems affirm that they appear to reflect this phenomena of criticality (Buckley, 1968; Collins, 2000; G. Thomas, 1997). If we are going to increase our understanding of and possible agency within social systems, we will need to account for complex systems dynamics in research design, models, and interpretive frameworks (Byrne, 1998). Policy is just such a form of intervention.

5. Networks

CRITICAL REALISM >>> COMPLEXITY SCIENCE >>> NETWORKS >>> SOCIAL CAPITAL >>> SPATIAL DATA

Figure 4

The critical dynamics that comprise complex behavior and which gives rise to their profound behavior is the way that elements are related to, and interact with, each other. Formal insight on this aspect of systems has led to the development of the science of networks. Networks provide the linkage between critical realism, complex systems, and the empirical aspects of social capital.

The means by which we can begin to understand many complex systems is through the simplification of complex dynamics. In networks, the nomenclature of nodes and edges are used as key descriptors. Nodes are the entities that comprise a system (people, books, papers, and so on) and edges are the relationships that connect the entities (trust, social ties, citations, and so on). The structure of nodes and edges gives a topology that can be studied and modeled in ways ranging from simple visualizations to highly complex mathematical and statistical analyses (Snijders, 2011).

A second critical aspect of network analytics is the dynamics that occur on the network structures as movements of influence, resources, or information. In the case of social networks, friendship, neighborhood and family ties form systems of nodes and ties that are complex but analyzable. Even a few dozen nodes with very simply dynamic qualifiers can become highly complex very quickly and are surprisingly difficult to analyze. The advent of mathematics supported by computation has enabled significant growth in the application of network analysis to a wide range of phenomena; however, one of the significant boundaries network scientists face are the in-principle non-computable problems owing to exponential increases in computational calculations with network size and dynamic complexity (Newman, 2010).

The highly complex realities that arise from topology and dynamics interactions require critical assessment of how much detail can be included in analysis. In planning environments, transportation has made significant use of network analysis to understand the dynamics of how people and vehicles move on roads, sidewalks, and other spatial structures and the role these structures play in large scale social and cultural dynamics (Little, 2002; Omrani, 2015; Papinski, Scott, & Doherty, 2009). In the case of social capital investigation where trust, relational connections, and proximity all interact in significantly subtle and powerful ways, network analysis becomes an obvious and important means of investigating the dynamics of social structures. The social infrastructure of cities is a highly complex network of relationships between people, groups, associations, institutions and a myriad of other structures (Bettencourt, 2013; Portugali, 2011; Zhou, Sornette, Hill, & Dunbar, 2005). The challenges of understanding these structures is compounded by their virtual invisibility in most cases and may include ongoing expert debate over the use of statistical methods for spatial analysis (Dubin, 1998; LeSage, 1997) and the relationship of standard statistics to machine learning approaches (Breiman, 2001). These are important elements of the challenges that social capital analysis in urban contexts has begun to take on and will need to continue to invest in. Although not detailed here, the two primary applications of network science within the proposed framework are respondent-driven descriptions of their social networks and trust, alongside mathematical descriptions of their GPS travel patterns.

6. Social Capital

Critical Realism >>> Complexity Science >>> Networks >>> Social Capital >>> Spatial Data

Figure 5

Community-level measurement of social capital represents well the kinds of problems that critical realism is suited to meaningfully approach. Complexity science operating out of a critical realist approach provides a framework where specific techniques can be employed. In the case of social capital investigations, this could include network descriptions of social ties, spatial networks (GIS), statistical analysis (R), and dynamic modeling (NetLogo) as examples (Papinski & Scott, 2011; Savitz & Raudenbush, 2009; Snijders, 2011). Social capital is a complex set of phenomena where there is no singular mechanism and no clear boundary between dynamics and where interacting mechanisms, agents, and other variables are at best partly understood and often unknown (Janssen, Holahan, Lee, & Ostrom, 2010; Ostrom, 1986).

It is not necessary to understand all of the underlying mechanisms of social capital in order to make provisional assertions about meaningful knowledge of social resources held among a number of actors—we can gain insight about social dynamics without proof of a causal link (Cushing & McMullin, 1989) between a given variable and social capital.

Measurement approaches in this study are designed to detect possible correlations between device-generated spatial data (Abarbanel, Brown, Sidorowich, & Tsimring, 1993) and social capital survey data (Weinberger, 2012). Correlation among specified variables is a means of testing hypotheses, while more formal causation (of the sort imagined in mechanistic interactions of the Newtonian variety—a given change in (x) always causes a given change in (y) —is more effective for physical systems without agency. Inference and probability rather than causation and certainty shape social dynamics hypothesis formulation and are consistent with a critical realist framework within which complex dynamics are examined. The partial nature of knowledge and causes means that any given phenomena can be scrutinized empirically from a variety of non-exclusive angles (Mir & Watson, 2001). Fragmented or incomplete knowledge is important and is the primary means by which we understand the dynamics of physical and social worlds.

The variety and nature of human social interactions in high density locations like cities are extremely complex and new forms of synthetic research design and analysis will undoubtedly lead to new insights about these phenomena (Dandekar, 2005).

7. Spatial Data

CRITICAL REALISM >>> COMPLEXITY SCIENCE >>> NETWORKS >>> SOCIAL CAPITAL >>> **SPATIAL DATA**

Figure 6

GPS data provides a concrete linkage between human behavior and survey data (social capital) that can be analyzed using network science. This is consistent with our understanding of complex systems in the context of a critical realist philosophical framework.

Recording the movement patterns of humans in their home territories provides an opportunity to examine how individual agency interacts with constraining structures related to geography, income, education, institutional experience, and a range of other perceptions. Knowledge can be legitimate as both homeostasis (stationary stability) and homeorhesis (evolutionary stability) (Sieweke, 2014), which has two direct implications for designing spatial data collection methods that explore complex social capital phenomena.

First, it means that it is possible to learn from other phenomena that are better understood than the one in question. We understand a complex phenomenon by using a known measurement method that corresponds to it. This learning is facilitated through an interplay of deduction, induction, abduction (Hintikka, 1998), and replication (Mir & Watson, 2001). Deduction is most suited to settings where defined logical relationships between all variables are possible, such as in mathematics, controlled laboratory settings, formalized philosophical argumentation—contexts where we are filling gaps in knowledge within a well-known space (Carnap, 1970). Induction is better suited to the exploration of phenomena that are not as well-known as it better serves an exploratory mode where understanding (generalization) grows through observation of instances and patterns (Chomsky, 1996). Proceeding in this way, explanations may be partial, but useful, and need not require direct cause and effect conclusions or logical formalisms (Henkin, 1967; Mir & Watson, 2001). By collecting data about movement patterns and calculating the distinct features of each participant, the Social Imaging Project explores how these generalizations relate to social capital levels gleaned from a newly developed social capital survey instrument (Friesen, 2018a).

As noted earlier, critical realism affirms the possibility of acquiring real knowledge of the external world, including other human beings, through observation and experience (Acemoglu, Johnson, & Robinson, 2004; Bhaskar, 1978). This does not require formal comparison in the sense of logical deduction, but may proceed through induction, whereby signals (data) can be identified, collected, and analyzed in a regular way (Abarbanel et al., 1993; Assad, 1999). Collecting spatial data is a valid means of affirming that something might be known about a mind-independent reality: "While science is indeed a social production process, it is also knowledge 'of' things which exist and act independently of science" (Steinmetz, 1998, p. 175). This process includes the comparison of lesser-known phenomena to better-known phenomena, which allows the scaffolding of hard-won and incomplete provisional knowledge to increase.

Social capital in particular requires integration and synthesis, in this case comparing survey and spatial data so that new knowledge, a 'third way' is possible: "[W]isdom requires us to invent a third curriculum, which will weave the warp of the rediscovered humanities to the woof of expert exactitude" (Serres, 1995, p. 184). This third way is consistent with the practice of scientific progress and the approach I have outlined:

> We don't select theories based on deduction, having seen them all and then deciding on the best—the options would quickly run a greater number than all the atoms of the universe. I would suggest that we choose theories based on coherence, whether intuited or consciously identified, between sets of problems and sets of possible solutions spaces. Our inquiry is aimed at correlations or probable causations rather than mechanistic certainty (whatever that is). (H. Putnam, 1988, p. 128)

8. Critical Realism and Complex Systems for Planning Policy

The foregoing discussion of the progression of critical realism, complex systems, networks, social capital, and spatial data leads logically to a consideration of the implications for planning, municipal policy, and civil society development. Social structures arising from relationship networks and spatial use comprise and may even give rise to the physical form of our cities and communities. Planning faces an increasingly fragmented theoretical and practical working space due to the fading of rational comprehensive assumptions; this difficulty is compounded by the significant range of professional, social science, political, and land use issues that planning endeavors to engage and order (Fainstein & Campbell, 2011). The value of the current research will increase to the extent it can support meaningful integration rather than increased fragmentation. By their nature, planning and policy are undertakings that operate at the intersection of a significant number of competing interests and enterprises, such as engineering, politics, ecology, sociology, commerce, and so on. It is critical that new research and practice enable diverse, but coherent, integration in order to make progress on perennial challenges (e.g., the complex relationships among transportation, land use, and social policy) (Irwin, 2010). The division of practice and theory in planning can be coherently bridged by recognizing that systems of social interaction have independent existence in a critical realist philosophical framework.

There are patterns for planning practitioners to identify and learn alongside theorists who develop additional questions for investigation (H. Putnam, 1988). These patterns merit scientific attention that can lead to new knowledge and insight, even if the systems display stochastic features. The Social Imaging Project, therefore, is not an esoteric exercise. A science of cities has the potential to grow fresh impetus not as a non-reductive, over-simplifying enterprise, but as a knowledge-driven process of gathering intelligence, identifying patterns of systems, and forming potential solutions with creative policy applications. This will need ongoing investment in theory, hypothesis formation, and testing focused on a synthesis of diverse and new data sources (Serres, 1995). If policy is guided by reductive paradigms of investigation, however, it is likely that the public appetite for the knowledge we desperately need will wane and we will fail to meet the demand for increased ingenuity:

> The experimental method is neither a self-contained nor a self-sufficient technique for discovering causal laws. The strict controls which scientists use to elicit nature's law-like properties produce only limited, idealized knowledge. Positivist canons can suffice only in the closed domain of the experimental setting. These law-like regularities with their clarity and order often disappear when taken from the laboratory and used to explain outcomes in the open world of everyday life. (Reed & Harvey, 1992, p. 356)

Cities and the social structures that constitute them are certainly part of "the open world of everyday life" (op cit). Developing a more integrated, sophisticated, and open approach to science that is transparent about contingencies and open to real learning will lead to concrete gains in understanding difficult phenomena, including social systems phenomena (Batty, 2012). Global urban demands require these gains if we are to succeed in providing for greater human flourishing, rather than compounding human misery (Burdett & Sudjic, 2011).

Critical realism provides a clear rationale for experimental investment to support planners and planning researchers. The rational comprehensive method leveraged control, reductive analysis, and expert power to build freeways through downtowns, build public housing, and invest in transportation, with results that have often been troubling (Scott, 1999). A new type of control-oriented planning practice is gaining ground through technical, data-driven approaches built on assumptions that big data will lead to the solutions we need. Big data systems and those that control them, however, are as likely to create new problems as they are to solve old ones (Borgman, 2015; Derman, 2011; Friedmann, 2000; Grimmer, 2015; O'Neil, 2016). Smart cities and big data are useful but over-reliance on technical solutions may turn out to be the downtown freeways of our time if significant supporting research is not matched to practices that support the common good.

One of the tests of the efficacy of this research is the potential that it will support generative approaches to planning. The study of complex systems dynamics has taught us that relatively simple core rules that function effectively can lead to positive outcomes and that more bureaucratic structures fail (Innes & Booher, 2010; Ostrom, 2005; Sanders, 1998; Snowden & Boone, 2007). The balance of control and permission may be most clearly seen in settings where informal development is common (Gouverneur, 2014; Graham & McFarlane, 2015) and where a more open and experimental tone is set for urban development: for example, think about tactical urbanism, guerilla urbanism, flexibility on mother-in-law suites in suburbs, and so on (Berger, Wong, & Rhode Island School of Design, 2014; Montgomery, 2014). Designing processes that feed a changing context back into the decision-making and building cycle can lead to the right kinds of change at the right times. Direct, problem-oriented experimentation can bridge practice and theory if the experimentation leads to improvement. Long term success and the accumulation of knowledge require sophisticated thinking and more complex, not just complicated, forms of social organizing (Homer-Dixon, 2001). Good ideas and sound thinking are no guarantee that new practices will follow. There is hope that understanding complex systems can seed the conditions for new strategies and practices that are more effective, not just more cumbersome, over time. We know that the arrangement of social structures, institutions, and cultural patterns has long-term effects on societies for good or ill: "The planning of institutions of both types —for the realization of planned change, and for subsequent control—is an important aspect of integrative planning. This means, for example, that planning for technological innovation ought to include planning for new social institutions" (Jantsch, 1972, p. 137). If new institutions are not included in a context of growing knowledge, we may fail to learn the lessons of history and constrain our urban growth possibilities through inadequately adaptive institutions (Schumpeter, 2011) and inattention to the social dimensions of our collective challenges will continue:

> The very rapid growth of the field of industrial relations as a professional specialty dramatizes the fact that our larger social systems, whether organizations or communities, are becoming more and more aware of their problems in the area of social progress in human relations and are turning more and more often to sources of outside professional help in solving them (Lippitt, Watson, & Westley, 1958, pp. 275-276).

I have argued that using a critical realist philosophical framework provides a rationale for empirical work through complex systems, network science, and the interactions of socio-spatial data. This framework enables us to enlarge our understanding of the dynamics of the social infrastructure of our cities at across scales. New knowledge about these social dynamics is increasingly critical as we contend with the simultaneous dynamics of decreasing stocks of social capital and emerging forms of social generation that are shaping our cities and communities. Our ability to describe and interact with these dynamics is essential if we are to continue to meet the needs of the full range of citizens that comprise our rapidly urbanizing world.

References

Abarbanel, H., Brown, R., Sidorowich, J., & Tsimring, L. (1993). The analysis of observed chaotic data in physical systems. *Reviews of Modern Physics, 65*(4), 1331-1392. doi:10.1103/RevModPhys.65.1331

Abbott, R. (2009). The reductionist blindspot. *Complexity, 14*(5), 10–22. doi:10.1002/cplx.20274

Acemoglu, D., Johnson, S., & Robinson, J. (2004). *Institutions as the fundamental cause of long-run growth* (Working Paper No. 10481). Retrieved from National Bureau of Economic Research website: http://www.nber.org/papers/w10481

Adler, P. S., & Kwon, S-W. (2002). Social capital: Prospects for a new concept. *The Academy of Management Review, 27*(1), 17-40. doi:10.2307/4134367

Albert, R. Z., & Barabási, L. (2001). *Statistical mechanics of complex networks.* Retrieved from http://citeseer.ist.psu.edu/viewdoc/summary?doi=10.1.1.25.5619

Alexander, C. (2001). *The nature of order: The phenomenon of life* (Vol. 1). CES Publishing.

Alexander, C. (2003a). *New concepts in complexity theory arising from studies in the field of architecture: An overview of four books of the nature of order with emphasis on the scientific problems which are raised.* Retrieved from http://

www.katarxis3.com/SCIENTIFIC%20 INTRODUCTION.pdf

Alexander, C. (2003b). *The nature of order: An essay on the art of building and the nature of the universe, book 2—the process of creating life* (Vol. 2). Center for Environmental Structure.

Allmendinger, P. (2009). *Planning theory*. New York, NY: Palgrave Macmillan.

Aristotle. (2012). *Aristotle's Nicomachean ethics* (R. C. Bartlett & S. D. Collins, Trans.). Chicago, IL/London, England: University Of Chicago Press.

Assad, M. L. (1999). *Reading with Michel Serres*. Albany, NY: State University of New York.

Badash, L. (1972). Completeness of nineteenth-century science. *Isis, 63* (216), 48–58. doi:10.1086/350840

Baker, W. E. (1990). Market networks and corporate behavior. *American Journal of Sociology, 96*(3), 589-625.

Batty, M. (2012). Building a science of cities. *Cities, 29(Supplement 1),* S9-S16. doi:0.1016/j.cities.2011.11.008

Baudelaire, C. P. (1981). *Paris spleen*. New York: New Directions.

Bechard, M., & Marchand, I. (2006). *General Social Survey Cycle 19: Time use (2005)* (No. Catalogue no. 12M0019GPE). Retrieved from Statistics Canada website: http://data.library.utoronto.ca/datapub/codebooks/cstdli/gss/gss19/gssc19gidv2.pdf

Belliveau, M. A., O'Reilly, C. A., & Wade, J. B. (1996). Social capital at the top: Effects of social similarity and status on CEO compensation. *The Academy of Management Journal, 39*(6), 1568-1593. doi:10.2307/257069

Berger, M., Wong, L., & Rhode Island School of Design. (2014). *Resilience and adaptability*. Retrieved from https://www.degruyter.com/view/product/428107

Bernard, H. R., Killworth, P., Kronenfeld, D., & Sailer, L. (1984). The problem of informant accuracy: The validity of retrospective data. *Annual Review of Anthropology, 13*, 495-517.

Bethune, B. (2014, August 8). The end of neighbours. Retrieved from Macleans website: http://www.macleans.ca/society/the-end-of-neighbours/

Bettencourt, L. M. A. (2013). *The kind of problem a city is: New perspectives on the nature of cities from complex systems theory*. Retrieved from http://www.santafe.edu/media/workingpapers/13-03-008.pdf

Bhaskar, R. (1978). Possibility of social scientific knowledge and limits of naturalism. *Journal for the Theory of Social Behaviour, 8*(1), 1-28. doi:10.1111/j.1468-5914.1978.tb00389.x

Blais, P. (2010). *Perverse cities: Hidden subsidies, wonky policy, and urban sprawl*. Vancouver, BC: UBC Press.

Boneham, M. A., & Sixsmith, J. A. (2006). The voices of older women in a disadvantaged community: Issues of health and social capital. *Social Science & Medicine, 62*(2), 269-279. doi:10.1016/j.socscimed.2005.06.003

Borgman, C. L. (2015). *Big data, little data, no data: Scholarship in the networked world*. Cambridge, MA: The MIT Press.

Bourdieu, P. (2008). The forms of capital. In N. W. Biggart (Ed.), *Readings in economic sociology* (pp. 280-291). Retrieved from http://onlinelibrary.wiley.com/doi/10.1002/9780470755679.ch15/summary

Bourdieu, P., & Wacquant, L. (1992). *An invitation to reflexive sociology*. Retrieved from http://www.press.uchicago.edu/ucp/books/book/chicago/I/bo3649674.html

Boxman, E. A. W., De Graaf, P. M., & Flap, H. D. (1991). The impact of social and human capital on the income attainment of Dutch managers. *Social Networks, 13*(1), 51-73. doi:0.1016/0378-8733(91)90013-J

Brehm, J., & Rahn, W. (1997). Individual-level evidence for the causes and consequences of social capital. *American Journal of Political Science, 41*(3), 999-1023. doi:10.2307/2111684

Breiman, L. (2001). Statistical modeling: The two cultures (with comments and a rejoinder by the author). *Statistical Science, 16*(3), 199-231. doi:10.1214/ss/1009213726

Brody, B. A. (Ed.). (1970). *Readings in the philosophy of science*. Englewood Cliffs, NJ: Prentice Hall.

Browning, C. R., Feinberg, S. L., & Dietz, R. D. (2004). The paradox of social organization: Networks, collective efficacy, and violent crime in urban neighborhoods. *Social Forces, 83*(2), 503-534. Roi:10.1353/sof.2005.0006

Buchanan, M. (2000). *Ubiquity: The science of history ... or why the world is simpler than we think*. New York, NY: Crown Publishers.

Buckley, W. (1968). Society as a complex adaptive system. In W. Buckley (Ed.), *Modern systems research for the behavioral scientist* (pp. 490-513).

Burdett, R., & Sudjic, D. (Eds.). (2011). *Living in the endless city: The urban age project by the London School of Economics and Deutsche Bank's Alfred Herrhausen Society*. Phaidon Press.

Burt, R.S. (1997). The contingent value of social capital. *Administrative Science Quarterly, 42*(2), 339-365. doi:10.2307/2393923

Byrne, D. (1998). *Complexity theory and the social sciences: An introduction* (1st ed.). New York, NJ: Routledge.

Campbell, S. D. (2013). Sustainable development and social justice: Conflicting urgencies and the search for common ground in urban and regional planning.

Michigan Journal of Sustainability, 1. doi:10.3998/mjs.12333712.0001.007

Carnap, R. (1970). Statistical and inductive probability. In B. A. Brody (Ed.), *Readings in the philosophy of science.* Englewood Cliffs, NJ: Prentice-Hall.

Caro, D. H., Sandoval-Hernandez, A., & Luedtke, O. (2014). Cultural, social, and economic capital constructs in international assessments: An evaluation using exploratory structural equation modeling. *School Effectiveness and School Improvement, 25*(3), 433-450. doi:10.1080/09243453.2013.812568

Carpiano, R. M., & Fitterer, L. M. (2014). Questions of trust in health research on social capital: What aspects of personal network social capital do they measure? *Social Science & Medicine, 116*, 225-234. doi:10.1016/j.socscimed.2014.03.017

Chomsky, N. (1996). Language and the problems of knowledge. In A. P. Martinich (Ed.), *The Philosophy of Language* (3rd ed., pp. 558-557). London, England: Oxford University Press.

Chow, W .S., & Chan, L. S. (2008). Social network, social trust and shared goals in organizational knowledge sharing. *Information & Management, 45*(7), 458-465. doi:10.1016/j.im.2008-06.007

Christensen, C. (2011). *The innovator's dilemma: The revolutionary book that will change the way you do business* (Reprint). New York, NY: Harper Business.

Christensen, C. M., Baumann, H., Ruggles, R., & Sadtler, T. M. (2006). Disruptive innovation for social change. *Harvard Business Review, 84*(12), 94–101.

Christensen, C. M., & Eyring, H. J. (2011). *The innovative university: Changing the DNA of higher education from the inside out* (8th Revised edition). New York, NY: Jossey-Bass.

Chung, S., Choi, H., & Lee, S. S. (2014). Measuring social capital in the Republic of Korea with mixed methods: Application of factor analysis and fuzzy-set ideal type approach. *Social Indicators Research, 117*(1), 45-64. doi:10.1007/s11205-013-0341-8

Cohen, N. (2011, March 26). Cellphones track your every move, and you may not even know. *The New York Times.* Retrieved from http://www.nytimes.com/2011/03/26/business/media/26privacy.html

Cohen, R., & Havlin, S. (2010). *Complex networks: Structure, robustness and function.* Cambridge, England: Cambridge University Press.

Coleman, J. (1994). *Foundations of social theory.* Cambridge, MA.: Belnap Press.

Coleman, J. S. (1988). Social capital in the creation of human capital. *American Journal of Sociology, 94*, S95-S120.

Collins, R. (2000). *The sociology of philosophies: A global theory of intellectual change* (Revised ed.). Cambridge, MA.: Belknap Press.

Crandall, D. J., Backstrom, L., Cosley, D., Suri, S., Huttenlocher, D., & Kleinberg, J. (2010). Inferring social ties from geographic coincidences. *Proceedings of the National Academy of Sciences, 107*(52), 22436-22441. doi:/10.1073/pnas.1006155107

Cushing, J. T., & McMullin (Eds.). (1989). *Philosophical consequences of quantum theory: Reflections on Bell's Theorem*. Notre Dame, IN: University of Notre Dame Press.

Dandekar, H. C. (2005). Qualitative methods in planning research and practice. *Journal of Architectural and Planning Research, 22*(2), 129-137.

de Tocqueville, A. (2001). *Democracy in America* (R. C. Heffner, Ed.). Signet Classics.

Derman, E. (2011). *Models. Behaving. Badly.* New York, NY: Free Press.

Dubin, R. A. (1998). Spatial autocorrelation: A primer. *Journal of Housing Economics, 7*(4), 304-327. doi:10.1006/jhec.1998.0236

Dugundji, E., Scott, D. M., Carrasco, J. A., & Paez, A. (2012). Urban mobility and social-spatial contact-introduction. *Environment and Planning A, 44*(5), 1011-1015. doi:10.1068/a45183

Dunkelman, M. J. (2014). *The vanishing neighbor: The transformation of American community* (1st edition). W. W. Norton & Company.

Eagle, N. N. (2005). *Machine perception and learning of complex social systems* (Dissertation, MIT). Retrieved from http://reality.media.mit.edu/pdfs/thesis.pdf

Edwards, R. W. (Series Ed.). (2004). *Measuring social capital: An Australian framework and indicators.* Retrieved from http://www.ausstats.abs.gov.au/Ausstats/free.nsf/Lookup/13C0688F6B98DD45CA256E360077D526/$File/13780_2004.pdf

Fainstein, S. S., & Campbell, S. (Eds.). (2011). *Readings in planning theory* (3rd ed.). West Sussex, England: Wiley-Blackwell.

Fairfield, P. (2003). Review: "A house divided: Comparing Analytic and Continental Philosophy" by C. G. Prado, ed. *Symposium, 7*(2), 251-253.

Farr, J. (2004). Social capital: A conceptual history. *Political Theory, 32*(1), 6–33.

Feigenbaum, M. (1983). Universal behavior in non-linear systems. *Physica D, 7*(1-3), 16-39. doi:10.1016/0167-2789(83)90112-4

Feyerabend, P. K. (1970). How to be a good empiricist - Ag. In B.A. Brody (Ed.), *Readings in the philosophy of science* (pp. 319-342). Englewood Cliffs, NJ: Prentice-Hall.

Finsveen, E., & van Oorschot, W. (2008). Access to resources in networks: A theoretical and empirical critique of networks as a proxy for social capital. *Acta Sociologica, 51*(4), 293-307. doi:10.1177/0001699308097375

Fischler, R. (2000). Linking planning theory and history: the case of development control. *Journal of Planning Education and Research, 19*(3), 233-241.

Franke, S. (2005). *Measurement of social capital: Reference document for public policy research, development, and evaluation*. Ottawa, Canada: Policy Research Institute.

Friedmann, J. (2000). The good city: In defense of Utopian thinking. *International Journal of Urban and Regional Research, 24*(2), 460-472. doi: 10.1111/1468-2427.00258

Friesen, M. J. (2013a). *Is social capital measurement still relevant? A roundtable policy and social impact assessment white paper*. Hamilton, Canada: Cardus.

Friesen, M. J. (2013b). Social infrastructure: Underpinning the success of cities. *Municipal World, 123*(12), 11-14.

Friesen, M. J. (2018a). Advancing social capital measurement: Using general social survey cycles to develop an efficient survey instrument. *The American Sociologist, 49*(3), 392-413. doi:10.1007/s12108-018-9380-6

Friesen, M. J. (2018b). *Navigating social capital scholarship: A Meta-Review of 9164 Web of Science Sources on social capital* (p. 44).

Fukuyama, F. (1996). *Trust: The social virtues and the creation of prosperity* (1st ed.). New York, NY: Free Press.

Fukuyama, F. (1997). Social capital and the modern capitalist society: Creating a high trust workplace. *Stern Business Magazine*, 4.

Fukuyama, F. (2002). Social capital and development: The coming agenda. *SAIS Review, 22*(1), 23-37. doi:10.1353/sais.2002.0009

Gadamer, H.-G. (1960). *Truth and method* (2nd ed.; J. Weinsheimer & D. G. Marshall, Trans.). New York, NJ: Continuum.

Garcia, F. P., Martinez, L. S., & Radoselovics, J. F. de G. (2008). *Estimation of social capital in the world* (p. 82). Bilboa, Spain: BBVA Foundacion.

Gesthuizen, M., van der Meer, T., & Scheepers, P. (2009). Ethnic diversity and social capital in Europe: Tests of Putnam's Thesis in European countries. *Scandinavian Political Studies, 32*(2), 121-142. doi:10.1111/j.1467-9477.2008.00217.x

Gilson, E. (1988). *Linguistics and philosophy*. Notre Dame, IN: Notre Dame University Press.

Goldspink, C. (1999). *Social attractors: An examination of the applicability of complexity theory to social and organisational anslysis* (Doctoral dissertation, University of Western Sydney-Hawkesbury).

Gouverneur, D. (2014). *Planning and design for future informal settlements: Shaping the self-constructed city* (1st edition). Abingdon, England/New York, NY: Routledge.

Graham, S., & McFarlane, C. (Eds.). (2015). *Infrastructural lives: Urban infrastructure in context* (1st ed.). New York, NY: Routledge.

Grimmer, J. (2015). We are all social scientists now: How big data, machine learning, and causal inference work together. *PS: Political Science & Politics, 48*(1), 80-83. doi:10.1017/S1049096514001784

Gunderson, L. H., & Holling, C. S. (2002). *Panarchy: Understanding transformations in human and natural systems*. Washington, DC: Island Press.

Henkin, L. (1967). Formal systems and models of formal systems. In P. Edwards (Ed.), *The encyclopedia of philosophy* (Vol. 8). New York, NY: Macmillan and The Free Press.

Hintikka, J. (1998). What is abduction? The fundamental problem of contemporary epistemology. *Transactions of the Charles S Peirce Society, 34*(3), 503-533.

Homer-Dixon, T. (2001). *The ingenuity gap: Can we solve the problems of the future?* (1st ed.). Vintage Canada.

Hu, C. (2014). Life and death in the open system. *On Site Review, 32*, 12-14.

Humphreys, P. (2016). *Emergence* (1st ed.). Oxford, England: Oxford University Press.

Inglehart, R. (1997). *Modernization and postmodernization: Cultural, economic, and political Change in 43 Societies.* Princeton, NJ: Princeton University Press.

Innes, J. E., & Booher, D. E. (2010). *Planning with complexity: An introduction to collaborative rationality for public policy* (1st ed.). Routledge.

Irwin, E. G. (2010). New directions for urban economic models of land use change: Incorporating spatial dynamics and heterogeneity. *Journal of Regional Science, 50*(1), 65-91.

Jacobs, J. (1959). *The Death and life of great American cities* (Revised ed.). New York, NY: Vintage.

Janssen, M. A., Holahan, R., Lee, A., & Ostrom, E. (2010). Lab experiments for the study of social-ecological systems. *Science, 328*(5978), 613-617. doi:10.1126/science.1183532

Jantsch, E. (1972). *Technological planning and social futures*. New York, NY: John Wiley & Sons.

Kawachi, I., Kennedy, B. P., Lochner, K., & ProthrowStith, D. (1997). Social capital, income inequality, and mortality. *American Journal of Public Health, 87*(9), 1491-1498. doi:10.2105/AJPH.87.9.1491

Kim, J. (1999). Making sense of emergence. *Philosophical Studies, 95*(1-2), 3-36. doi:10.1023/A:1004563122154

Knoke, D. (1999). Organizational networks and corporate social capital. In R. T. A. J. Leenders & S. M. Gabbay (Eds.), *Corporate Social capital and liability* (pp. 17-42). doi:10.1007/978-1-4615-5027-3_2

Kojima, K. (2014). Crafting space: Generative processes of architectural configurations. *Architectural Design, Profile No. 231*(Emphatic Space), 38-45.

Kripke, S. (1996). On rules and private language. In A. P. Martinich (Ed.), *The philosophy of language* (3rd ed., pp. 524-537). New York, NY: Oxford University Press.

Kuhn, T. (1962). *The Structure of scientific revolutions* (3rd ed.). Chicago, IL: University of Chicago Press.

Kuhn, T. (1970). The function of dogma in scientific research. In B. A. Brody (Ed.), *Readings in the philosophy of science* (pp. 356-373). Englewood Cliffs, NJ: Prentice-Hall.

Kwan, M.-P. (2007). Mobile communications, social networks, and urban travel: Hypertext as a new metaphor for conceptualizing spatial interaction. *Professional Geographer, 59*(4), 434-446. doi:10.1111/j.1467-9272.2007.00633.x

LeSage, J. P. (1997). Regression analysis of spatial data. *The Journal of Regional Analysis and Policy, 27*(2), 83-94.

Lewin, R. (1999). *Complexity: Life at the edge of chaos*. Chicago, IL: University of Chicago Press.

Lin, N., Cook, K. S., & Burt, R. S. (2001). *Social capital: Theory and research*. Piscataway, NJ: Transaction Publishers.

Lindblom, C. E. (1959). The science of "muddling through." *Public Administration Review, 19*(2), 79-88. doi:10.2307/973677

Lippitt, R., Watson, J., & Westley, B. (1958). *Planned change: A comparative study of principles and techniques*. New York, NY: Harcourt, Brace and Company.

Little, D. (2002, September). *Transportation as a large historical factor: A case study in new philosophy of history*. Colloquium presented at the Humanitas Colloquium, University of Michigan-Dearborn. Retrieved from https://www.google.ca/url?sa=t&rct=j&q=&esrc=s&source=web&cd=1&cad=rja&uact=8&ved=0ahUKEwjWi4mao8zSAhVC2IMKHf27DWQQFggcMAA&url=http%3A%2F%2Fwww-personal.umd.umich.edu%2F~delittle%2FTransport%2520as%2520a%2520causal%2520factor%2520in%2520history%2520short%2520version.htm&usg=AFQjCNFHLTaQ0fxei4nMhvnbVaAA0JZWPQ&sig2=OK2tJuBN8hnFTVDoS3NbCw

Lochner, K., Kawachi, I., & Kennedy, B. P. (1999). Social capital: A guide to its measurement. *Health & Place,*

5(4), 259-270. doi:10.1016/S1353-8292(99)00016-7

Logan, J. R. (2012). Making a place for space: Spatial thinking in social science. *Annual Review of Sociology, 38*, 507-524.

Logan, R. K. (2007). *The extended mind: The emergence of language, the human mind, and culture*. Toronto, Canada: University of Toronto Press.

Lorenz, E. N. (1963). Deterministic nonperiodic flow. *Journal of the Atmospheric Sciences, 20*(2), 130-141. doi: 10.1175/15200469(1963)020<0130:DNF>2.0.CO;2

Loury, G. (1992). The economics of discrimination: Getting to the core of the problem. *Harvard Journal for African American Public Policy, 1*, 91-110.

Margolis, M. (2012). *Arduino cookbook* (2nd ed.). Beijing, China: O'Reilly.

Martinich, A. P. (Ed.). (1996). *The philosophy of language* (3rd ed.). New York, NY: Oxford University Press.

May, R. (1976). Simple mathematical-models with very complicated dynamics. *Nature, 261*(5560), 459-467. doi:10.1038/261459a0

McDoom, O. S. (2014). Predicting violence within genocide: A model of elite competition and ethnic segregation from Rwanda. *Political Geography, 42*, 34-45. doi:10.1016/j.polgeo.2014.05.006

McPherson, M., Smith-Lovin, L., & Brashears, M. E. (2006). Social isolation in America: Changes in core discussion networks over two decades. *American Sociological Review, 71*(3), 353-375.

Mir, R., & Watson, A. (2001). Critical realism and constructivism in strategy research: Toward a synthesis. *Strategic Management Journal, 22*(12), 1169-1173.

Montgomery, C. (2014, October). Charles Montgomery: Welcome to Happyville: How we can improve our lives by designing smart cities. *National Post*. Retrieved from http://fullcomment.nationalpost.com/2014/10/11/charles-montgomery-welcome-to-happyville-how-we-can-improve-our-lives-by-designing-smart-cities/

Moray, N. (1963). *Cybernetics*. In *Twentieth Century encyclopedia of Catholicism: XIII Catholicism and science* (Vol. 131). New York, NY: Hawthorne Books.

Murphy, N. (1997). *Anglo-American postmodernity*. Boulder, CO: Westview Press.

Nahapiet, J., & Ghoshal, S. (1998). Social capital, intellectual capital, and the organizational advantage. *The Academy of Management Review, 23*(2), 242-266. doi:10.2307/259373

Newman, M. E. J. (2010). *Networks: An introduction*. Oxford: Oxford University Press.

Omrani, H. (2015). Predicting travel mode of individuals by machine learning. *Transportation Research Procedia, 10*(Complete), 840-849. doi: 10.1016/j.trpro.2015.09.037

O'Neil, C. (2016). *Weapons of math destruction: How big data increases inequality and threatens democracy*. New York, NY: Crown.

Ostrom, E. (1986). An agenda for the study of institutions. *Public Choice, 48*(1), 3-25.

Ostrom, E. (2005). *Understanding institutional diversity*. Princeton, NJ: Princeton University Press.

Ostrom, E., & Ahn, T. (2003). *Foundations of social capital*. Northhampton, MA: Edward Elgar Pub.

Paldam, M. (2000). Social capital: One or many? Definition and measurement. *Journal of Economic Surveys, 14*(5), 629-653. doi:10.1111/1467-6419.00127

Papinski, D., Scott, D. M., & Doherty, S. T. (2009). Exploring the route choice decision-making process: A comparison of planned and observed routes obtained using person-based GPS. *Transportation Research Part F-Traffic Psychology and Behaviour, 12*(4), 347-358. doi:10.1016/j.trf.2009.04.001

Papinski, D., & Scott, D. M. (2011). A GIS-based toolkit for route choice analysis. *Journal of Transport Geography, 19*(3), 434-442. doi:10.1016/j.jtrangeo.2010.09.009

Pennar, K. (1997, December 15). The ties that lead to prosperity: The economic value of social bonds is only beginning to be measured. *Business Week*, 153-153.

Pentland, A. (2014). *Social physics: How ideas turn into action*. New York, NY: Penguin Books.

Pinker, S. (2014). *The village effect: How face-to-face contact can make us healthier, happier, and smarter*. New York, NY: Spiegel & Grau.

Portes, A. (1998). Social Capital: Its origins and applications in modern sociology. *Annual Review of Sociology, 24*, 1-24. doi:10.1146/annurev.soc.24.1.1

Portes, A. & Sensenbrenner, J. (1993). Embeddedness and immigration: Notes on the social determinants of economic action. *American Journal of Sociology, 98*(6), 1320-1350.

Portugali, J. (2011). *Complexity, cognition and the city*. Berlin, Germany: Springer.

Putnam, H. (1988). *Representation and reality* (6th Printing). Cambridge, MA.: The MIT Press.

Putnam, R. D. (1995). Bowling alone: America's declining social capital. *Journal of Democracy, 6*(1), 65–78.

Reed, M., & Harvey, D. (1992). The new science and the old - Complexity and realism in the social-sciences. *Journal for the Theory of Social Behaviour, 22*(4), 353-380. doi:10.1111/j.1468-5914.1992.tb00224.x

Richardson, K. A., Snowden, D., & Allen, P. M. (2006). *Emergence: Complexity & organization 2005 annual.* Isce Publishing.

Richey, S. (2007). Manufacturing trust: Community currencies and the creation of social capital. *Political Behavior, 29*(1), 69-88. doi:10.2307/4500234

Rorty, R. (1979). *Philosophy and the mirror of nature.* Princeton, NJ: Princeton University Press.

Rorty, R. (1998). *Truth and progress.* In *Philosophical Papers (Vol. 1).* Cambridge, MA.: Cambridge University Press.

Rostila, M. (2011). The facets of social capital. *Journal for the Theory of Social Behaviour, 41*(3), 308-326. doi:10.1111/j.1468-5914.2010.00454.x

Sanders, T. I. (1998). *Strategic thinking and the new science: Planning in the midst of chaos, complexity, and change.* Free Press.

Savitz, N. V., & Raudenbush, S.W. (2009). Exploiting spatial dependence to improve measurement of neighborhood social processes. *Sociological Methodology, 39,* 151-183.

Scheffer, M., Bascompte, J., Bjordam, T. K., Carpenter, S. R., Clarke, L. B., Folke, C., ... Westley, F. R. (2015). Dual thinking for scientists. *Ecology and Society, 20*(2). doi:10.5751/ES-07434-200203

Schiff, M. (1992). Social capital, labor mobility, and welfare: The impact of uniting states. *Rationality and Society, 4*(2), 157-175. doi:10.1177/1043463192004002003

Schumpeter. (2011, January 29). The crescent and the company. *The Economist.* Retrieved from https://www.economist.com/business/2011/01/27/the-crescent-and-the-company

Scott, J. C. (1999). *Seeing like a state: How certain schemes to improve the human condition have failed* (New ed.). New Haven, CT: Yale University Press.

Sekar, A., & Rai, V. (2018). Inferring latent constructs from passive datasets: Significance and opportunities. *SSRN Electronic Journal,* 1-19. doi:10.2139/ssrn.3285417

Sekara, V., Stopczynski, A., & Lehmann, S. (2016). Fundamental structures of dynamic social networks. *Proceedings of the National Academy of Sciences of the United States of America, 113*(36), 9977-9982. doi:10.1073/pnas.1602803113

Serres, M. (1995). *Conversations on science, culture, and time: Michel Serres with Bruno LaTour.* Ann Arbor, MI: University of Michigan Press.

Sieweke, J. (2014). Preserving the natural flow: Natural disasters in ignorance. In *Interventions adaptive reuse*: *Vol. resilience and adaptability. IntAR* (Vol. 5). Providence, RI: Rhode Island School of Design.

Simon, H. A. (1962). The architecture of complexity. *Proceedings of the American Philosophical Society, 106*(6), 467-482.

Snijders, T. A. B. (2011). Statistical models for social networks. *Annual Review of Sociology*, *37*, 131-153.

Snowden, D., & Boone, M. E. (2007). Leader's framework for decision making. *Harvard Business Review*. Retrieved from https://hbr.org/2007/11/a-leaders-framework-for-decision-making

Stanley, M. (2007). So simple a thing as a star: The Eddington–Jeans debate over astrophysical phenomenology. *The British Journal for the History of Science*, *40*(1), 53-82. doi:10.1017/S0007087406008740

Steinmetz, G. (1998). Critical realism and historical sociology. A review article. *Comparative Studies in Society and History*, *40*(1), 170-186.

Taleb, N. N. (2010). *The Black Swan: Second edition: The impact of the highly improbable: With a new section: "On Robustness and Fragility"* (2nd ed.). New York, NY: Random House Trade Paperbacks.

Taylor, C. (2004). *Modern social imaginaries*. Duke University Press Books.

Thomas, C. Y. (1996). Capital markets, financial markets, and social capital (An essay on economic theory and economic ideas). *Social and Economic Studies*, *45*(2/3), 1-23.

Thomas, G. (1997). What's the use of theory? *Harvard Educational Review*, *67*(1), 75-104.

Tod, A. M., Kennedy, F., Stocks, A.-J., McDonnell, A., Ramaswamy, B., Wood, B., & Whitfield, M. (2016). Good-quality social care for people with Parkinson's disease: A qualitative study. *BMJ Open*, *6*(2), e006813. doi:10.1136/bmjopen-2014-006813

Trofimova, I. (2000). Principles, concepts and phenomena of ensembles with variable structure. In *Nonlinear Dynamics in Life and Social Sciences*. Amsterdam, Netherlands: IOS Press.

Uphoff, N., & Wijayaratna, C.M. (2001). *Demonstrated benefits from social capital: The productivity of farmer organizations in Gal Oya, Sri Lanka* (SSRN Scholarly Paper No. ID 252837). Retrieved from Social Science Research Network website: https://papers.ssrn.com/abstract=252837

van der Gaag, M. (2002, February 13). *The resource generator: Measurement of individual social capital with concrete items*. Presented at the XXII Sunbelt International Social Networks Conference, New Orleans.

van Oorschot, W., & Arts, W. (2005). The social capital of European welfare states: the crowding out hypothesis revisited. *Journal of European Social Policy*, *15*(1), 5-26. doi:10.1177/0958928705049159

Varnava, C., Stevenson, R. M., Nilsson, J., Skiba-Szymanska, J., Dzurňák, B., Lucamarini, M., ... Shields, A. J. (2016). An entangled-LED-driven quantum relay over 1 km. *Npj Quantum Information*, *2*, 16006. doi:10.1038/npjqi.2016.6

Veenstra, G. (2002). Explicating social capital: Trust and participation in the civil space. *The Canadian Journal of So-*

ciology/Cahiers Canadiens de Sociologie, 27(4), 547-572. doi:10.2307/3341590

Waldrop, M. M. (1993). *Complexity: The emerging science at the edge of order and chaos*. Simon & Schuster.

Weaver, W. (1948). Science and complexity. *American Scientist, 36*(4), 536-544. doi:10.2307/27826254

Weinberger, D. (2012). *Too big to know: Rethinking knowledge now that the facts aren't the facts, experts are everywhere, and the smartest person in the room is the room*. Basic Books.

Westley, F., Zimmerman, B., & Patton, M. (2006). *Getting to maybe: How the world is changed*. Toronto, Canada: Random House Canada.

Wheatley, M. J. (2006). *Leadership and the new science: Discovering order in a chaotic world* (3rd ed.). San Francisco, CA: Berrett-Koehler Publishers.

Woolcock, M. (1998). Social capital and economic development: Toward a theoretical synthesis and policy framework. *Theory and Society, 27*(2), 151-208.

Woolcock, M. (2001). The place of social capital in understanding social and economic outcomes. *Canadian Journal of Policy Research, 2*(1), 11-17.

Woolcock, M., & Narayan, D. (2000). Social capital: Implications for development theory, research, and policy. *The World Bank Research Observer, 15*(2), 225-249.

Zhou, W-X., Sornette, D., Hill, R. A., & Dunbar, R. I. M. (2005). Discrete hierarchical organization of social group sizes. *Proceedings: Biological Sciences, 272*(1561), 439-444.

Appendix 1

Social Capital Definitions

There are earlier core lists of definitions that are useful (Adler & Kwon, 2002) but given ongoing development, incomplete. Below is a list of more than three-dozen definitions provided to give context for each definition, which has been developed for use in the current paper. It should be understood as representative rather than exhaustive. With the number of academic papers on social capital increasing beyond 14,000 (2018) it is clear that more variations exist.

ID	Definition	Source
1	the density and quality of human relational networks both formal and informal	Current paper definition
2	a resource that actors derive from specific social structures and then use to pursue their interests; it is created by changes in the relationship among actors	(Baker, 1990, p. 619)
3	an individual's personal network and elite institutional affiliations	(Belliveau, O'Reilly, & Wade, 1996, p. 1572)
4	the aggregate of the actual or potential resources which are linked to possession of a durable network of more or less institutionalized relationships of mutual acquaintance or recognition	(Bourdieu, 2008, p. 248) - 1986
5	made up of certain obligations ('connections') which are convertible, under certain conditions, into economic capital and may be institutionalized in the form of a title of nobility	(Bourdieu, 2008, p. 243) - 1986
6	the sum of resources, actual or virtual, that accrue to an individual or a group by virtue of possessing a durable network of more or less institutionalized relationships of mutual acquaintance and recognition	(Bourdieu & Wacquant, 1992, p. 119)
7	the number of people who can be expected to provide support and the resources those people have at their disposal	(Boxman, De Graaf, & Flap, 1991, p. 52)
8	the web of cooperative relationships between citizens that facilitate resolution of collective action problems	(Brehm & Rahn, 1997, p. 999)
9	friends, colleagues, and more general contacts through whom you receive opportunities to use your financial and human capital	(Burt, 1997, p. 9)

10	the brokerage opportunities in a network	(Burt, 1997, p. 355)
11	defined by its function...it is not a single entity but a variety of different entities having two characteristics in common: they all consist of some aspect of social structure, and they facilitate certain actions of individuals who are within the structure	(Coleman, 1994, p. 302)
12	in its basic understanding...people's access to resources in their networks	(Finsveen & van Oorschot, 2008, p. 295)
13	the ability of people to work together for common purposes in groups and organizations	(Fukuyama, 1996, p. 10)
14	the existence of a certain set of informal values or norms shared among members of a group that permit cooperation among them	(Fukuyama, 1997)
15	an instantiated informal norm that promotes cooperation between two or more individuals. The norms that constitute social capital can range from a norm of reciprocity between two friends all the way up to complex and elaborately articulated doctrines like Christianity or Confucianism. They must be instantiated in an actual human relationship...the norm of reciprocity exists in potential in my dealings with all people, but it is actualized only in my dealings with my friends	(Fukuyama, 2002, p. 1)
16	a culture of trust and tolerance in which extensive networks of voluntary association emerge	(Inglehart, 1997, p. 188)
17	These [neighborhood] networks are a city's irreplaceable social capital. When capital is lost, from whatever cause, the income from it disappears, never to return unless new capital is slowly and chancily accumulated.	(Jacobs, 1959, p. 180)
18	the network of associations, activities, or relations that bind people together as a community via certain norms and psychological capacities, notably trust, which are essential for civil society and productive for future collective action or goods in the manner of other forms of capital	(Farr, 2004, p. 9)
19	the process by which social actors create and mobilize their network connections within and between organizations to gain access to other social actors' resources	(Knoke, 1999, p. 18)
20	investment in social relationships with expected returns	(Lin, Cook, & Burt, 2001, p. 6)
21	resources embedded in a social structure which are accessed and/or mobilized in purposive actions	(Lin et al., 2001, p. 32)

22	a feature of the social structures, not of the individual actors within the social structure: it is an ecologic characteristic. In this way social capital can be distinguished from the concepts of social networks and social support, which are attributes of individuals	(Lochner et al., 1999, p. 260)
23	naturally occurring social relationships among persons which promote or assist the acquisition of skills and traits valued in the marketplace...an asset which may be as significant as financial bequests in accounting for the maintenance of inequality in our society	(Loury, 1992, p. 100)
24	the sum of the actual and potential resources embedded within, available through, and derived from the network of relationships possessed by an individual or social unit. Social capital thus comprises both the network and the assets that may be mobilized through that network.	(Nahapiet & Ghoshal, 1998, p. 243)
25	networks, together with shared norms, values, and understandings which facilitate cooperation within or among groups	(Australian Bureau of Statistics, 2004)
26	inclusive civic engagement with democratic governance, generally agreed rules, sanctioning of non-compliance behavior, and resolving of conflicts	(Ostrom, 2005, pp. 255-288)
27	the web of social relationships that influences individual behavior and thereby affects economic growth	(Pennar, 1997, p. 154)
28	the ability of actors to secure benefits by virtue of membership in social networks or other social structures	(Portes, 1998, p. 6)
29	those expectations for action within a collectivity that affect the economic goals and goal seeking behavior of its members, even if these expectations are not oriented toward the economic sphere	(Portes & Sensenbrenner, 1993, p. 1323)
30	features of social organization such as networks, norms, and social trust that facilitate coordination and cooperation for mutual benefit	(R. D. Putnam, 1995, p. 67)
31	the social resources that evolve in accessible social networks or social structures characterized by mutual trust	(Rostila, 2011, p. 321)
32	the set of elements of the social structure that affects relations among people and are inputs or arguments of the production and/or utility function	(Schiff, 1992, p. 160)
33	those voluntary means and processes developed within civil society which promote development for the collective whole	(C. Y. Thomas, 1996, p. 11)

34	resources embedded in inter-personal relationships, essential glue for society	(Uphoff & Wijayaratna, 2001)
35	the information, trust, norms or reciprocity inhering in one's social networks	(Woolcock, 1998, p. 158)
36	merely the structure of networks and social relations that lead to mutual benefit through cooperation, but not the adjoining behavioral dispositions that often accompany these, such as trust, reciprocity, honesty, and institutional quality measures	(Woolcock, 2001, p. 12)
37	the basic idea of social capital is that one's family, friends, and associates constitute an important asset, one that can be called upon in a crisis, enjoyed for its own sake, and/or leveraged for material gain...those communities endowed with a rich stock of social networks and civic associations will be in a stronger position to confront poverty and vulnerability, resolve disputes and/or take advantage of new opportunities	(Woolcock & Narayan, 2000, p. 3)
38	the quality of communities and their institutional networks	(Campbell, 2013, p. 80)

When Well-Intentioned Legal Reform Goes Awry: A Case Study of Legal Loopholes and Challenges to Anti-Corruption Reform of Russia's Complex Procurement System

Moskaleva Anastasia

Director of Moscow Research Institute for Standardization and Innovative Technologies

director@mniisit.ru

Nada M Zohdy

Director of Open Gov Hub

nada.zohdy@globalintegrity.org

Abstract

This case study examines Russia's public procurement system as an example of a complex system, and explores the social implications of attempts to reform this system. It highlights a key reality of complex social systems: the original intention of systems established to promote social order is often not fulfilled in practice. The same law meant to ensure healthy competition over government contracts in Russia is being manipulated by actors to restrict which companies win contracts in order to best suit their own personal interests. It explores the gap between what may appear to be an effective reform on paper, versus the actual implementation of this law and how human behavior functions in this complex system. By understanding the manipulation of legal loopholes, this case study then concludes by offering key lessons for other transparency reform efforts and considerations for how they will actually operate in practice within complex systems.

Keywords: Russian public procurement system; complex social systems; competition restriction; legal loopholes in Russia; Russian anti-corruption reform

Cuando la reforma legal bien intencionada sale mal: un estudio de caso de lagunas legales y desafíos para la reforma anticorrupción del complejo sistema de adquisiciones de Rusia

Resumen

Este estudio de caso examina el sistema de contratación pública de Rusia como un ejemplo de un sistema complejo y explora las implicaciones sociales de los intentos de reformar este sistema. Destaca una realidad clave de los sistemas sociales complejos: la intención original de los sistemas establecidos para promover el orden social a menudo no se cumple en la práctica. Los actores manipulan la misma ley destinada a garantizar una sana competencia por los contratos del gobierno en Rusia para restringir qué compañías ganan contratos para satisfacer mejor sus propios intereses personales. Explora la brecha entre lo que puede parecer una reforma efectiva en papel, versus la implementación real de esta ley y cómo funciona el comportamiento humano en este complejo sistema. Al comprender la manipulación de las lagunas legales, este estudio de caso concluye ofreciendo lecciones clave para otros esfuerzos de reforma de transparencia y consideraciones sobre cómo operarán realmente en la práctica dentro de sistemas complejos.

Palabras Clave: Sistema ruso de contratación pública; sistemas sociales complejos; restricción de competencia; lagunas legales en Rusia; Reforma anticorrupción rusa

当善意的立法改革变得扭曲：俄罗斯复杂的政府采购体系的立法漏洞和反腐改革挑战——一项案例研究

摘要

本案例研究将俄罗斯政府采购体系作为一种复杂系统进行分析，同时探究了为改革该体系所做的尝试的社会意义。本文强调了复杂社会系统的一个关键现实：用于推动社会秩序的系统原始目的，时常未付诸实践。同样，用于确保俄罗斯政府合同的良性竞争的法律被行动者操纵，以限制哪些企业能获得合同，进而最有利于自身的私人利益。本文探究了，那些看似是有效改革的书面内容，和法律的实际执行以及人类行为如何在这一复杂系统中发挥作用，之间的差距。通过理解对立法漏洞的操纵，本案例研究作出结论，为其他关乎透明性的改革努力提供了重要经验，为改革努力将在复杂系统中如何实际操作提供了考量。

关键词：俄罗斯政府采购体系；复杂社会系统；竞争限制；俄罗斯立法漏洞；俄罗斯反腐改革

Introduction

The public procurement system—through which the government hires private companies to perform public projects (from building schools and roads, to providing medical supplies and offering other national services) —in Russia is still very young. Only five years have passed after its qualitative reform, whereas in many other countries it has existed for decades. It is obvious that, despite its well-developed work, it has several problem areas. The main goal of the public procurement institution is to ensure the economical use of public budget funds, subject to the purchase of high-quality goods, works and services for the needs of state and municipal customers. The system is meant to ensure healthy competition between private companies seeking business contracts from the government and thus, the efficient spending of public tax money. In this regard, researchers and practitioners of the institution of state order are faced with a large number of issues as they need to ensure a balance between quality and minimization of costs in this area.

It is obvious that such a balance is achieved in a highly competitive market, where a contract is received by a company that is able to offer the best quality at the lowest price. In this regard, one of the most acute and problematic issues of the public procurement system is the problem of ensuring competition in this market. On the one hand, it is important for customers to prevent the conclusion of a contract with unscrupulous companies that are unable to fulfill their obligations under the contract and only waste time of the customer. In a situation where customers implement important state functions, their time is especially valuable since the quality and speed of their service realization affects large segments of the population. On the other hand, only admitting the maximum number of companies to participate in the public procurement process can make this market truly open and transparent. However, this is not happening in Russia today: local officials are more likely to be interested in entering into contracts with "friendly" firms that will personally share part of their profits in exchange for the opportunity to get a contract at a high price.

Context of the Russian Procurement System

The total volume of purchases for state and municipal needs in Russia exceeds $ 125 billion per year. Purchases are made through competitive procedures—most often these are electronic auctions. They are held incognito; the contract is given to the company that has offered the lowest price for the execution of works or the delivery of goods. There are other forms of procurement applied in strictly defined cases—quotation requests, contests, direct purchases. Conflict of interest invariably arises at the point where it is profitable for the state/national budget to purchase at the lowest price, and a particular official wants to get as much reward as possible for securing a contract from a particular company, which he will give preferences as a result of legal manipulations and loopholes available to him. To do this, he needs to maximize the purchase price, and in addition to prevent anyone to a competitive procedure except the "friendly" company. This is the essence of the paradoxical restriction of competition in practice.

According to Antirutina's 2018 calculations, budget losses from unfair overpricing just in the open area are 16% on average, 21% for food, 17% for maintenance and property management, 27% for office equipment, 29% for educational services, in health care and construction it sometimes reaches 40% (Antirutina, 2018; Kommersant, 2018). At the same time, the 2018 calculations of Antirutina did not take into consideration the overestimation of the tricks of customers to restrict competition.

The system of state order of Russia is governed mainly by the special Federal Law No. 44-FZ of April 5, 2013 (SMB, 2016a). It states: "On the contract system in the field of procurement of goods, works, services for state and municipal needs". As an independent branch of law, the public procurement industry is based on a number of principles. The principle of ensuring competition is enshrined in Art. 8 of the Law 44. It reads: "1. The procurement contract system is aimed at creating equal conditions for ensuring competition between procurement participants. Any interested person has the opportunity in accordance with the legislation of the Russian Federation and other regulatory legal acts on the contractual system in the field of procurement to become a supplier (contractor, performer)."

From the outside, the 44th Law looks very regulated and describes in detail every step of all participants of the process. From the outside, it seems that there is no place for corruption at all. However, in practice, everything is different.

Key Challenges of the Russian Procurement System

The term "competition" received its legislative definition in Federal Law No. 135-FZ of July 26, 2006 "On Protection of Competition" (Section 7, Article 4): "Competition is defined as a rivalry between economic entities, in which independent actions of each of them are excluded or the ability of each of them to unilaterally influence the general conditions of circulation of goods in the relevant product market is limited." (SMB, 2016b)

In the same law in paragraph 17 of Art. 4 the indications of competition restriction are identified (SMB, 2016b). Despite the rather wide list of signs of restriction of competition, in our opinion, it does not include all possible cases, and the list is closed, it does not imply the possibility of expansion by other cases. With regard to the activities of state and municipal customers, there is directly listed only one option for their possible actions to limit competition: the establishment of requirements for goods or economic entities that are not provided by law.

For example, government procurement of goods at overpriced or undervalued prices is in fact an increase or decrease in the price of the goods, not due to market circumstances. However, this wording presents the result of unfair actions of officials, but not their essence, and this result is rather difficult to identify. The reduction in the number of entities involved in public procurement, of course, can serve as a sign of restricting competition, but in reality, this effect can only be assessed by the results of a long period of time, which makes it difficult to apply measures here and now. In addition, this formulation deals with the product market as a whole, which makes it difficult for one specific customer to analyze whether all interested participants have the opportunity to take part in the procurement process. The statements related to the definition of the general conditions for the circulation of goods in the market or the creation of other circumstances that give individual business entities to influence this market also do not take into consideration the possible actions of individual customers, despite the fact that the general conditions of commodity circulation in the market can also be formed from such separate actions.

Thus, the wording of the signs of restriction of competition, available in the legislation, does not make it possible to realistically assess the specific actions of individual officials that limit competition, assess their individual effect and make its practical application difficult, including by regulatory authorities.

An analysis of the Federal Law 44 immediately makes clear that the rights and obligations of procurement participants and customers, as well as the ways to protect their rights, are very asymmetric (SMB, 2016a). For example, procurement participants who do not fulfill their duties in the public procurement process are punished seriously enough. They are entered in the register of unscrupulous suppliers. In accordance with Part 2 of Art. 104

"the register of unscrupulous suppliers includes information on procurement participants who evaded contracting, as well as suppliers (contractors, performers) with whom contracts were terminated by a court decision or in case of unilateral refusal of the customer to execute the contract due to a substantial violation of the conditions contracts."

In accordance with Part 9 of Art. 104 information on such procurement participants is put into the register for a period of 2 years (SMB, 2016a). So, procurement participants in case of violations are excluded from the public procurement process for 2 years, since, in accordance with part 1.1 of Art. 31, customers have the right to require the absence of information about the procurement participant in the above registry, which they do in most cases. Thus, there is an unofficial term "*dishonest supplier*"—this is a procurement participant who avoided signing a contract, or a contract with which was terminated by the court or unilaterally due to significant breach of the terms of the contract. At the same time, the special law does not contain the term "*unscrupulous official of the customer*" for those who commit certain offenses in this area and, in particular, restricts competition.

Researchers pay most attention to the procedural and economic problems of government customers in studying government procurement. There are quite a lot of publications on this topic, many of which are distinguished by an integrated approach and a wide coverage of issues. This is understandable, since the main objective of this legal institution is to ensure efficient, cost-effective purchases of high-quality goods and services at minimal cost. In this regard, the scientific problem of saving labor costs for customers in the implementation of Federal Law No. 44, providing opportunities for them to purchase high-quality goods, but not at high prices, is very serious. The problems of restricting competition in the public procurement market are perceived by scientists mainly as secondary, since the main purpose of this institution is not to expand the business opportunities of entrepreneurs per se, but instead to provide public budget savings while adequately meeting the needs of government customers.

In most developed countries, the federal contractual system aims not only to meet the needs of the state for goods and services at the lowest price, but is also used as a powerful regulator of the market that sets the trend for supporting innovative producers and small businesses. The influence of the state order system on the development of small business in the country is difficult to overestimate.

In this regard, there is a very interesting regression model by Fukina, Gafurova, and Notfullina (2016): $\ln(OBOR) = 12.934 + 0.884 \times \ln(ZAK\_SMP)$, where OBOR is the average regional annual turnover of Russian small enterprises, and ZAK_SMP is the number of state and municipal customers who placed orders for small businesses per year. The adjusted R-square model of 52% showed that the cash flow of small enterprises by 52% depends on the number of state and municipal customers who place their orders within them.

The democratic community pinned great hopes on the system of public commenting on procurements, but this method of protecting the interests of the participants was not highly effective. The participants' activeness in the discussions is often not large (0-10 comments per purchase), while in most cases comments are reduced to an emotional discussion of the need for such a purchase in general. In such discussions, the participants' arguments about violations in these purchases, signs of misuse of funds and so on are far less common.

However, this method of finding public opinion is very important and necessary. In our opinion, it needs to be popularized through a large-scale social advertising campaign. It is also important to increase the number of cases when public discussion of procurement is necessary, or to make it mandatory and open to all procurement.

Justifying the initial maximum contract price gives customers more opportunities to pursue their personal interests. In this regard, there are two options for violation of state interests by customers. On the one hand, the initial maximum contract prices are often inflated. This allows participants, who, through the use of certain methods of restricting competition, obtains a state contract at such an inflated price, receive additional profit, a part of which they can share with the official contributing to them in the form of a so-called "*kickback*". However, in itself, overstating the initial maximum contract price is not a way to restrict competition, rather, on the contrary, such contracts attract more participants, so here unscrupulous customers are forced to use additional tricks.

Another option is less common, but no less interesting. Often, the initial maximum contract price is, on the contrary, underestimated. However, this does not always indicate that these customers are too thrifty. This method is used by unscrupulous officials to exclude all unwanted participants from participating in the purchase, who immediately see that participation in the purchase is unprofitable for them for such a small amount of money.

The only organization that takes part in such a purchase knows in advance that the customer does not really need a part of the work, services or goods. This often happens when the so-called "empty" works are included in the estimates. For example, it may be cleaning work, which according to the documents is made more often than in fact. Often such things are found in repair contracts, when additional layers of screed, plaster, paint or repair of objects that have recently been repaired are included in the estimate. Also, such phenomena are not uncommon for contracts of compensated provision of services, in which a larger volume of services is included than is required, for example, consulting services, repair of office equipment, and so on. A good example is also the contract for the supply of goods that are quickly consumed, but not normalized: paper or printer cartridges, food, building materials, and so on.

Another way to illegally restrict competition at the pre-contract stage is to impose unnecessary requirements on procurement participants not provided by the law. Given the fact that Art. 31 quite clearly regulates the list of permissible requirements for procurement participants, this kind of violations is getting smaller, but there are still examples. Most often this is the requirement for license to work that is not actually provided by the contract. Such requirements are sometimes made by customers by mistake, but sometimes deliberately.

There are also other cases when customers mix in one purchase work that requires and does not require a license. In the autumn of 2016, an electronic auction was held in the city of Saratov for the amount of about three million rubles for the repair work of a cultural heritage object, which requires a license. The customer did not consider that part of the work must be carried out in a hospital, the building of which is an object of cultural heritage, and part of it in a building which is not an object of cultural heritage, therefore, in fact, the repair of its facade should be allocated to a separate purchase with no license requirements. The contract was concluded at almost the initial maximum contract price.

Often, customers try to limit the deadline for submission of applications for participation in procurement. The law establishes a minimum period during which the notice of the procurement should be posted in a single information system. However, most often, customers try to minimize this period by setting the deadline for filing applications on a non-working day, or the deadline for submitting applications to early morning or night. This approach is contrary to the meaning of the provisions of the Civil Code of the Russian Federation on the terms defined in Art. 193 and Part 2 of Art. 194 of the Civil Code.

A very common method of limiting the number of participants is to set unrealistic terms of contract execution. For example, carrying out repair work within two days after the conclusion of the contract. In this situation, it is necessary to understand each case: if it is possible to perform work for such a period, if it is really possible that such tight deadlines are justified by the needs of the customer, and why the customer did not place such a purchase in a single information system earlier, if he knew that it is necessary to complete the work by a certain date. Such tricks of customers can often be easily recognized, for example, when the deadlines for the performance of work or the delivery of goods that are not common on the market and are purchased only by an order. However, it is often difficult to prove the unreality of such terms.

The position of the regulatory authorities in this matter is not unified. Sometimes such requirements are recognized as restriction of competition, and sometimes Federal Antimonopoly

Service (FAS) stands on the side of the customer, arguing that the purpose of government procurement is not only to obtain the lowest contract price, but also to receive quality services, and the quality of the service is determined, including, by a short time of its rendering. This position was formulated in the Decree of the Presidium of the Supreme Arbitration Court of the Russian Federation of 12/28/2010 No 11017/10 in case No. A06-6611 / 2009.

The most common violation of the interests of public procurement participants is, of course, legal linguistic uncertainty, ambiguity, entanglement, or excessive detail in describing the quality, volume, composition of the work and services required and the quality of the goods required. In this regard, unscrupulous customers come up with many tricks. The most common option is to entangle the technical part of the documentation, use a mass of punctuation marks that have different meanings for the procurement participant, use the words "more", "less" in different combinations, sometimes replacing them with different signs and words-synonyms, putting these words in different columns and in the most unexpected places, sometimes small or even barely visible font. Also, one of the very common tricks of customers is the placement of information about the purchased goods and their requirements in an unreadable format or in a format that does not allow copying and searching for text. With a small amount of goods, this is not so critical. However, such technical assignments often include several hundred items and occupy several hundred sheets.

For example, in the purchase of 0372200258515000337 requirements for goods took 86 sheets of paper (Russian Federal Treasury, 2018). In the purchase of 0373200173915001449 requirements for goods took 70 sheets (Russian Federal Treasury, 2018). In the purchase of 0373200041515000502-130 sheets (Russian Federal Treasury, 2018). But the greatest surprise was the purchase of 0172200000416000002, there were 679 commodity items in it (Russian Federal Treasury, 2018). Whether such a vast number of requirements for goods is a real need of the customer or his trick to get rid of unnecessary suppliers, that is necessary to understand objectively in each particular case.

P. 2 of Part 1 of Art. 33 has given customers a great imagination to compile the technical part of the procurement documentation. In the descriptions of the goods, it is now increasingly possible to meet numerous riddles on the knowledge of many documents of the national standardization system. It is obvious that it is much easier for the customer himself to simply specify the requirements for the goods to meet one or another specific standard, than to rewrite a huge number of conditions from it to the technical part, sometimes replacing specific values with ranges that the purchaser must turn again into specific values to receive a right of participating in the auction. It is worth noting that this empty labor of specialists of the contractual services of the customer is also paid from the budget. For a procurement participant, filling out such an application turns into an examination of the knowledge of the documents of the national standardization system in great details for a huge amount of goods, which does not correlate with the firm's actual qualifications.

Also, customers often shy away from accurately specifying the scope of work or the quantity of goods purchased, directly indicating their possible un-limitedness. In our opinion, this approach directly contradicts Part 2 of Art. 42, moreover, without a clear definition of the scope of the purchased works or goods, such a state contract can be considered as non-concluded in accordance with the provisions of the Civil Code of the Russian Federation. However, in the purchase no. 0394100001014000001 the scope of work on creating courses was formulated as "at least 1,008" (Russian Federal Treasury, 2018). This means that there may be 2,000 or more courses, which naturally will scare away many bona fide participants. Or in the purchase of 0360100015616000115 "the daily amount of work must be at least 500 square meters per day." (Russian Federal Treasury, 2018).

An important sticking point between customers and suppliers is the question of the legality or illegality of the admission of a procurement participant to view the object for which work is required. This is especially true for repairs. Customers most often refuse to participants in the inspection of repaired objects before the conclusion of the contract and even at the stage of its conclusion, although this is not directly prohibited by law.

Despite the fact that the most frequent and common ways of restricting competition in public procurement are various tricks of customers at the supplier determination stage, there are many different ways to get rid of unwanted participants after determining the winner, who will be contracted. These methods are often aimed at relieving the participant from the desire to participate in the procurement of this customer afterwards, or in some way to terminate the contract.

Very often, procurement participants with whom a contract is made, face excessive claims from customers. These claims can be aimed not only at real quality assurance of goods and works, but also at creating additional obstacles for the bidder. In this situation, the contractor has virtually no opportunity to resolve this issue in the legal framework. For example, during the execution of the procurement contract 0360300298216000014, the customer sent claims to the contractor daily several hours after the daily work was completed (Russian Federal Treasury, 2018). Considering that the essence of the work was street cleaning of monuments, it was extremely difficult to prove the quality of work to the contractor, since the street garbage can occur at any time. The customer required the contractor to provide video evidence of the fact of the work, despite the absence of such a condition in the contract. For the contractor, this meant hiring a videographer with the same contract budget. As a result, the customer greatly reduced the amount of payment under the contract.

Also, customers often violate the procedure of accepting work, goods, services under a contract, evading acceptance and signing the documents, carrying out this procedure not within the deadlines specified in the contract, or refusing to sign documents for formal reasons for their allegedly incorrect design. Often, customers require contractors to schedule the execution of the contract, even in cases where it is not provided for in paragraph 12 of Art. 34. In this regard, we propose to add to the law clear rules for accepting goods, works, and services under a contract, the terms of this procedure, and also to establish the responsibility of customers for violation of this procedure.

On the other hand, in practice, the right of the procurement participants to reduce the penalty for the delay in the execution of individual stages of contract execution in proportion to the volume of obligations fulfilled is practically not implemented. In clause 6 of the Rules established by the Government Decree of November 25, 2013 No. 1063, it is stated that such obligations may be confirmed by documents on the acceptance of goods, the results of works and the provision of services. In fact, in practice, when performing contract work, only acts of work performed are used as such documents. At the same time, their signing is impossible outside the contract execution stages. However, the absence of such documents does not mean that part of the work was not completed by the contractor. In our opinion, such supporting documents can also be acts of inspection, acts of hidden works and other documents and evidence.

As you can see, although violations at the contractual and post-contractual stage are somewhat less common than at the pre-contractual stage, they are very diverse and least regulated by current law. Moreover, it is precisely the difficulties of contract execution, often created by customers, that lead to a decrease in the authority of the public procurement system in the country and the fear of many bona fide organizations to take part in this process. Only the provision of adequate measures to protect the interests of the procurement participants can make this market truly transparent, interesting for the participants, and therefore competitive and economical.

Russian Procurement System as a Complex Social System

Russian law in general is distinguished by a very high formalization and overregulation. It seems from the outside that this creates significant barriers to corruption and any other violations. Never will an official in Russia will deviate one step from what is written on paper, also he will never do even one extra action not written down in documents—even if common sense requires it. This is the reason why in Russia a person who does not have an insurance policy with him can be thrown outside the hospital walls, simply because he or she is not supposed to be accepted without documents. For this reason, officials in

Russia are not responsible for their real actions: their main task is to submit the correct statements on paper. In Russia, a well-formed document always prevails over common sense. This comes from the judicial system, in which the judge is not obliged to rely on his own to collect evidence and study the case. The tasks of the Russian judge include only an assessment of the evidence presented, that is, a comparison of paper documents. For any official in Russia, repairs are done qualitatively, if there is an examination document that confirms this, and not at all if the ceiling did not fall.

Entrepreneurs who are able to integrate into this system, make friends with officials, agree on remuneration and provide the necessary documentation, are able to survive in this system. Entrepreneurs who prioritize quality, speed and common sense do not stand up to it. In Russia, an enormous stratum of entrepreneurs has actually been formed, who never participate in the public procurement system, considering it to be corrupt, dishonest and dangerous. At best, without agreements with officials, they will have to fulfill a hard labor contract at a super low price. In the worst case, they will receive huge fines, and possibly a prison for any violations found. For them this market is cut off, just as state institutions are completely cut off from their services.

There is also a stratum of entrepreneurs who consider this system normal, because they have a friendly approach to officials. In their picture of the world, kickbacks, bribes, technical tasks written only for them are the norm. They justify this by the fact that they have been working with the customer for a long time and know how to do everything quickly and efficiently for them, while the rest allegedly cannot. As a rule, such companies rarely work in the real consumer market: they do not withstand the requirements for quality, attitude, service. They do not understand how such high costs of quality and service can be more profitable than a well-executed act of completed work.

Officials are much more pleasant to work with the second category of entrepreneurs, because they can provide them with closing documentation in time, they will bring a gift for the holiday. In essence, how a hospital room looks like after such a repair is a secondary issue. Moreover, a serving of a product or a result of work for too long is not beneficial to the officials. After all, a damaged product is a pledge of getting a budget from the state for a new one, and these are new gifts and kickbacks. In conditions when the salary of officials is not high not to annoy citizens, this is their main source of income.

Any of the most regulated Russian law operates according to the principle "everything that is not prohibited is allowed". On the other hand, the Russian people are strongly accustomed to survive. They are able to find loopholes in any laws, and so that the judge, who looks at any case strictly formally without any assessment of real justice, will be forced to agree. And this means that schemes of unfair circumvention of the law will always be found, and the process of their local blocking must occur all the time.

Key Lessons to Increase Transparency and Combat Corruption

In our opinion, the public procurement system should be as open as possible for entrepreneurs, and the ideas of many researchers about introducing additional barriers to procurement participants who are inexperienced or not having certain resources contradict the very principle of market competition, because the basic postulates of a market economy is the idea of creating perfect competition (Andreeva, 2014; Belov, 2014; Chernyakova, 2014; Medvedeva, 2015; Morozyuk, 2015; Podrechnev, 2015). The elimination of unscrupulous market participants should be carried out not by applying formal requirements to them, but by high and documented requirements to the quality of the goods supplied or services provided.

The process of increasing transparency should be built simultaneously in two directions. On the one hand, we cannot escape the need to constantly block illegal circuits of circumvention of the law at the legislative level. And we have prepared a number of specific amendments to the law.

However, this process will be endlessly patching holes without working with underlying value orientations in society. In the review, it is necessary to carry out work on restructuring with an overly formalized approach to bearing responsibility for one's own actions. Complex systems should be studied and designed with a realistic prediction of human behavior—we should expect that human behavior will drive individual actors to manipulate even the best law to serve their personal interests. Thus, it is necessary to start from this assumption, then apply it to the procurement system or any other complex social system—*as they exist in the real world, not on a theoretical basis.* In this case, we believe it is necessary to introduce such concepts as "*procurement efficiency*", "*fair competition*", "*nudity official*", "*unfair restriction of competition*" in everyday life and into legislation. The use of these terms is not only in the formal document flow, but, to be more exact, in the value settings of society, without which it is really impossible to build an honest system of public procurement.

For comparison, we can add that much less formalized European public procurement laws provide far lower levels of corruption in these countries due to the fact that corruption is considered not a normal phenomenon, but something really shameful and blamed in society. Only when people stop to communicate with corrupt officials in a friendly way, stop to congratulate them on holidays, stop inviting them into communities, stop to respect them, only then even an imperfect law can bear fruits.

References

Andreeva, L. (2014). Government procurement as a tool for innovative socio-economic development of Russia. *DNA of Law, 1*, 3-8.

Antirutina. (2019). *Public procurement with 44 Federal Law prices analysis.* Retrieved from https://antirutina.net/fz-rating-goszakupok.php.

Belov, V. (2014). On the issue of qualification requirements in the field of procurement of goods, performance of works, provision of services for state and municipal needs. *Business in Law. Economic and legal journal, 5*, 24-28.

Chernyakova, S. (2014). Ensuring the fulfillment of contractual obligations under a contract for state needs. *Service in Russia and abroad, 9,* (56), 195-206.

Fukina, S., Gafurova, G., & Notfullina, G. (2016). Government procurement as a tool for the development of small and medium-sized businesses in Russia. *Economy of the region, 4*, 1233-1243.

Kommersant. (2018, January 28). Honesty map. *Dengi.* Retrieved from https://www.kommersant.ru/doc/3196321.

Medvedeva, N. (2015). Problems of legal support in the sphere of state and municipal procurement management. *Innovation science, 5*(5), 115-119.

Morozyuk, Y. (2015). The impact of open auctions in electronic form on business processes in construction projects. *Management sciences in the modern world, 1*, 724-728.

Podrechnev, V. (2016). The main problems of public procurement management: optimization mechanisms. *Spiritual situation of time. Russia XXI century, 1*(6), 30-33.

Russian Federal Treausury (2018). Retrieved from http://www.zakupki.gov.ru.

SMB (2016a). *On the contract system in state and municipal procurement of goods, works and services.* Retrieved from en.smb.gov.ru/support/regulation/44fz/.

SMB (2016b). *On protection of competition.* Retrieved from http://en.smb.gov.ru/support/regulation/135fz/.

Error Reasoning in Complex Systems: Training and Application Error for Decision Models

Brian J. Goode*

Fralin Life Sciences Institute of Virginia Tech, Arlington, VA, USA

Corresponding author: bjgoode@vt.edu

Bianica Pires

Fralin Life Sciences Institute of Virginia Tech, Arlington, VA, USA

Abstract

A conventional approach to assessing the feasibility of a predictive model is to compare the predictive performance using withheld training data to a baseline model. Colloquially termed a "dummy model", the baseline model relies only on prior training outcomes (e.g., always choose the mean outcome) and is not based on input features. Trained models that perform better than the baseline in terms of error demonstrate better predictive performance than random guessing based on prior outcomes. In the ideal case, this property will also be present when the model has finished training and is implemented. Although generally a useful threshold for model selection, we question if it is indeed enough of a guarantee when implemented in complex systems of high consequence, e.g., social systems. This article presents a preliminary exploration of a scenario where a decision model is trained using one type of error, but the application is more aligned with another. Such circumstances arise when the convergence properties of training a model require convex loss functions, but the desired error is non-convex. A stylized classroom assignment simulation is presented where a machine learning model is trained to optimize for mean square error. Individual, student level, observations are used for training the model, but non-independent hierarchical effects compound the error at the class and school grouping levels. We demonstrate the case where a model might perform better than a conventional baseline, but still under- perform relative to the requirements of an application. Methods for using complex system modeling to establish a new baseline approach are explored.

Keywords: training error; complex systems; machine learning; social system modeling; decision making

复杂系统中的误差推理：决策模型的训练误差和应用误差

摘要

评估预测模型可行性的传统方法是对基准模型使用预留的训练数据，进而比较预测表现。基准模型口头上被称为假体模型(dummy model)，其仅依赖于之前取得的训练结果（比如，始终选择平均结果）且不基于输入特征。训练后的模型在误差方面比基准模型的表现更好，证明其预测表现优于基于先前结果的随机估计 。在理想状态下，这种特质在当模型完成训练、投入实施后依然存在。尽管总体上这对模型挑选而言是一个有用的门槛标准，但我们对该标准是否能提供充分保障提出质疑，尤其是当这一标准投入到具备重大后果的复杂系统，例如社会系统中时。本文针对一个场景进行了初步探究，在这个场景中，决策模型通过一种误差进行训练，但模型应用却更多地与另一误差相一致。当模型训练的收敛特性要求凸损失函数，但期望的误差是非凸时，这类场景便会出现。本文提出一种程式化的课堂作业模拟建模，其中机器学习模型通过训练后被用于均方误差的最优化。个体层面、学生层面的观察结果被用于训练该模型，但“非独立等级效果”（non-independent hierarchical effects）从课堂层面和学校团体层面上使误差复杂化。我们证明的案例则是，一种模型可能比传统基准模型表现更好，但在模型应用要求方面依然表现不佳。探究了如何用复杂系统建模来建立一种新基准方法。

关键词：训练误差；复杂系统；机器学习；社会系统建模；决策

Razonamiento de errores en sistemas complejos: error de capacitación y aplicación para modelos de decisión

Resumen

Un enfoque convencional para evaluar la viabilidad de un modelo predictivo es comparar el rendimiento predictivo utilizando datos de capacitación retenidos con un modelo de referencia. Coloquialmente denominado "modelo ficticio", el modelo de referencia se basa solo en resultados de entrenamiento anteriores (por ejemplo, siempre elige el resultado medio) y no se basa en las características de entrada. Los modelos entrenados que funcionan mejor que la línea de base en términos de error demuestran un mejor desempeño predictivo que las suposiciones aleatorias basadas en resultados previos. En el caso ideal, esta propiedad también estará presente cuando el modelo haya terminado la capacitación y se implemente. Aunque generalmente es un umbral útil para la selección del modelo, nos preguntamos si es realmente una garantía suficiente cuando se implementa en sistemas complejos de alta consecuencia, por ejemplo, sistemas sociales. Este artículo presenta una exploración preliminar de un escenario en el que se entrena un modelo de decisión utilizando un tipo de error, pero la aplicación está más alineada con otro. Tales circunstancias surgen cuando las propiedades de convergencia del entrenamiento de un modelo requieren funciones de pérdida convexa, pero el error deseado es no convexo. Se presenta una simulación de asignación de aula estilizada donde se entrena un modelo de aprendizaje automático para optimizar el error cuadrático medio. Las observaciones individuales, a nivel de estudiante, se utilizan para entrenar el modelo, pero los efectos jerárquicos no independientes agravan el error en los niveles de agrupación de clase y escuela. Demostramos el caso en el que un modelo podría funcionar mejor que una línea de base convencional, pero todavía tiene un rendimiento inferior en relación con los requisitos de una aplicación. Se exploran métodos para utilizar modelos de sistemas complejos para establecer un nuevo enfoque de línea de base.

Palabras clave: error de entrenamiento; sistemas complejos; aprendizaje automático; modelado del sistema social; Toma de decisiones

1. Introduction

We are seeing a confluence of the social and data sciences around social system modeling and prediction. Much work has been accomplished on the research front. Challenges have been developed for machine learning (ML) models to predict social well-being indicators of children (Lundberg, Narayanan, Levy, & Salganik, 2018). Protests events are being predicted using surrogates in social media and other open source indicators (Ramakrishnan & et al., 2014). Machine learning is also finding utility in applications as well. Predicted risk influences police action in child protective services calls (Church & Fairchild, 2017; Cuccaro-Alamin, Foust, Vaithianathan, & Putnam-Hornstein, 2017). Algorithms determine parole (Berk, 2017).

Methods to decision making for data-driven or evidence-based policy have the benefit of increased transparency and provenance. However, models interacting with complex systems, like those seen in the social sciences face huge challenges to replicability, reproducibility and model evaluation (c.f., Collaboration (2015)). Well-trained models, if placed in situ, may still reveal unintended consequences. There are multiple sides to these issues, and there is no one clear solution. In what follows, we simply advance the idea that downstream applications of the model should affect the way error measures are constructed and represented contextually. Borrowing a metaphor from the logistics community, we can think of it as "final mile" analysis. Our work is motivated by the following research questions:

1. How does an intended application differ from and effect model training error?

2. Can complex modeling be used to refine baselines that define acceptable levels or error?

To address these questions, we have constructed a stylized scenario where a machine learning model is used to make decisions about student placement in classrooms at a hypothetical school. The model predicts a student's GPA that is then binned into three different levels of classroom rigor. Students are then placed into their assigned classrooms, but given model error, the assignment may be incorrect and have a significant negative impact on the student's GPA performance. Here, there are two interesting factors that play into the success of the implementation. First, we assume that the model is trained to closely approximate a student's GPA performance as possible. Therefore, a probabilistic error measure (distance measure, see Ferri, Hernández-Orallo, and Modroiu (2009)) is used for model training. Second, the model is trained on individual observational data of prior student performance and that assumption is maintained during this data repurposing. However, we add in hierarchical effects at the classroom and school levels that are not captured by the available data. These effects take the form of "disruptors" that deter learning throughout the school and are modeled through a simple contagion process. Students that are more susceptible are those that are placed incorrectly in their class, thereby making it more likely that the entire school performs at a lower level.

Although stylistic in nature, this example illustrates how an application can influence the way model training error is interpreted and refined. In what follows, we will present the scenario in more detail. Different types of error will be discussed, and error type constraints will be established from application. The focus will be to establish methods for adjusting model baselines for acceptable levels of error. These methods will leverage complex systems modeling better anticipate predictive performance in the context of application. In addition, we will hint at possible implications for a more holistic evaluation of a social modeling system wherein applications of policy frameworks can be adjusted based on model performance. We note that this a preliminary work with interesting findings and is anticipated to lead to further investigations of increased rigor.

2. Background

The interaction of a predictive model with an application such as a social system is itself a complex system. Complex systems are composed of numerous interacting entities whose aggregate behavior is nonlinear. It is argued that generating these macro-behaviors requires that we model the individual components of the system (Miller & Page, 2007; Schelling, 2006). Agent-based modeling (ABM), which is a computational method that allows for the modeling of autonomous, heterogeneous, and interacting agents, is well suited for simulating such systems (Gilbert & Troitzsch, 2005; Manson, Sun, & Bonsal, 2012). Within a computer simulation, agents interact with each other and the environment (Macal & North, 2010). Whereas the interactions are known and specified, the cumulative outcomes are often not obvious.

In such a modeling environment, we can observe the impact that varying changes to a system have on meso- and macro-level outcomes. Examples of such changes might include new zoning plans or policies related to land use, the dismissal of poor performing employees within an organization, or strategies for determining student placement in a school where different class levels are available (e.g., honors, regular, advanced placement). Because ABMs account for the inter-dependencies and feedback in a system, we may find that such changes in policies or strategies may in fact result in unintended consequences. For instance, the removal of a poor performing employee may hinder communication because of their prominent position in the organization's social network. A machine learning approach to placing students in class may optimize for improved aggregate level measures of error but offer fewer guarantees of individual classification performance that impact a student's ability to realize their full potential.

Making predictions about or within complex systems spanning multiple levels of inter- action is not a straightforward task. There can be different motives for model training and model implementation. Aggregate error methods are useful, because individual errors con- tribute to the overall error but allow enough robustness to outliers to prevent over-fitting (c.f., outside of the computer sciences (Arya, Fellingham, & Schroeder (2004)). This gives higher confidence that the model features are indeed useful and increase the chance that a model may be applicable in multiple implementation scenarios. However, applications can be high risk when individual predictions carry large consequences if incorrect (e.g., predictions related to human lives).

Further clouding the problem is that error has different meaning based on type. Ferri et al. (2009) identifies the interpretability of error metrics as: 1.) qualitative metrics, 2.) probabilistic metrics, and 3.) ranking metrics. Qualitative metrics such as accuracy require thresholds and count the number of occurrences of correct or incorrect classifications. Probabilistic metrics (e.g., mean square error, MSE) represent the degree of incorrectness as a distance. Ranking metrics focus on order but will not be discussed here. Despite different meanings, experimental evidence (Gaudette & Japkowicz, 2009; Ferri et al., 2009) shows a high degree of correlation between error measures like MSE and accuracy. Often, one type of error is chosen out of convenience for model training (i.e., convexity, Tseng (2010)). However, there is no guarantee of in situ performance if the application considered is sensitive to another type of error. Therefore, our approach is to recast conventional baselines of performance in terms of the needs of intended applications.

Many classic agent-based models (e.g., Schelling, 1969; Epstein, 2002) have demonstrated the value of developing simple, stylized models of social phenomena. By uncovering some new relationship or testing some hypothesis, these models have shown the advantages of a computational approach. More recently, these classic models have also provided fruitful groundwork for more realistic, empirically-driven models (e.g., Pires & Crooks, 2017). In this paper, we present a stylized model of student placement at a school. We seek to demonstrate how methodological improvements in error representation can impact outcomes. Given the stylized nature of the scenario, we do not consider validation of the agent-based model itself. We can however simplify assumptions in the ABM to match those of the ML model and compare results, which is a form of validation.

3. Framework

The model and simulation framework will be presented in terms of a dynamical system as shown in Figure 1. We define a school as a bipartite graph that consists of N students, $s \in \{s_1, s_2, \ldots s_N\}$ paired with K classes $c \in \{c_1, c_2, \ldots, c_K\}$. Each student is defined as a tuple, $s := (\mathbf{x}, y^*)$ where $\mathbf{x}$ is a vector of input features and y^* is the "true" resulting GPA of the student. In practice, the "true" GPA is only accessible for analysis during the training phase of model development and assumes that assumptions of correct class placement have been verified during the data collection process. Similarly, each class is a tuple, $c := (L, S)$ that consists of a class level, L, and a set of students, $S \subseteq \{s_1, s_2, \ldots, s_N\}$.

Predictive Model (Machine Learning). Central to the social system model is that the student placement into classes is adjudicated by the prediction of a student's GPA, $\mathrm{M}_P : \mathbf{x} \; 1\!\!\rightarrow y$ During ML training, the parameter vector, P , is optimized according to some convex loss function, $l(\cdot)$. Therefore, the chosen

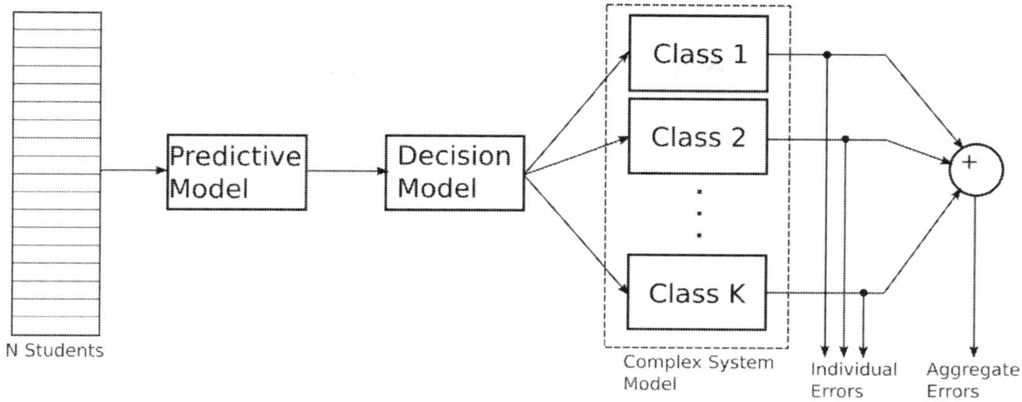

Figure 1. Social Modeling System. A group of N students is labeled with a set of features, x and true GPA outcomes y*. A predictive model takes the features as input and generates a student-level GPA prediction, y. This prediction is then fed into a decision function that determines the class that the student should be placed into. The class dynamics are then modeled and GPAs are now assigned to each student in the class. We assume that the student GPA performance is a combination of the student's innate ability (captured by "True GPA"), class assignment, and the number of disruptors in the class. Finally, the error of the performance is measured both in aggregate and individually.

P during training is directly a result of the choice of minimizing training error. For this scenario, we want the model to minimize the distance between predictions and true GPA outcomes in training data using MSE

$$e_{mse} = \frac{1}{N}(y_i - y_i^*)^2 \tag{1}$$

This is a probabilistic type of error that penalizes heavily for outliers which works to correct for overfitting. In this example, we do not specify the predictive model exactly, but identify predictions based on the error of the model. In other words, we assume that the model has been trained and validated to have a certain MSE.

Given a single MSE value, there are many combinations of residuals, $r_i = y_i - y_i^*$, that could be constituted to form that value. These residuals all form an N-Sphere of radius $\sqrt{e_{mse}N}$. To produce a realization of the predictive model, then one only needs to select a residual vector from this spherical manifold. Methods for doing so are discussed in Krauth (2006).

Decision Model. Ultimately, the decision to place the students in a particular class falls to a decision model, $D_\Delta : y \mapsto$

L. Here, the measure of student performance is mapped to a set of discrete classes. This can be an automated process or even be the result of policy given to a school administrator. Although in real applications there are multiple factors that go into class assignment, in this stylized model we propose a simple partitioning of GPA performance to make that decision. For this model, we will assume that the decisions form a cover of uniform intervals over the performance domain,

$$D^{\Delta}(y) = \frac{y}{\Delta} \tag{2}$$

In this case, the GPA domain is split into intervals of width, Δ, which determines the number of class partitions. For this scenario, Δ = 1. This function is surjective in that multiple GPA values map to class assignments. Class assignment is performed for each student by randomly assigning over the set of qualifying classes of the identified level,

$$\hat{c} = U(\cdot) \tag{3}$$

Complex System Model (Application). The classroom performance model roughly has the form

$$n_d \sim N, \varphi_1, \varphi_2, \theta \tag{4}$$

where the number of disruptors, n_d, is dependent on the number of students in the school (N), the proportion of students that are off by 1 class level, φ_1, and the proportion of students that are off by 2 class levels, φ_2 and the initial proportion of disruptors in the classroom, θ. The model form is a simple ABM of student placement using NetLogo, a multi-agent modeling environment (Wilensky, 1999). Whereas the training data does not explicitly encode the student arrangements and compounding effects resulting from decisions, these can be simulated. In an ABM, we can account for the local interactions of students (agents) over a physical space. In this case, we use a regular lattice (or grid) to create simple peer networks. In other words, students may be influenced to become disruptors by other students in their "network". The localized interactions that occur through these simple network structures are critical to generating the dynamic processes behind the social system. Figure 2 shows the modeling interface.

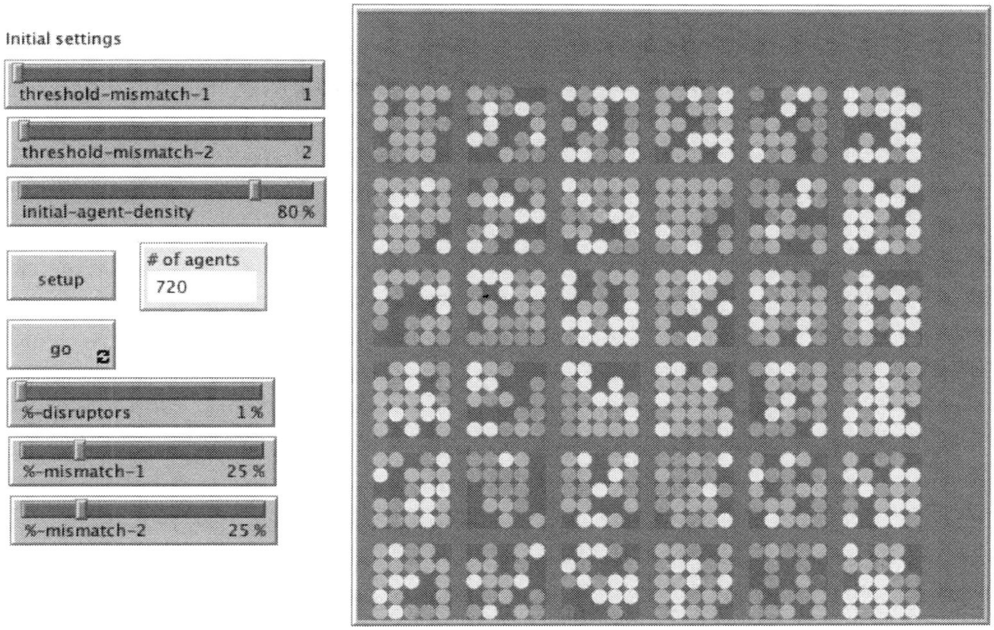

Figure 2. The user interface of the agent-based model in NetLogo. The dark blue cells represent the classrooms. The circles represent the student agents. The different colors represent the agents' "true" class level (cyan agents' true class level is 1, green agents true class level is 2, and yellow agents true class level is 3).

The "school" has 36 classrooms with a capacity of 25 students each. We set the total number of students at the school to be 720 (80% of total school capacity). Each classroom is provided a class level and students are given a "true" class level *TrueL*. Students who are placed in a classroom that matches their true class level are said to have a class mismatch of 0 (*TrueL* == *AssignedL*). Students placed in a classroom that does not match their true class level are said to be mismatched by |*TrueL* – *AssignedL*|. At model initialization, students are placed in classrooms based on a predetermined percentage of students to be mismatched by 1 and by 2, φ_1 and φ_2, respectively. In the event that no classroom space is available that meets a student's mismatch criteria, the student will be randomly placed in an available space. A specified percentage of students, θ are then randomly selected to be "disruptors". Table 1 outlines the model's input parameters.

At each tick of the simulation, students can be influenced to become disruptors. A student's decision to become a disruptor is a function of their mismatch and vision threshold. A student with a mismatch of 1 or 2 will "look" at its neighbors within its vision. If another student within this vision is a disruptor, the student will be "influenced" to also become a disruptor. The greater the student's mismatch, the larger the vision threshold. The model out-

Table 1. Input Parameters for the Agent-Based Model

Parameter	Range	Default value	Description
Students			
True class level	1, 2, 3	1, 2, 3	The student's true class level *TrueL*.
Assigned class level	1, 2, 3	1, 2, 3	The student's assigned class level *AssignedL*.
Vision threshold if mismatched by 1	0-5	1	The distance a student with 1 mismatch will search for a disruptor.
Vision threshold if mismatched by 2	0-5	2	The distance a student with 2 mismatches will search for a disruptor.
Classroom			
Class level	1, 2, 3	1, 2, 3	The class level assigned to the classroom.
Population and Environment			
Student density	0-100%	80%	This determines the number of students at the school. If student density is 100% all classrooms are at full capacity.
Percent disruptors	0-100%	1%	Percentage of total students that are disruptors at model initialization.
Percent mismatched by 1	0-100%	0-100%	Percentage of total students with $\lvert TrueL - AssignedL \rvert = 1$.
Percent mismatched by 2	0-100%	0-100%	Percentage of total students with $\lvert TrueL - AssignedL \rvert = 2$.

puts a set of aggregate statistics at each tick of the simulation, including the count of students by the three potential mismatch values (0, 1, 2), the total number of disruptors, n_d, and the count of students by each class level, *TrueL* and *AssignedL*.

Realized GPA. The GPA of the students resulting from the predictive model, decision model, and classroom model is dependent on the true potential GPA of the student, the number of disruptors in the school, and the level of mismatch in the classrooms. The latter two variables are additional hierarchical considerations in the application at the classroom and school levels. These are not guaranteed to be in training data if the focus of the training data is on individual level performance. Variables such as the proliferation of the number of disruptors in the school is completely application dependent and contextually dependent on the predictive model outcomes. In this stylized example, calculation of individual *i*'s realized GPA is a function of both individual and group-level effects (e.g., peer influence) captured only in the complex system model

$$GPA_i = y_i^* - \underbrace{[w_1 n_d + w_2 \lvert TrueL - AssignedL \rvert]}_{\text{group / application error}} \qquad (5)$$

Once the classroom dynamics have been calculated, a predictive model is selected as de- scribed above to produce a set of residuals, r_i. Then the GPA for each student is calculated where w_1 and w_2 are weights on the school-wide disruptors and the assignment mismatch, respectively.

Application Error. In addition to the training error (MSE) discussed above, there is an additional error requirement induced by the choice of application. We can immediately see that the binning accuracy of the classroom assignments is going to be important as it impacts both the number of disruptors, n_d and the individual class assignment $|TrueL - AssignedL|$.

In this case Accuracy is defined as

$$e_{acc} = \frac{1\,(TrueL == AssignedL)}{N} \tag{6}$$

where $1\_(\cdot)$ is the indicator function. Because it is not a convex function, it is more difficult to train a predictive model to maximize accuracy than the chosen MSE. It also does not penalize outliers as much as MSE. However, it is important for the application, because it directly factors into the GPA calculation. One could argue that the MSE also factors into the application as well, but despite having correlation to Accuracy, it is not as representative. Therefore, we seek to find an MSE baseline of acceptance for model training that satisfies certain Accuracy constraints.

4. Analysis & Results

Our goal is to arrive at a formulation described by,

$$P(l\,|\,e_{mse}, \Delta) = \underbrace{P(l\,|\,e_{acc})P(e_{acc}\,|\,e_{mse}, \Delta)}_{\text{complex system}} \tag{7}$$

where l is an application outcome. For this example, let us define the application outcome to be the mean GPA of the entire school,

$$l = \frac{y_i}{N} \tag{8}$$

and let us set a target threshold of $l^* = 2.25$. This target threshold is the minimum GPA we would like to see for the entire school. The distinction is made between $P\,(l|e_{acc})$ and $P\,(e_{acc}|e_{mse}, \Delta)$ because the former is including effects that extend beyond individual observations such as group level events, path dependency, and renewal effects. In contrast, $P\,(e_{acc}|e_{mse}, \Delta)$ is subjugated to having

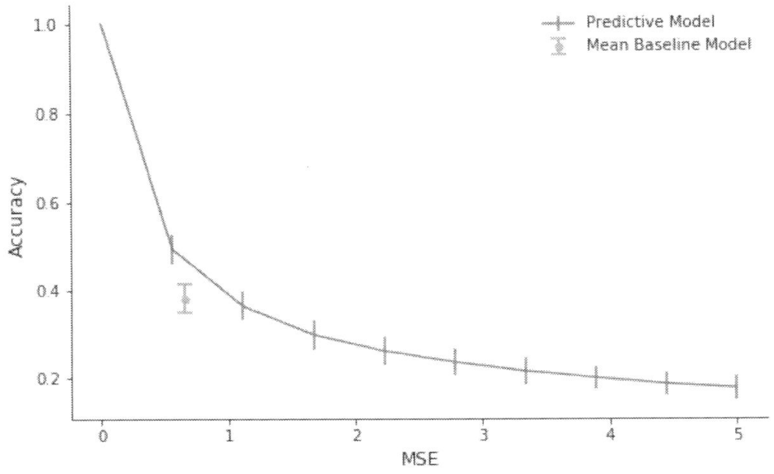

Figure 3. Empirically derived Accuracy as a function of Mean Square Error (MSE). This figure compares two different types of error measures: qualitative and probabilistic. Qualitative error here is Accuracy and represents the proportion of individuals that are correctly assigned to a given class. Probabilistic error is mean square error and represents the aggregate distance that all of the samples are away from the 'true' value. In terms of computation, MSE is a convex function that allows for ease of training machine learning algorithms. However, in complex systems the choice of error metric depends on the interaction hierarchy of the agents. As shown in this figure, a single choice of MSE threshold for implementation can result in multiple realized accuracy values. Therefore, in developing an implementation, one has to decide not only the minimum desired accuracy, but that which is best suited to the application to which it is applied.

independent outcomes for training. Therefore, this framework enables one to simulate a variety of $P\ (l|e_{acc})$ given an underlying process or set of assumptions.

For determining model training error, parameters $N = 720$ and decision model threshold, $\Delta = 1$ were set, and the result for $P\ (e_{acc}|e_{mse}, \Delta)$ is shown in Figure 3. This figure shows the expected value of accuracy given MSE, but is also subject to some error around the expected value. The Accuracy distributions were generated by sampling an N-sphere of radius $e_{mse}N$ as described in Krauth (2006). As N decreases for smaller populations we expect this distribution to exhibit wider variances of Accuracy. This distribution is important because it gives meaning to model training error (MSE) in qualitative terms relevant to the application by assigning several expected incorrect observations to a given probabilistic error measure. Figure 3 also shows the expected accuracy of the mean baseline model which always predicts the mean GPA of the training data.

The ABM was run over range of parameter values of 100 replications each. We varied the percentage of students mismatched by 1 and 2, respectively, between 0% and 100% in increments of 1%. The values of the other parameters were maintained as outlined in Table 1. We are now able to calculate the first set of distributions, P ($l|e_{acc}$) using the ABM. Additionally, we will assume that the population has a true GPA potential defined by a normal distribution

$$y^* \sim \max\{1, \min\{N(2.5, 1.5), 4.0\}\} \quad (9)$$

with mean 2.5 and standard deviation 1.5.

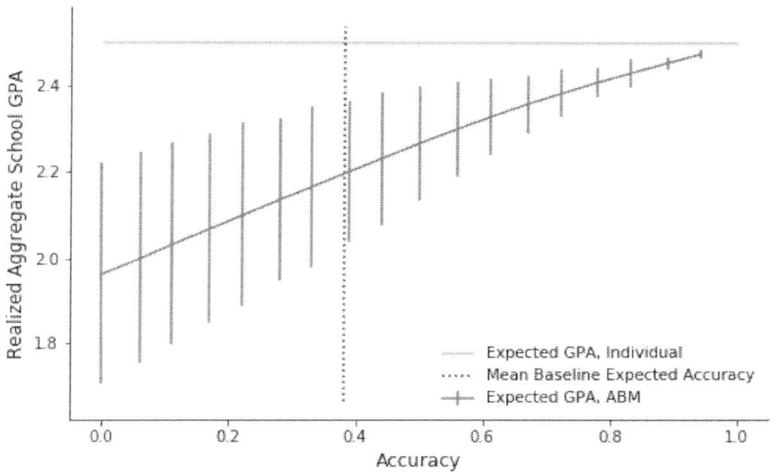

Figure 4. Probability of Outcome, P ($l|e_{acc}$).

The result of the ABM simulations with parameters $w_1 = .25$, $w_2 = .5$ is shown in Figure 4. Because this is a stylistic model, the choice of weights is arbitrary and chosen only to be illustrative of the baseline choice argument. The blue line in the figure shows the expected value of GPA given group effects of the students at varying degrees of model accuracy. We see that each value of accuracy can result in a distribution of expected aggregated school GPAs, *l*. Error bars indicate the 95% confidence intervals of these distributions.

5. Discussion & Conclusions

We are now able to address the research questions directly. In the first question, we see that application error and model training error are not necessarily coincident. Figure 4 shows the expected model GPA by the orange horizontal line. This is the error when only individual GPA discrepancies are considered, and class-level and school-level effects are left out. In contrast, the application error measuring the same outcome, aggregate GPA, shows a decline with accuracy and an increase in uncertainty.

In response to the first research question, it is not entirely surprising that training error measures and application error measures are different. However, what is surprising is that in terms of our framework, the differences between the errors is a result of compounding error of model predictions. More prediction error leads to more incorrect class assignments and more disruptors at the school. If observations are treated independently, as is common, then this information is inaccessible to model training. This seems to suggest a need for adaptive feedback mechanisms to ensure model stability when placed in situ and not just error performance.

In the second research question, we can also evaluate baseline refinement as an acceptance criterion for model training. In Figure 4, the vertical dashed line represents the expected accuracy resulting from a mean baseline model. Given the distribution of y^*, the mean baseline model has an MSE of .62 which translates to an expected accuracy of about 38%. Choosing this as a baseline for model evaluation does not define a useful point of reference if our goal is defined as $l^* = 2.25$, because models performing better than the baseline can still have a high probability of going below this mark. Instead, a better baseline would be to select an accuracy value of 70% which translates to an MSE of .2. Therefore, the target training error of the model should aim to have an MSE of 0.2 or better in order to reach the application goals.

In total, this paper presents a framework for analyzing predictive models in the context of complex systems. The need for such a framework is illustrated using a simple stylistic model of classroom assignments and we begin to explore the differences and relations between model training error and application error. There is evidence that these two can be related more rigorously but will be application dependent. Our future efforts will be twofold: 1.) to make this framework more mathematically rigorous to establish bounds on expected application error given errors in predictive model training and 2.) to use more realistic scenarios and datasets. Of interest will be including multiple operationalized models of theories in the social sciences to better anticipate outcomes of implementing predictive models in complex systems.

References

Arya, A., Fellingham, J. C., & Schroeder, D. A. (2004). Aggregation and measurement errors in performance evaluation. *Journal of Management Accounting Research, 16* (1), 93–105.

Berk, R. (2017). An impact assessment of machine learning risk forecasts on parole board decisions and recidivism. *Journal of Experimental Criminology, 13* (2), 193–216.

Church, C. E. & Fairchild, A. J. (2017). In search of a silver bullet: Child welfare's embrace of predictive analytics [article]. *Juvenile and Family Court*

Journal, (Issue 1), 67.

Collaboration, O. S. (2015). Estimating the reproducibility of psychological science. *Science, 349* (6251).

Cuccaro-Alamin, S., Foust, R., Vaithianathan, R., & Putnam-Hornstein, E. (2017). Risk assessment and decision making in child protective services: Predictive risk modeling in context. *Children and Youth Services Review, 79,* 291 - 298.

Epstein, J. M. (2002). Modeling civil violence: An agent-based computational approach. *Proceedings of the National Academy of Sciences, 99* (suppl 3), 7243–7250.

Ferri, C., Hernández-Orallo, J., & Modroiu, R. (2009). An experimental comparison of performance measures for classification. *Pattern Recognition Letters, 30* (1), 27–38.

Gaudette, L. & Japkowicz, N. (2009). Evaluation methods for ordinal classification. In *Advances in Artificial Intelligence, 22nd Canadian Conference on Artificial Intelligence, Canadian AI 2009, Kelowna, Canada, May 25-27, 2009, Proceedings*, (pp. 207–210).

Gilbert, N. & Troitzsch, K. (2005). *Simulation for the social scientist*. New York, NY: Open University Press.

Krauth, W. (2006). *Statistical Mechanics: Algorithms and Computations*. London: Oxford University Press.

Lundberg, I., Narayanan, A., Levy, K., & Salganik, M. J. (2018). Privacy, ethics, and data access: A case study of the fragile families challenge. Retrieved from https://arxiv.org/abs/1809.00103.

Macal, C. M. & North, M. J. (2010). Tutorial on agent-based modeling and simulation. *Journal of Simulation, 4,* 151–162.

Manson, S., Sun, S., & Bonsal, D. (2012). Agent-based modeling and complexity. In A. J. Heppenstall, A. T. Crooks, L. M. See, & M. Batty (Eds.), *Agent-based models of geographical systems* (pp. 125–139). New York, NY: Springer.

Miller, J. H. & Page, S. E. (2007). *Complex adaptive systems: An introduction to computational models of social life.* Princeton, NJ: Princeton University Press.

Pires, B. & Crooks, A. T. (2017). Modeling the emergence of riots: A geosimulation approach. *Computers, Environment and Urban Systems, 61*, 66–80.

Ramakrishnan, N., Butler, P., Muthiah, S., Self, N., Khandpur, R., Saraf, P.,... Mares, D. (2014). 'beating the news' with embers: Forecasting civil unrest using open source indicators. In *Proceedings of the 20th ACM SIGKDD International Conference on Knowledge Discovery and Data Mining*, KDD '14, (pp. 1799–1808)., New York, NY, USA. ACM.

Schelling, T. C. (1969). Models of segregation. *The American Economic Review, 59* (2), 488–493.

Schelling, T. C. (2006). *Micromotives and macrobehavior.* New York. NY: WW Norton & Company.

Tseng, P. (2010). Approximation accuracy, gradient methods, and error bound for structured convex optimization. *Mathematical Programming, 125* (2), 263–295.

Wilensky, U. (1999). Netlogo. http://ccl.northwestern.edu/netlogo/. Center for Connected Learning and Computer-Based Modeling, Northwestern University, Evanston, IL.

Confronting Model Uncertainty in Policy Analysis for Complex Systems: What Policymakers Should Demand

Paul K. Davis (corresponding author)
Principal Researcher, RAND (retired adjunct);
Professor, Pardee RAND Graduate School
pdavis@rand.org

Steven W. Popper
Senior Economist, RAND Corporation;
Professor, Pardee RAND Graduate School

ABSTRACT

Good policy analysis needs to improve in *routinely* addressing not only uncertainty about model inputs to the model used, but also uncertainty about the model itself and disagreements about perspective affecting the model. This is especially true when analyzing complex systems. Progress will depend on analysts and modelers understanding how to proceed and, significantly, on policymakers demanding that they do so. Methods for doing so now exist, but culture changes will be necessary. In the future, analysis that fails to address uncertainties about both models and their inputs may come to be regarded as fatally flawed.

Keywords: uncertainty analysis; deep uncertainty; policy analysis; model uncertainty; complex adaptive systems

Confrontación a la incertidumbre del modelo en el análisis de políticas para sistemas complejos: Lo que los responsables políticos deberían exigir

RESUMEN

Un buen análisis de políticas debe mejorar al abordar de manera rutinaria no solo la incertidumbre sobre las entradas del modelo al modelo utilizado, sino también la incertidumbre sobre el modelo en sí y los desacuerdos de perspectiva que lo afectan. Esto es especialmente cierto cuando se analizan sistemas complejos. El progreso dependerá de que los analistas y modeladores comprendan cómo proceder y, de manera significativa, de los encargados de formular políticas que exijan que lo hagan. Ahora existen métodos para hacerlo, pero serán necesarios cambios culturales. En el futuro, el análisis que no aborde las incertidumbres sobre ambos modelos y sus aportes de manera efectiva puede considerarse fatalmente defectuoso.

Palabras Clave: Análisis de incertidumbre; incertidumbre profunda; análisis de políticas; incertidumbre del modelo; sistemas adaptativos complejos

直面复杂系统政策分析中模型的不确定性：决策者应要求什么

摘要

一个好的政策分析不仅需要在“照例”应对模型输入（数据）的不确定性，还要在模型自身的不确定性、以及影响模型的不一致观点等方面上取得进步。这一点在分析复杂系统时尤为正确。进步将取决于分析师和建模者对如何取得进展的理解，但更取决于决策者要求前者执行这一过程。现下已存在执行方法，但文化改变将不可或缺。未来，那些无法有效应对自身模型和模型输入的不确定性的分析，将有可能被视为存在根本缺陷。

关键词：不确定性分析；深度不确定性；政策分析；模型不确定性；复杂适应系统

1. Introduction: Analysis When the Model is Uncertain

This paper is written for the modeling and analysis communities, for policy analysts more generally, and for policymakers who commission studies. While addressing uncertainty analysis more broadly, we highlight a specific challenge: “How do we conduct policy analysis when we lack confidence in the model, i.e., when we disagree or are unsure about how the world works?” Methods exist for dealing with parametric uncertainty, but what if the model itself is problematic? That constitutes model uncertainty (also called structural uncertainty). Good policy analysis needs to confront it far better than in the past. The issue was recognized a half-century ago (Quade & Boucher, 1968). Nonetheless, it is common to place bets on the one model that somehow seems best, even when dealing with complex and poorly understood systems. We instead urge an approach that explores model uncertainty as a primary facet of analysis. Analysis that fails to do so may be perceived in the future as fatally flawed.

As stage setting, we note that policymakers often recognize that the analysis with which they are presented rests on arguable (often unstated) assumptions. Their reticence to accept the analysis is then warranted—it is a sign of wise skepticism, rather than parochialism or aversion to science or evidence. Their skepticism might be ameliorated if analysis dealt transparently with uncertainties and disagreements, but it seldom does.

Examples of where this might matter include evaluating tax-reform proposals (will the 2017 tax cuts pay their way by stimulating sustained growth?) and policies to mitigate effects of climate change (are they effective?). To be sure, some policymakers will be impervious to analysis if they don't like its implications, but others will engage and be influenced if only the analysis is more candid, intelligible, and helpful.

What follows discusses the importance of addressing model uncertainties (Section 2), its feasibility (Section 3), a way ahead (Section 4), examples showing feasibility (Section 5), and recommendations (Section 6).[1]

2. Importance of the Problem

Three examples illustrate the importance of dealing with model uncertainty.

2.1. The Financial Collapse of 2008

The financial crisis of 2008 was profound. Even today, America suffers from a lost decade of severely sub-par economic performance. A major factor underlying the crisis was the misrepresentation of human behavior in mental models and in corresponding financial-risk models (Financial Crisis Inquiry Commission, 2011; Krugman, 2009; Lewis, 2010; Thaler & Sunstein, 2008). As Alan Greenspan famously testified (U.S. House of Representatives, 2008), "Those of us who have looked to the self-interest of lending institutions to protect shareholders' equity, myself included, are in a state of shocked disbelief."

Before the crisis, lending institutions took exceptional risks, which

1 We discuss model uncertainty. Model validation is a separate and difficult subject. Model validity should be addressed for five separate dimensions: description, explanation, post-diction, exploration, and prediction, especially for complex-system phenomena (Davis, O'Mahony, & Pfautz, 2019, pp. 28-32). Other research has described techniques for building confidence in complex-system models (Howick, Eden, Ackermann, & Williams, 2008; Wallis & Johnson, 2018). These include cognitive or causal maps, interviews, and simulation. Wallis and Johnson (2018) referred to the method as Integrative Propositional Analysis (IPA), a method for evaluating the conceptual structure of theories and models.

were behaviorally incentivized by competition with other lenders promising high rates of return, the potential for extraordinary personal gain, and the belief that housing prices would always rise (Financial Crisis Inquiry Commission, 2011, p. 6). Perhaps they assumed that the government would bail them out if need be, or that they could move in or out of the market as needed. In any case, the risk models were poor matches for reality.

2.2. Debate about Limits To Growth

Details of model-based analysis seldom receive public attention, but a tumult followed publication of *The Limits of Growth* in the early 1970s (Meadows, Meadows, Randers, & Behrens III, 1972). The authors were associates of MIT professor Jay Forrester, the father of the method called System Dynamics. The book warned of civilizational collapse due to environmental and economic issues if business-as-usual trends continued. Criticisms were strenuous (Cole, Freeman, Jahoda, & Pavitt, 1973), with Forrester responding vigorously (Forrester, Low, & Mass, 1974). Later exchanges were more restrained (Nordhaus, 1992), but the debate was not always constructive, much less convergent (Bardi, 2011).[2]

The study's computer model embodied assertions about demographic, economic, technological, and political processes. Model parameters were treated as uncertain, but not so much the models themselves.[3] The model assumed exponential growth of population, although not in the naive way assumed by critics. Arguably, the model did not adequately allow for revolutionary changes in technology, energy production, agriculture, or birth rates (Kahn, 1983). For example, the authors did not fully anticipate the drastic changes that were to occur involving solar energy, tertiary recovery, and use of natural gas. Arguably, their model did not allow market forces to respond adequately as resource scarcity grew. Nor did it anticipate that worldwide energy production would increase less than proportionally to economic growth (Business Council for Sustainable Energy, 2017). The model also did not distinguish well among different regions and climates. The authors were sometimes seen as extreme advocates for environmentalism and slow growth.

For years, the conventional wisdom was that the Limits to Growth work had been discredited. In reality, it had had much to say that was important and usefully provocative. Moreover, several researchers have found remarkable agreement between empirical reality over time and many of the model's predictions (Bardi, 2011; Turner, 2008). Other authors have remarked on analogies between the debate about Limits to Growth and the more recent debate

2 Meadows (2012) noted the primary criticisms in a 40-year retrospective.

3 Some model uncertainties could be studied by varying model parameters jointly (Cole et al., 1973, p. 223; Forrester et al., 1974), but how to so was not intuitive to critics unaccustomed to system dynamic models. For example, the net population growth rate seemed like an input assumption, but was actually an output influenced by multiple factors.

about climate change (Eastin, Grundman, & Prakash, 2010).

A lesson from the Limits to Growth saga was to view computer models as something to use in exploring and contemplating, rather than in confidently predicting. The book presented valid danger signals about how bad the future would be *unless* major changes occurred. The contingent nature of this discussion was more clearly expressed in the 30-year update (Meadows, Randers, & Meadows, 2004), but was present from the outset. Regrettably, policymakers and people generally have a difficult time with contingent predictions. No, collapse was not inevitable, and the study said so (Gamino, 2012).

At the time of the publication of the *Limits to Growth*, scientists were doing well if they varied simulation parameters to generate diverse scenarios. To also vary the underlying conceptual models, and to do so in a comprehensible way enabling productive debate, was a bridge too far. Doing better is today feasible, but it is a grand challenge for policy analysts.

2.3. The 2003 Iraq War and the 2007 Surge Operation

As a further example of why models matter, consider a strategic-military decision with profound consequences. The decision to invade Iraq in 2003 depended on assessments of what would happen after an invasion, assessments based on war gaming, more detailed simulation, and other analysis. It was believed that the military operation would be fast and decisive.[4]

Some of the premises underlying the war proved wrong (Saddam did not have nuclear weapons), as did the planners' basic conceptual model of conflict (Gordon & Trainor, 2012; Kaplan, 2013). Instead of conflict being brief and decisive, what emerged was insurgency and civil war.

In 2007, after years of dismal results, President Bush authorized the surge, a last-ditch effort to salvage a losing war. Most observers opposed the surge, believing that it would either fail or be counterproductive (Gordon & Trainor, 2012), but President Bush was persuaded by arguments from a group of analysts that conducted map games that could foresee a road to victory (see Chapter 24 of Gordon & Trainor, 2012).

As it happened, the subsequent operations under the leadership of General David Petraeus were successful, although the surge in U.S. forces was only one of several reasons for the temporary success. In the so-called Anbar Awakening, Sunni tribal leaders concluded that it was in their interest to collaborate with Americans. Another factor was ethnic redistribution, as residents of mixed neighborhoods voted with their feet during the quasi-civil war, separating combatants. Also, President Maliki reluctantly recognized that Shia militias were a threat to his own

4 Some cautions were posted. Historical analysis warned about an invasion with such a small ground force (Quinlivan, 1995). Reflecting such experience, the Army Chief of Staff Eric Shinseki told Congress that a much larger ground force was needed, something immediately derided by political leaders.

power and allowed stabilizing actions that he had previously prohibited.

Most computer modeling in this period represented only force movements and combat—not the longer-run issues that were more quintessentially political, such as the parochial shortcomings of Nouri al-Maliki that led him to squander opportunities.[5]

U.S. troops departed over the period 2007-2011, as promised in a formal agreement reached under President Bush, which President Obama honored, despite calls for leaving forces in Iraq. Subsequently, Iraq fell again into sectarian struggle and the Islamic State emerged to fill the vacuum. We need not elaborate here on how the saga unfolded (and continues to unfold 16 years later). This case illustrates the profound importance of questioning the conceptual model behind reasoning, not just the values of parameters in a formalized model.

3. Myths and Realities about Uncertainty Analysis

Section 2 illustrated why analysis should consider model uncertainties, as has long been recognized. It has been widely believed, however, that confronting model uncertainty is not feasible and that it is more pragmatic to make assumptions and plunge on, rather than being paralyzed by uncertainty. That stance once had considerable basis in practical experience, but it is now a myth: uncertainty analysis—even about model uncertainties—can be very helpful.

Pioneering work on uncertainty analysis in the 1980s was pulled together in a textbook (Morgan & Henrion, 1992). Subsequently, two streams of research evolved at the RAND Corporation: one focused primarily on defense planning (Davis, 1994; Davis, 2014), the other primarily on broader social-policy issues (Bankes, 1993). These efforts have led to the methodology now called robust decision-making (RDM) (Lempert, Popper, & Bankes, 2003; Lempert, Groves, Popper, & Bankes, 2006; Popper, Lempert, & Bankes, 2005). Interest in decision-making under deep uncertainty now has strong international interest (Marchau, Walker, Bloemen, & Popper, 2019), as evidenced by important contributions from the Technical University of Delft (Haasnoot, Kwakkel, Walker, & Maat, 2013) and a vibrant professional society (see http://www.deepuncertainty.org).

Uncertainties can be addressed with the more sophisticated approaches and policymakers can—without paralysis—be assisted in making well hedged decisions. The approaches, however, are more advanced for parametric uncertainties than for model uncertainties. What follows suggests a way ahead, described for uncertainty analysis generally so that our discussion of model uncertainty fits into that larger context.

5 An exception was work with the political simulation model, Senturion (Abdollahian, Barnick, Efird, & Kugler, 2006).

4. Elements of a Way Ahead

4.1. A Framework for Uncertainty Analysis in Complex Policy Problems

Simulating consequences of policy actions depends on inputs to the simulation (including the models to be used). When each such input is specified, the result is a scenario, run, or case. Assessments from such work must obviously consider the uncertainties in those inputs. But how should those uncertainties be organized?

We have used two similar frameworks. The first conceives the "scenario space" implied by uncertainties in groups labeled Context, Objectives and Strategies, Resources, Effectiveness, Environment, and Other Model Assumptions (Davis, 1994, p. 82). The second uses a framework and terminology, called XLRM (Lempert, Popper, & Bankes, 2003) which refers to uncertainty factors X, levers of policy L, models and relationships R, and performance metrics M. For the purposes of this paper focused on model uncertainty, we have amended the XLRM framework as shown in Figure 1. The stack of clouds at the top left of the diagram indicates "meta models," fundamentally different models of the problem (referred to as alternative *perspectives* in some past work (Davis, Gompert, Johnson, & Long, 2008; Davis, Shaver, & Beck, 2008)).

For *each* meta model, it is possible to specify X, L, R, and M, and to then explore by varying their values systematically. This may involve scores of variables and hundreds of millions of runs. Uncertainties can be represented with a range of discrete values, probability distributions, or both. The cases generated may be comprehensive or based on Monte Caro sampling.

Uncertainty factors (X)
Uncertain factors not controlled by planning organization (i.e., exogenous factors)

Policy levers (L)
Factors that can be adjusted as part of a planning organization's strategy

Models and relationships (R)
Models, including relationships among variables for evaluating outcomes, using metrics M, from using levers L across ensembles of assumptions about uncertain factors X

Performance metrics (M)
Multi-attribute framework consisting of both metrics and acceptable/unacceptable values for those metrics as set by policy

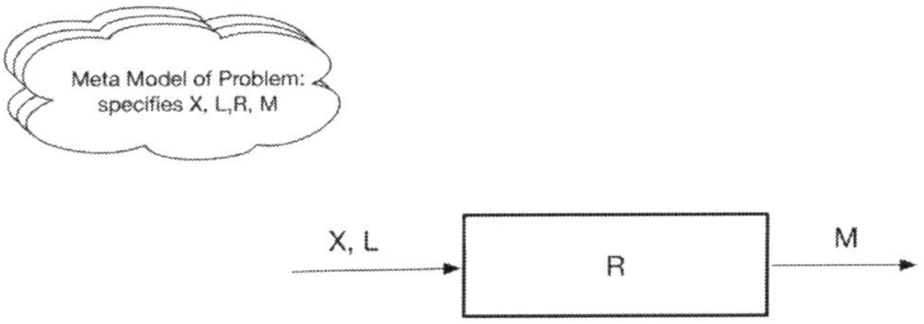

Figure 1. An adaptation of the XLRM Framework highlighting model uncertainty.

Since the R of XLRM already refers to models and relationships, why do we need the meta models? The reason is practical: once we allow for fundamentally different models of the problem, it affects "everything": the uncertainty factors, the policy levers, the computational model, and the measures of effectiveness. Thus, in practice, it is useful to show these separately for each meta model. Fortunately, addressing just two or three substantially different views of the problem often suffices.

4.2. Methods for Dealing with Model Uncertainty

Let us now ask about specific mechanisms for considering model uncertainty. We suggest the methods in Table 1, all of which we have used. Some have led to different meta models, some to alternative formulations within a single meta model.

Table 1. Methods for Addressing Model Uncertainty

Method	Description
Scenarios	Use scenarios to group alternative assumption sets. *Example*: strategic planning that describes the world as potentially unfolding by a no-surprises scenario or a scenario with technological breakthroughs and economic growth
Competitive Models	Use competing models. Often, the most important disagreements or other uncertainties can be grouped into two or three clumps. This sharpens issues. *Example*: in contemplating coercive strategy, use alternative cognitive models of how the adversary reasons. Is the adversary fearfully attempting to deter or is the adversary contemptuous of others and planning aggression?[6]
Bounding Models	Identify models that bound the range of not-implausible model-uncertainty consequences (easiest if the issue has only one primary dimension).[7] *Example*: in estimating outcome of a group's internal debates, one model might assume an outcome compromising across factions; another might assume that the outcome is the strident outcome of the winning faction.
Ensemble of Models	Elicit diverse alternative models and consider all of them. *Example*: in the study of climate-change, consider results of models from different universities, government laboratories, and private institutions.[8]

6 An early example used competing "red agents" in a simulation to study Cold War deterrence (Davis, 1989). Later, competing models of Saddam Hussein helped anticipate Saddam's 1990 aggression against Kuwait (Davis & Arquilla, 1991; National Research Council, 2014). These efforts reflected cognitive biases and misperceptions. Later, competing models of Kim Jong Il were used to study possible negotiation options, although the study concluded that Kim was very unlikely (across plausible models) to truly give up his nuclear program (Arquilla & Davis, 1994). Recent studies compare alternative social-science theories in agent-based modeling of social systems (Gunaratne & Garibay, 2018; Hadzikadic & Whitmeyer, 2019).

7 The method was used for a model of public support for terrorism (Davis & O'Mahony, 2013) and in a study of heterogeneous fusion of information, bearing on whether an individual should be judged as a potential terrorist threat given inconsistent information (some of it wrong or deceptive) (Davis, Perry, Hollywood, & Manheim, 2016).

8 See the Intergovernmental Panel on Climate Change (IPCC; 2010, 2014).

"Models" Inferred from Causal Statements	Have experts affirm important causal relationships among variables comprising a system lacking a formal model. Each set of statements acts as an alternative model. *Example*: in assessing the value of the United States supplying equipment to a regional security partner, require explicit statements about the perceived benefits and drawbacks for such objectives as joint effectiveness and human and institutional capacity building. Ask for estimates of the signs and magnitudes of effects, and for the shape of the combined-effect curve (e.g., linear, decreasing returns, or sigmoid) (O'Mahony et al., 2018).
Aggregate Parameters	Forego modeling *mechanisms* and instead focus on aggregate consequences represented by parameters (a type of minimalist modeling). *Example*: New technologies could mitigate effects of climate change as characterized by sea level rise. Other aggregate measures are the decoupling rate between growths of the economy and energy production, and the decoupling rate between the growth of the economy and greenhouse gas emissions (Lempert et al., 2003).

Even with these methods, we cannot be comprehensive, but we can aspire to due diligence by considering model uncertainties of which we are or should be aware. That does not mean tossing in every possibility someone can think of. To do so would lead to paralysis. The practitioner analyst must employ a mix of art and science and must subjectively omit some possibilities (e.g., invasions from Mars).

4.3. Broadening the Concept of Analysis Campaign

Given methods for varying model structures, as above, the next element for a way ahead is approaching analysis with a multifaceted "analysis campaign," perhaps with elements, as in Table 2. We use the first column to indicate classic aspects of operations analysis (Greenberger, Crenson, & Crissey, 1976; Walker, 2000), the second column to note features now coming into acceptance, and the third column to indicate additional features relating to *model* uncertainty.

Table 2. Increasingly Ambitious Treatments of Uncertainty in Analysis Campaigns

Early	*Advanced (primarily parametric uncertainty)*	*More Advanced, Routinely Addressing Model Uncertainty and Multiple Perspectives*
Identify problem	Understand system and problem area	+ Recognize parties, stakeholders, and views + Understand broadened system, issues, questions, and tradeoffs + Recognize emergent phenomena[9]

9 This is crucial for "wicked problems," the norm in higher-level policy problem areas (Rosenhead & Mingers, 2002). How to represent emergence with generative models is a frontier challenge in social-behavioral modeling (Davis et al., 2019).

Build relatively narrow model	Start building evolving system model addressing phenomena, issues, and questions	+ Include alternative model constructs + Allow for alternative perspectives + Represent emergent phenomena
Identify objectives and possible goals	Recognize multiple objectives (often in tension) and possible constraints of and on parties. Represent underlying values.	+ Allow objectives to vary across models and perspectives + Reflect emergent phenomena, including changes of value systems
Choose evaluation criteria	Choose criteria, including "soft" criteria reflecting qualitative values.	+ Allow criteria to vary across models and perspectives
Plan sensitivity analysis on a few primary variables	Plan broad parametric exploration across all significant variables	+ Broaden exploration to cut across model structure and alternative perspectives
Select policy alternatives	Construct policy options, including creative options not offered initially	Include options that allow for changes of system or processes
Analyze alternatives; compare by criteria above	Analyze with multi-criteria methods (e.g. scorecards). Do not "add up" scores prematurely.	+ Extend to address model uncertainties and alternative perspectives
Choose the best option (optimization) and implement it	Identify options that are relatively robust to parametric uncertainties, i.e., options that are flexible, adaptive, and robust to shocks.	+ Extend to reflect treatment of model uncertainty and alternative perspectives +Anticipate the likely need for major adaptations
Monitor results	Monitor and adapt, sometimes on the margin and sometimes with major shifts	+ Extend to include adaptations changing primary model or perspective

Figure 2 suggests how an analysis campaign can affect results. It recognizes that analysis should have both deep and shallow components: deep, so that critical phenomena are understood, and shallow, to permit good communication, explanation, and persuasion. Policymakers and those receiving decisions need to understand the reasoning. This requires simple conceptual models and compelling stories. A feature of the analysis campaign is that it anticipates being able to report the top-level story (or conflicting stories), also providing in-depth explanation as necessary. This means zooming into detail as necessary to support findings and recommendations (Davis, 2014).

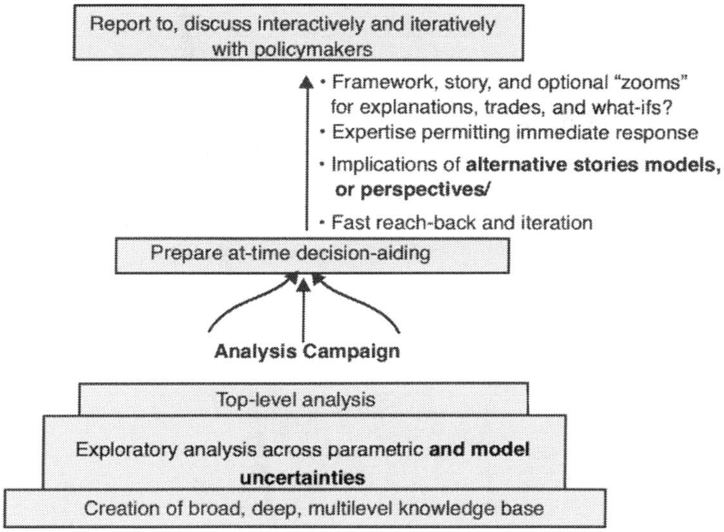

Figure 2. Analysis campaign.

4.4 Improving the Communication of Insights

All readers will agree on the need to improve communication among modelers, analysts, and policymakers. Doing so, however, is notoriously difficult. Authors in the *Limits to Growth* controversy had labored to make their model and study understandable, but misunderstandings were common. We have attempted the same in our own work, but—to our chagrin—have only sometimes succeeded. Nonetheless, modern concepts and technology make success increasingly feasible. Some admonitions that we offer are as follows, some of which are especially important when addressing model uncertainty.

- Elevator Speech. Be sure always to prepare an elevator speech on results and insights, but also highlight crucial model uncertainties.
- Conceptual Model. Provide a clear conceptual model and simplified depictions of results. Causal diagrams, logic tables, and game-theory tables can all be helpful, as can simplified charts briefly depicting key points about dynamics. Showing multiple complex charts of simulation trajectories is counterproductive.
- Multi-Resolution Layering. Convey complex models with a multi-resolution approach, since one-layer diagrams are too difficult to comprehend. This is valuable not only in the final presentation, but also in the analysis campaign itself.
- Qualitative Models. Reject the classic obsession with quantification and alleged rigor, which is often false, and instead embrace qualitative models, especially for description and explanation. Examples include system diagrams, factor trees, influence diagrams, and social-network diagrams.

- Region and Tradeoff Plots. Emphasize charts showing how outcomes vary with combinations of causal-factor values and model structures. Instead of showing results and waiting for the recipient's "What if?" questions, preemptively show results across the assumption space.

We illustrate this last approach in the next two figures. The top pane in Figure 3 shows a conventional comparison of two options for some standard case. The lower pane is a region plot that is much richer, showing *when* Option 1 or Option 2 is better. For simplicity, it uses only two dimensions (mission difficulty and timeliness required). Option 2, not Option 1, is better unless the standard case is assuredly correct. It is possible to show some audiences results with six to 10 independent variables (Davis, 2014) or to project multi-dimensional uncertainty analysis onto two dimensions (Davis, Bankes, & Egner, 2007; Lempert et al., 2006).

Figure 4 conveys a similar story for a more complex case that highlights model uncertainty. It compares simulated outcomes with four different strategies (called plans in the figure) given uncertainty and disagreement about which of two models, M1 or M2, is correct. Reflecting myriad simulations, Figure 4 shows the expected outcome in terms of regret for each alternative strategy as a function of the odds that the first model is correct. "Regret" measures how much better one might have done with a different decision. In Figure 4, strategy B performs best (*lowest* regret) when M2 is correct (bottom left) and strategy D has the least expected regret when M1 is most likely correct (right side). Strategy A is dominated at every point by other strategies. Strategy C is interesting; although it is never the best, it places a close second everywhere, with low expected regret. That is, it hedges well. Adopting Strategy C could avoid a costly blunder (the result of guessing wrong about which model to assume).

As mentioned earlier, decision-makers have a hard time dealing with contingent predictions for reasons that lie deep in neuropsychology, but we know from personal experience that analysts and senior leaders *can* learn to think in terms of region charts and tradeoff charts, such as in Figures 3 and 4. They can then internalize the contingent nature of outcomes. Thus, analyses need to be simplistic, and displays must be intuitive.

5. Existence Proofs

This paper stems from concern that analysis does not routinely address model uncertainty. Nonetheless, enough past examples exist to demonstrate feasibility and value. We mention a few briefly.

1. Planning Military Capabilities. In recent decades, the U.S. Department of Defense (DoD) has moved away from planning based on single scenarios toward an approach that seeks to assure that capabilities are adequate to deal with a broad range of possible conflicts and crises (Rumsfeld, 2001) and an understanding of a broad range of ways in

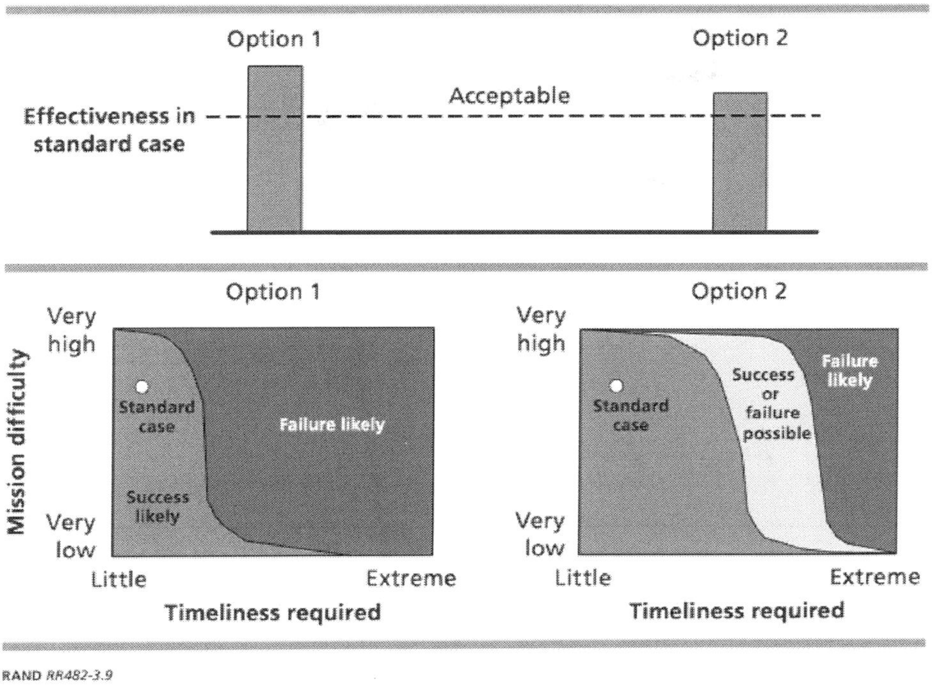

Figure 3. Illustrating region plots for parametric uncertainty.

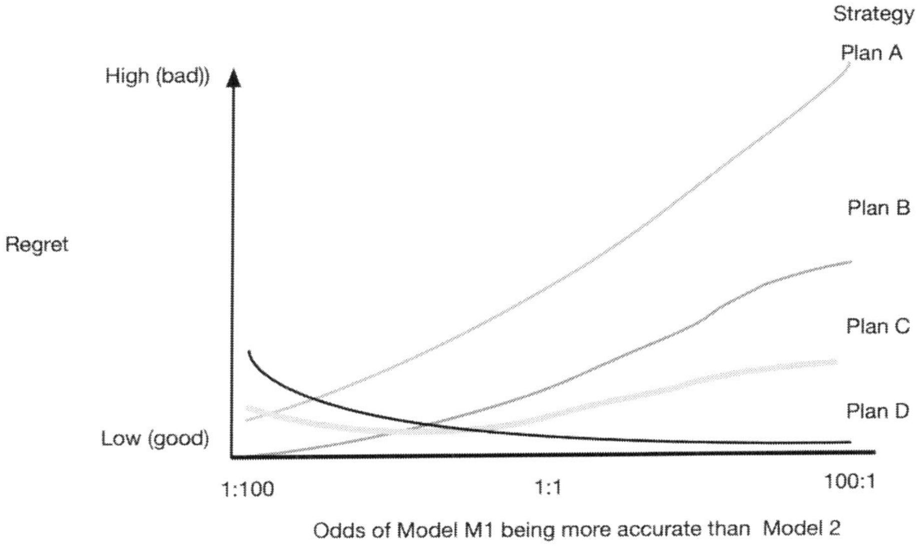

Figure 4. Using a measure of "regret" to assess an option's robustness in relation to assumptions. (Source: adapted from Popper, Griffin, Berrebi, Light, & Min, 2009).

which any particular conflict might unfold (e.g., different friendly and enemy tactics, different degrees of warning) (Davis, 2002).

2. Studies of Counterterrorism and Counterinsurgency. The DoD concluded in the late 2000s that its traditional models were unsuited for counterterrorism and counterinsurgency, subjects on which great disagreements exist about cause-effect relationships and the potential effectiveness of interventions. The DoD asked for a review of the underlying base in social science that should inform modeling and simulation. The resulting work generated mostly qualitative models, with an emphasis on being able to deal with model uncertainty (Davis & Cragin, 2009; Davis & O'Mahony, 2017).

3. Industrial Transformation and Sustainability of Emission Control Policies. Although many aspects of climate change are largely settled, policy prescriptions remain controversial. Understanding the issues requires thinking about possible transformational effects on commercial, energy, and transformation systems. One study discussed adaptive co-evolutionary possibilities for technology, political coalitions, industry, and government. It highlighted the need for experiments and iterations of policy as the future unfolds (Isley, Lempert, Popper, & Vardavas, 2013).

4. International Investment in Clean-Energy Technology. The United Nations agreed in 2010 to the creation of the Green Climate Fund (GCF). A new organization was tasked with directing over $100 billion dollars per year toward investments in clean energy technologies. Deep model uncertainties exist in attempting to understand these issues. As shown in a recent study, however, much can be done to confront these and to find a robust set of policies (Molina-Perez, 2016).

5. Water Management Planning. Water resources managers and their partners have begun to use methods of decision-making under deep uncertainty to account for uncertain changes in hydrology and other drivers of supply and demand. Early work involved case studies in California (Groves & Lempert, 2007; Tingstad, Groves, & Lempert, 2014). Similar methods have been used subsequently to evaluate the vulnerability of complex U.S. water systems (Groves, Fischbach, Bloom, Knopman, & Keefe, 2013; Lempert & Groves, 2010) and international water management issues (Kalra et al., 2015; Ray et al., 2018).

6. Conclusions and Recommendations

Our basic recommendation is that policy analysts and those who commission their work should prioritize serious uncertainty analysis, to include addressing uncertainty and disagreement about conceptual models that underlie the analysis.

This will mean analysis to find strategies that are flexible, adaptive, and robust (often called robust for short)—i.e., strategies that are expected to do well across the range of assumptions about inputs, how the world works, and how alternative policies would affect outcomes over time. The need to do so should become a basic ethic for analysts of choice under uncertainty (Davis, 2014).

Success will require basic cultural changes in the analytic and policymaker communities using analysis. Table 3 characterizes the needed culture changes. The first column shows common current-day questions asked by policymakers and by people developing terms of reference for studies. The second column indicates the better types of question that would represent a shift in analytic culture.

Table 3. Culture Changes Needed for Analysis Under Uncertainty

Current Type of Question Asked by Policymakers	Better Questions for Policy Under Uncertainty
What's your best prediction? What should we prepare for?	What are the things I can do now that will best position us to deal with whatever arises down the pike?
Which option is best?	How do I make a robustly good decision? What is necessary to have a strategy that is as flexible, adaptive, and robust as possible given budgetary and other considerations?
Whose options are you going to look at?	Where will your options come from? Are you talking to everyone? Are you going beyond the options that the bureaucracy provides? Will there be new ideas?
What data are you using?	What is your campaign plan for analysis? Will you be addressing the fundamental uncertainties and disagreements, as well as the uncertainties of so-called data (are the right variables being measured is the data credible)?
Do you have a steering group with reps from the relevant offices?	Do you plan to have a "Red team" to ask the hard questions? Do you plan to have an Advisory Group to assure that you're covering all the bases—a group of not just the "official" stakeholders, but of everyone who should be heard?
	Will implementation be part of the campaign of analysis or will that be an afterthought?
Are you using a validated model and data?	How is your campaign plan for analysis going to assure that your modeling and analysis are valid for the purposes intended, whether to "describe and explain," to "explore to find insights and the ingredients of robust decisions," or prediction? What model(s) are you going to consider?

Can I ask *what if* questions about results under different scenarios?	Are you going to give me intelligible big-picture estimates as a function of major variables? Tradeoff plots? Measures of robustness (e.g., regret)? Will I have to just listen, or can I interact? Will there be real-time responses to questions or requests for another six months?
How long do you need for your brief-out? 30 minutes? More?	How am I going to interact along the way? Initial plan, interim discussion, final discussion? Are you going to have results in layers of detail so that I (or my staff) can get into details where necessary? Will the study be documented intelligibly?
Oh, how do I monitor to assure that my decision is implemented?	Recognizing that our action will be an experiment and that we will likely learn from experience and must adapt, perhaps in a major way, how should we plan to monitor and anticipate such adaptations if needed?

It is not the role of analysis and analysts to create deus ex machina in the form of analyses that will resolve policy choices. That is rightly the job of elected officials and their appointees. But analysts can illuminate the policy trade-off space: which short-term actions (and preparation for later adaptations) will likely achieve long-term policy objectives despite uncertainties and disagreements now and the likelihood of unexpected developments? If analysts can do this, they may help bring about a needed shift in culture.

Acknowledgements

This paper was possible thanks to support from the RAND Center for Decision Making under Uncertainty, within the Pardee RAND Graduate School. We thank Andrew Parker, David Groves, and two anonymous reviewers for comments on the draft.

References

Abdollahian, M., Barnick, M., Efird, B., & Kugler, J. (2006). *Senturion: A predictive political simulation model.* Washington, DC: National Defense University. Retrieved from http://www.ndu.edu/CTNSP/docUploaded/DTP%2032%20Senturion.pdf

Arquilla, J., & Davis, P. K. (1994). *Modeling decision-making of potential proliferators as part of developing counterproliferation strategies (MR-467).* Santa Monica, CA.: RAND Corporation. Retrieved from http://www.rand.org/pubs/monograph_reports/MR467.html

Bardi, U. (2011). *The limits to growth revisited.* New York, NY: Springer.

Business Council for Sustainable Energy. (2017). *Sustainable energy in America Factbook: Understanding the U. S. energy transformation.* Retrieved from http://www.bcse.org/wp-content/uploads/BCSE-2017-Sustainable-Energy-in-America-Factbook-Brochure.pdf

Cole, H. S. D., Freeman, C., Jahoda, M.,

& Pavitt, K. L. R. (Eds.). (1973). *Models of doom: A critique of 'limits to growth'*. New York, NY: Universe Books.

Davis, P. K. (Ed.). (1994). *New challenges in defense planning: Rethinking how much is enough*. Santa Monica, CA: RAND. Retrieved from http://www.rand.org/pubs/monograph_reports/MR400.html

Davis, P. K. (2002). *Analytic architecture for capabilities-based planning, mission-system analysis, and transformation (MR1513)*. Santa Monica, CA: RAND. Retrieved from http://www.rand.org/pubs/monograph_reports/MR1513.html

Davis, P. K. (2014). *Analysis to inform defense planning despite austerity*. Santa Monica, CA: RAND. Retrieved from http://www.rand.org/pubs/research_reports/RR842.htm

Davis, P. K., & Arquilla, J. (1991). *Deterring or coercing opponents in crisis: Lessons from the war with Saddam Hussein* (R-4111-JS). Santa Monica, CA: RAND. Retrieved from https://www.rand.org/content/dam/rand/pubs/reports/2007/R4111.pdf

Davis, P. K., Bankes, S. C., & Egner, M. (2007). *Enhancing strategic planning with massive scenario generation: Theory and experiments (TR-392-OSD)*. Santa Monica, CA: RAND.

Davis, P. K., & Cragin, K. (Eds.). (2009). *Social science for counterterrorism: Putting the pieces together*. Santa Monica, CA: RAND. Retrieved from http://www.rand.org/pubs/monographs/MG849.html

Davis, P. K., Gompert, D. C., Johnson, S., & Long, D. (2008). *Developing resource-informed strategic assessments and recommendations* (April 8, Trans. MG-662). Santa Monica, CA: RAND. Retrieved from http://www.rand.org/pubs/monographs/MG703.html

Davis, P. K., & O'Mahony, A. (2017). Representing qualitative social science in computational models to aid reasoning under uncertainty: National security examples. *Journal of Defense Modeling and Simulation, 14*(1), 1-22. doi:10.1177/1548512916681085

Davis, P. K., O'Mahony, A., & Pfautz, J. (Eds.). (2019). *Social-behavioral modeling for complex systems*. Hoboken, NJ: John Wiley & Sons. doi:10.1002/9781119485001

Davis, P. K., Perry, W. L., Hollywood, J. S., & Manheim, D. (2016). *Uncertainty-sensitive heterogeneous information fusion: Assessing threat with soft, uncertain, and conflicting evidence*. Santa Monica, CA: RAND.

Davis, P. K., Shaver, R. D., & Beck, J. (2008). *Portfolio-analysis methods for assessing capability options* (August 11, Trans. MG-662-OSD). Santa Monica, CA: RAND. Retrieved from http://www.rand.org/pubs/monographs/MG662.html

Eastin, J., Grundman, J., & Prakash, A.

(2010). The two limits debates: "Limits to growth" and climate change. *Futures, 43*(1), 16-26. Retrieved from https://www.sciencedirect.com/science/article/pii/S0016328710000352

Financial Crisis Inquiry Commission. (2011). *Financial crisis inquiry report.* Washington, DC: GPO.

Forrester, J. W., Low, G. W., & Mass, N. J. (1974). The debate on world dynamics: A response to Nordhaus. *Policy Sciences, 5*, 169-190.

Gamino, M. (2012). Is it too late for sustainable development? Interview with Dennis Meadows. *Smithsonian.* Retrieved from http://www.smithsonianmag.com/science-nature/is-it-too-late-for-sustainable-development-125411410/

Gordon, M. R., & Trainor, B. E. (2012). *The endgame.* New York, NY: Pantheon Books of Random House.

Greenberger, M., Crenson, M. A., & Crissey, B. L. (1976). *Models in the policy process: Public decision making in the computer era.* New York, NY: Russell Sage Foundation.

Groves, D. G., Fischbach, J. R., Bloom, E., Knopman, D., & Keefe, R. (2013). *Adapting to a changing Colorado River (RR-242-BOR).* Santa Monica, CA: RAND.

Groves, D. G., & Lempert, R. J. (2007). A new analytic method for finding policy-relevant scenarios. *Global Environmental Change, 17*(1), 78-85. Retrieved from http://www.rand.org/pubs/reprints/2007/RAND_RP1244.pdf

Gunaratne, C., & Garibay, I. (2018). *Evolutionary model discovery of factors for farm selection by the artificial Anasazi.* Retrieved from https://arxiv.org/abs/1802.00435v1.

Haasnoot, M., Kwakkel, J. H., Walker, W. E., & Maat, J. T. (2013). Dynamic adaptive policy pathways: A method for crafting robust decisions for a deeply uncertain world. *Global Environmental Change, 23*(2), 485-498.

Hadzikadic, M., & Whitmeyer, J. (2019). Lessons from a project on agent-based modeling. In P. K. Davis, A. O'Mahony, & J. Pfautz (Eds.), *Social-behavioral modeling for complex systems* (pp. 655-671). Hoboken, NJ: John Wiley & Sons.

Intergovernmental Panel on Climate Change (IPCC). (2010). *IPCC expert meeting on assessing and combining multi model climate projections.* Boulder, CO: National Center for Atmospheric Research. Retrieved from https://www.ipcc.ch/publication/ipcc-expert-meeting-on-assessing-and-combining-multi-model-climate-projections/

International Panel on Climate Change. (2014). *Climate change 2014: Synthesis report.* Geneva, Switzerland: Author.

Isley, S. C., Lempert, R. J., Popper, S. W., & Vardavas, R. (2013). *An evolutionary model of industry transformation and the political sustainability of emission control policies (TR-1308-NSF).* Santa Monica, CA: RAND.

Kahn, H. (1983). *The coming boom: Economic, political, and social.* New York, NY: Simon & Schuster.

Kalra, N. R., Groves, D. G., Bonzanigo, L., Molina Perez, E., Ramos, C., Brandon, C.J., & Cabanillas, I. R. (2015). *Robust decision-making in the water sector: A strategy for implementing Lima's long-term water resources master plan (Policy Working Paper 7439).* Washington, DC: World Bank. Retrieved from http://documents.worldbank.org/curated/en/617161468187788705/pdf/WPS7439.pdf

Kaplan, F. (2013). The end of the age of Petraeus. *Foreign Affairs, 92*(1), 75-90.

Krugman, P. (2009). How did economists get it so wrong? *New York Times Magazine*, p. MM36. Retrieved from http://www.nytimes.com/2009/09/06/magazine/06Economic-t.html?pagewanted=all

Lempert, R. J., & Groves, D. G. (2010). Identifying and evaluating robust adaptive policy responses to climate change for water management agencies in the American west. *Technological Forecasting and Social Change, 77*(6), 960-974.

Lempert, R. J., Groves, D. G., Popper, S. W., & Bankes, S. C. (2006). A general analytic method for generating robust strategies and narrative scenarios. *Management Science, 4*, 514-528.

Lempert, R. J., Popper, S.W., & Bankes, S. C. (2003). *Shaping the next one hundred years: New methods for quantitative long-term policy analysis* (August 8, Trans.). Santa Monica, CA: RAND. Retrieved from https://www.rand.org/pubs/monograph_reports/MR1626.html

Lewis, M. (2010). *The big short: Inside the doomsday machine.* New York: W.W. Norton.

Marchau, V. A. W. J., Walker, W. E., Bloemen, P. J. T., & Popper, S. W. (Eds.). (2019). *Decision making under deep uncertainty: From theory to practice.* Cham, Switzerland: Springer.

Meadows, D. H., Randers, J., & Meadows, D. L. (2004). *The limits to growth: The 30-year update.* White River Junction, VT: Chelsea Green Publishing Company. Retrieved from http://www.loc.gov/Calif.tdir/toc/ecip0413/2004000125.html

Meadows, D. H., Meadows, D. L., Randers, J., & Behrens III, W. W. (1972). *The limits to growth: A report for the Club of Rome's project on the predicament of mankind.* New York, NY: Universe Books.

Molina-Perez, E. (2016). *Directed International Technological Change and Climate Policy.* Santa Monica, CA: RAND. Retrieved from https://www.rand.org/pubs/rgs_dissertations/RGSD369.html

Morgan, M. G., & Henrion, M. (1992). *Uncertainty: A guide to dealing with un-*

certainty in quantitative risk and policy analysis. New York, NY: Cambridge University Press.

National Research Council. (2014). *U.S. Air Force strategic deterrence analytic capabilities: An assessment of methods, tools, and approaches for the 21st century security environment* (December 20). Washington, DC: National Academies Press. Retrieved from http://www.nap.edu/openbook.php?record_id=18622

O'Mahony, A., Blum, I., Armenia, G., Burger, N., Mendelsohn, J., McNerney, M. J., ... Szayna, T. S. (2018). Assessing, monitoring, and evaluating Army security cooperation: A framework for implementation (RR-2165-A, 2018). Santa Monica, CA: RAND. Retrieved from https://www.rand.org/pubs/research_reports/RR2165.html

Popper, S. W., Griffin, J., Berrebi, C., Light, T., & Min, E. Y. (2009). *Natural gas and Israel's energy future: A strategic analysis under conditions of deep uncertainty.* Santa Monica, CA: RAND.

Popper, S. W., Lempert, R. J., & Bankes, S. C. (2005). Shaping the future. *Scientific American, 292*(4), 66-71.

Quade, E. S., & Boucher, W. I. (Eds.). (1968). *Systems analysis and policy planning: Applications for defense.* New York, NY: Elseveier Science Publishers.

Quinlivan, J. T. (1995). Force requirements in stability operations. *Parameters, Winter,* 59-69. Retrieved from http://Calif.rlisle-www.army.mil/usawc/parameters/1995/quinliv.htm

Ray, P. A., Bonzanigo, L., Wi, S., Yang, Y-C. E., Karki, P., Garcia, L. E., ... Brown, C. M. (2018). Multidimensional stress test for hydropower investments facing climate, geophysical and financial uncertainty. *Global Environmental Change, 48,* 168-181. Retrieved from https://www.researchgate.net/publication/322024347_Multidimensional_stress_test_for_hydropower_investments_facing_climate_geophysical_and_financial_uncertainty

Rosenhead, J., & Mingers, J. (Eds.). (2002). *Rational analysis for a problematic world revisited: Problem structuring methods for complexity, uncertainty and conflict* (2nd ed.) New York, NY: John Wiley & Sons.

Rumsfeld, D. (2001). *Report of the quadrennial defense review.* Washington, DC: Department of Defense.

Thaler, R., & Sunstein, C. R. (2008). Human frailty caused this crisis. *Financial Times.* Retrieved from https://www.ft.com/content/ac2839ac-b015-11dd-a795-0000779fd18c

Tingstad, A. H., Groves, D. G., & Lempert, R. J. (2014). *Paleoclimate scenarios to inform decision making in water resource management: Example from southern California's inland empire.* Santa Monica, CA: RAND. doi:10.1061/%28ASCE%29WR.1943-5452.0000403

Turner, G. (2008). *A comparison of the 'limits to growth' with thirty years of reality.* Canberra, Australia: Commonwealth Scientific and Industrial Research Organization.

U.S. House of Representatives. (2008). *The financial crisis and the role of federal regulators.* Retrieved from https://www.gpo.gov/fdsys/pkg/CHRG-110hhrg55764/html/CHRG-110hhrg55764.htm

Walker, W. E. (2000). Policy analysis: A systematic approach to supporting policymaking in the public sector. *Journal of Multi-Criteria Decision Analysis*, 9, 11-27.

This publication is available open access at:
http://www.ipsonet.org/publications/open-access

Thanks to the generosity of the American Public University System

APU American Public University

AMU American Military University

Featured Titles from Westphalia Press

Issues in Maritime Cyber Security Edited by Nicole K. Drumhiller, Fred S. Roberts, Joseph DiRenzo III and Fred S. Roberts

While there is literature about the maritime transportation system, and about cyber security, to date there is very little literature on this converging area. This pioneering book is beneficial to a variety of audiences looking at risk analysis, national security, cyber threats, or maritime policy.

The Death Penalty in the Caribbean: Perspectives from the Police Edited by Wendell C. Wallace PhD

Two controversial topics, policing and the death penalty, are skillfully interwoven into one book in order to respond to this lacuna in the region. The book carries you through a disparate range of emotions, thoughts, frustrations, successes and views as espoused by police leaders throughout the Caribbean

Middle East Reviews: Second Edition
Edited by Mohammed M. Aman PhD and Mary Jo Aman MLIS

The book brings together reviews of books published on the Middle East and North Africa. It is a valuable addition to Middle East literature, and will provide an informative read for experts and non-experts on the MENA countries.

Unworkable Conservatism: Small Government, Freemarkets, and Impracticality by Max J. Skidmore

Unworkable Conservatism looks at what passes these days for "conservative" principles—small government, low taxes, minimal regulation—and demonstrates that they are not feasible under modern conditions.

The Politics of Impeachment
Edited by Margaret Tseng

This edited volume addresses the increased political nature of impeachment. It is meant to be a wide overview of impeachment on the federal and state level, including: the politics of bringing impeachment articles forward, the politicized impeachment proceedings, the political nature of how one conducts oneself during the proceedings and the political fallout afterwards.

Made in United States
Troutdale, OR
11/03/2026

56845268R00120